Chromebook™

FOR

DUMMIES®

A Wiley Brand

by Mark LaFay

Chromebook™ For Dummies®

Published by: **John Wiley & Sons, Inc.,** 111 River Street, Hoboken, NJ 07030-5774, `www.wiley.com`

Copyright © 2015 by John Wiley & Sons, Inc., Hoboken, New Jersey

Media and software compilation copyright © 2015 by John Wiley & Sons, Inc. All rights reserved.

Published simultaneously in Canada

For general information on our other products and services, please contact our Customer Care Department within the U.S. at 877-762-2974, outside the U.S. at 317-572-3993, or fax 317-572-4002. For technical support, please visit `www.wiley.com/techsupport`.

Wiley publishes in a variety of print and electronic formats and by print-on-demand. Some material included with standard print versions of this book may not be included in e-books or in print-on-demand. If this book refers to media such as a CD or DVD that is not included in the version you purchased, you may download this material at `http://booksupport.wiley.com`. For more information about Wiley products, visit `www.wiley.com`.

Library of Congress Control Number: 2014941052

ISBN 978-1-118-95126-2 (pbk); ISBN 978-1-118-95127-9 (ebk); ISBN 978-1-118-95128-6 (ebk)

Manufactured in the United States of America

10 9 8 7 6 5 4 3 2 1

Contents at a Glance

Table of Contents

Introduction

• •

Currently, laptops are on the decline. This is largely due to the penetration of smartphones and tablets in the consumer market. Technology is getting smaller, faster, and more portable, so the world's dependence on full-featured computers with fixed connections has begun to decrease.

However, in this declining market, the rising star is the *Chromebook* — a kind of low-cost portable computer powered by Google's Chrome OS, an operating system inspired by and designed around the Chrome web browser. The Chromebook is designed to rely heavily on the Internet for the bulk of its functionality. Instead of a hard drive, then, Chromebook relies on cloud-based storage. And instead of resident applications, Chromebook uses web-based applications that are accessed and bookmarked through the Google Play store.

By offloading the bulk of the functionality to the omnipresent cloud, Google made it possible for hardware manufacturers to create computers with hardware configurations specifically optimized for life on the web. The result is an accessible, user-friendly computer with a low price point, making it a great option for schools, students, companies, and budget-conscious people in need of computing power.

About This Book

Sometimes the greatest hurdle in picking up a new technology is the fear that you won't be able to learn it fast enough for it to be useful to you. The good news is that this book is designed to alleviate the fear involved with using a Chromebook by removing all of the guesswork. *Chromebooks For Dummies* is designed to give you all the tips and tools you need to excel with your Chromebook.

You don't need to have any preexisting experience with Chromebooks, Chrome OS, or the Chrome browser to be able to use *Chromebooks For Dummies.* You don't even have to own a Chromebook: The first section of the book is designed to help you choose the Chromebook that's right for you! If you do have a Chromebook, this book guides you from the initial setup phase to the everyday features that make Chromebooks truly unique. Later sections of the book give you step-by-step instructions on installing popular apps that can make you productive on day one. By the time you hit the advanced settings and features section of the book, you'll probably consider yourself an advanced Chromebook user.

Many computer books get bogged down with technical jargon and mumbo jumbo. *Chromebooks For Dummies,* however, isn't written for the technical elite; it's written for the 99.9 percent of the population who just want a no-nonsense approach to using a Chromebook.

Currently, several hardware manufacturers make Chromebooks. You've probably heard of many of them: HP, Samsung, Dell, Acer, and Asus, to name a few. Google even has its own branded Chromebook called Chromebook Pixel. The only difference between these different devices is the hardware — not the operating system. For that reason, I wrote *Chromebooks For Dummies* without referencing any specific device.

Chromebooks are great devices, and their intuitive design makes for a very short learning curve. *Chromebooks For Dummies* can help ensure that you have all the info you need to use your Chromebook like a rock star!

Foolish Assumptions

When writing this book, I made some assumptions about you, the reader. My editor promptly slapped my hand and told me to knock that off. So I threw all assumptions out of the window. *Chromebooks For Dummies* requires no prior knowledge or experience. Of course, if you do have experience using PCs or Macs, you'll already be very familiar with many of Chromebook's features.

This book makes no assumptions about your skill level. *Chromebooks For Dummies* is as much an introductory tutorial on personal computing as it is on the Chromebook and Chrome OS.

Icons Used in This Book

As you read this book, you'll see icons in the margins that indicate material of interest (or not, as the case may be). This section briefly describes each icon in this book.

Tips are nice because they help you save time or perform some task without a lot of extra work. The tips in this book are timesaving techniques or pointers to resources that you should try so that you can get the maximum benefit from your Chromebook.

At the risk of sounding like an alarmist, anything marked with a warning is something you should pay close attention to. Proceed with caution if you must proceed at all.

Whenever you see this icon, think *advanced* tip or technique. You might find these tidbits of useful information just too boring for words, or they could contain the solution you need to get your Chromebook working just the way you want. Skip these bits of information whenever you like.

If you don't get anything else out of a particular chapter or section, remember the material marked by this icon. This text reminds you of meaningful content that you should file away. This icon might also draw your attention to something I already covered that's useful again.

Beyond the Book

A lot of extra content that you won't find in this book is available at www. dummies.com. Go online to find the following:

- **Online articles covering additional topics are at**

    www.dummies.com/extras/chromebook

    This page has information on how to customize your Chrome browser, set up Google Calendar on your iPhone and Android, use your Chromebook as a media center for your TV, print documents into files for printing at a later time, and more!

- **The Cheat Sheet for this book is at**

    www.dummies.com/cheatsheet/chromebook

    Here you'll find quick-reference information that might come in handy when you're in a pinch.

- **Updates to this book, if we have any, are also available at**

    www.dummies.com/extras/chromebook

Where to Go from Here

The time has come to dive into the wild world of Chromebooks and Chrome OS. If you're completely new to computers or maybe just a little timid with new computers, then start with Chapter 1. The first chapters of the book are designed to guide you through the process of powering on your device, logging in, navigating your new computing environment, and even getting familiar with some keyboard and touchpad features new to the Chromebook.

If you're a little more daring than others, you may consider skipping the first few chapters of the book and heading directly to the chapter on the Chrome browser. Regardless of how you fancy yourself, this book can serve as a great primer for life with a Chromebook.

Part I
Getting Started with Chromebook

In this part . . .

- ✔ Identifying the Chromebook that most closely matches your needs
- ✔ Getting familiar with the Chromebook desktop and Shelf
- ✔ Unleashing some of the Chrome's advanced features to make you a Chromebook power user
- ✔ Customizing keys, clicks, and swipes to maximize your Chromebook experience
- ✔ Getting acquainted with powerful apps that make your Chromebook a dream machine

Chapter 1

Choosing and Setting Up
Your Chromebook

. . . .

In This Chapter

▶ Understanding what makes a Chromebook tick

▶ Selecting your very own Chromebook

▶ Using your Chromebook for the first time

▶ Transitioning to Chromebook from Windows or Mac

. . . .

*I*f you've been keeping up with the technology news lately, you've probably heard about how Google is making yet another splash in the hardware market with their Chromebook. In 2013, they captured one percent of the laptop market in the U.S., which equates to roughly 2.5 million units sold, a number expected to grow.

In this chapter, I go over what makes the Chromebook unique when compared to other personal computers on the market. I also take an in-depth look at how to set up your Chromebook and prepare you to transition to Chromebook from Windows or the Mac.

Checking Under the Hood of the Chromebook

But what is a Chromebook? In short, a Chromebook is a laptop computer running Google's proprietary operating system, *Chrome OS*.

The *operating system (OS)* is the software that manages and schedules the basic tasks and functions of your computer. You might have a little experience with other popular operating systems like Microsoft Windows or Apple's Mac OS X.

Chrome OS is a new operating system developed by Google to work primarily with web-based software. Your experience using your Chromebook will be very similar to previous experiences you might have had surfing the web with the Chrome web browser. The Chrome web browser shares many similarities with other web browsers on the market like Internet Explorer, Firefox, and Safari. (See Figure 1-1.)

Figure 1-1:
The Google
Chrome web
browser.

With the exception of the Chromebook Pixel, Google isn't manufacturing Chromebooks directly. Instead, Google has licensed a number of major laptop manufacturers to create them. Manufacturers such as ACER, HP, Lenovo, Dell, Toshiba, and Samsung are all making their own Chromebooks with their own technical specifications.

The software

Almost everything you do on your Chromebook happens in the Chrome web browser. This is because all the applications you will use on your Chromebook actually reside on the Internet. This is one of the things that sets Chromebook apart from other computers: You don't install applications on a Chromebook; instead, you access them from the Internet. You find applications through the Chrome Web Store and add them to your App Launcher, which, in many cases, means nothing more than creating a bookmark for quick access through your Chrome web browser. This approach can be limiting in some cases, but these cases are rare. Thanks to the vast nature of Google's ecosystem, thousands of great applications are at your fingertips.

While some Chromebook applications offer offline features and functionality, you will need an Internet connection to be able to take advantage of everything your Chromebook has to offer.

The hardware

Unlike all other computers on the market that run Mac OS X or Windows, no software is installed on your Chromebook, which means that your Chromebook doesn't need to have vast amounts of hard drive space, memory, or processing power. Most Chromebooks have less than 2 gigabytes (GB) of memory, less than 64GB of hard drive space, and a low-power processor.

The reduced technical features mean that Chromebooks use less power, which means longer battery life. It also means that Chromebooks come with a drastically lower price tag compared to other computers available today. This explains why Google is gaining such a large share of the laptop market.

Choosing a Chromebook

Given the nature of Chrome OS, Chromebooks do not require extremely high-powered hardware to provide an excellent user experience. Even so, the great variety of manufacturers and hardware specifications available can make choosing a Chromebook somewhat difficult.

Screen

These days, the options available for computer screens are almost endless. They include

✔ **High-definition screens:** High-definition screens may be important if you use your computer to stream video. High definition will ensure the videos you stream look fantastic.

✔ **Touch screens:** You may be a tactile person or just used to working on a tablet. For you, the touchscreen will be of great value because you can interface with your Chromebook in much the same way you would a tablet or smartphone.

✔ **Screen sizes ranging from 10 to 15 inches or greater:** The most notable screen feature is its size. A larger screen may be ideal for you if you have a visual impairment or if you prefer having multiple windows open at once and simply need the extra screen real estate. On the other hand, maybe you travel quite a bit and dislike carrying a heavy, large-screen computer. In that case, a small-screen Chromebook is for you. Figure 1-2 shows several popular Chromebook models with different screen sizes.

Figure 1-2: Chromebook screens come in many shapes and sizes.

Processor

There are several key hardware features that impact the overall performance of your computer. The first is your *processor,* which is the brain of the computer. The overall speed of your processor is determined by a few factors:

✔ **Processor speed, measured in gigahertz (GHz):** This rating indicates how fast your processor can perform calculations. The higher the number, the faster the calculations.

✔ **Number of cores:** Each core can perform one operation at a time. Multiple cores means multiple processes can happen at once. Hence, more cores = a faster processor.

✔ **Processor cache, measured in kilobytes (K) or megabytes (MB):** Cache is ultra-fast memory. Whenever you ask your computer to do something, the instruction gets pulled from your computer memory and loaded into the processor cache. In essence, processor cache is like the on-deck batter in baseball.

These three components are key drivers in overall processor performance and more, in this case, is better.

The faster the processor, the more expensive the processor. Chromebooks don't need a lot of power, so the processor doesn't need to be out-of-control fast!

Memory

Another key driver in computer performance is the quantity of memory present. *Memory* is high-speed, short-term storage. When you open a program, the program is loaded into memory so that it can be run. Naturally, the more memory you have, the more programs can be run simultaneously. Chromebooks, however, don't load many programs into memory. The only real program that runs in memory is the Chrome web browser and the websites and applications that run within Chrome. Therefore, a large amount of memory is not necessary. Memory is measured in gigabytes (GB), and your Chromebook should have anywhere from 2GB to 4GB. Two gigabytes, however, will be adequate for the average user.

Hard drive

The *hard drive* is where all of your computer's data is stored. Hard drives are referred to as *non-volatile storage* — meaning they do not require a constant electrical charge to remember what is stored on them. Accessing data on a hard drive is much slower than it is with memory. Hard drives, however, are capable of storing vast amounts of data. The speed at which your hard drive can serve up the data is the third key driver in computer performance.

With most computers, a large hard drive is necessary to store all of your files — music, videos, and so on. Because you don't install software on a Chromebook, a large hard drive isn't important. Google offers *cloud storage* with Google Drive, which means that all of your music, documents, videos, and other files are stored on remote servers accessible via the Internet. This means that when selecting a Chromebook, 32GB to 64GB of hard-drive storage will be more than adequate. You will, however, want to make sure that the Chromebook you are buying also includes free use of Google Drive.

Most Chromebooks come with 100GB of Google Drive storage free for three years. Given the nature of the Chromebook, 100GB will be an adequate amount of storage for the average user. If you are above average, you also have the option to increase your Google Drive size. More on Google Drive in Chapter 6.

Internet connection

To be fully useful, all Chromebooks require an Internet connection. The connection can come in two forms:

- ✔ All Chromebooks have built-in Wi-Fi to connect to wireless networks.
- ✔ Some Chromebook models have cellular options so that you can activate a wireless Internet data plan with a national provider like Verizon or AT&T.

If you think you will not typically be in a place where there is accessible Wi-Fi, and you don't have a mobile hotspot or a phone that can produce a mobile hotspot, then you should consider purchasing a Chromebook with the cellular option built in.

Battery

Battery life, which is usually a major issue with portable devices, is a key feature of the Chromebook. If you compare the specifications of different devices, you'll find that the more powerful devices typically show a lower battery life. Although this is also the case with Chromebook, the Chromebook actually tends to have a *longer* battery life. This is because the Chromebook's operating system is small and streamlined and doesn't require ultra-powerful hardware.

Choosing a Chromebook with high battery life means you'll be able to work on your Chromebook longer before you need to plug it in. Battery life that is over seven hours is ideal. Battery life over 8½ or 9 hours is excellent.

SD card slot

SD cards are small portable storage devices that are typically found in digital cameras. They are handy for storing and transferring photos, among other file types, between devices. Some Chromebooks come with an SD card slot. Having the ability to quickly add external storage with an SD card is valuable, especially if you have a large collection of photos or other files that you want to access quickly.

HDMI support

HDMI is a type of interface primarily used for high-definition video and audio. If you want to use a high-definition external monitor, you should make sure your Chromebook comes with an HDMI port. More on this in Chapter 17.

HDMI ports make it possible to use your television as an external monitor. Connecting your Chromebook to your TV via HDMI turns your Chromebook into a portable media center!

USB ports

USB has become the standard for attaching devices to devices. It has also become the standard for digitally powering electronic devices. The question you need to ask yourself when selecting a Chromebook is not *if* there is a USB port, but *how many* USB ports it has. If you use a USB mouse and you need another port for a keyboard or external storage device, you should ensure that your Chromebook has more than one USB port.

Setting Up Your Chromebook

You really should have a wireless Internet service available when you set up your Chromebook. (If you don't know about the Internet service, it's time to bring in the person who does.) If you're using a stationary (home or public) wireless Internet network or a portable device with an Internet *hotspot,* you probably need to know

- ✔ The network name (like Smith Family WiFi or ATT034)
- ✔ The network password (usually a bunch of random letters and numbers)

If you don't already have a Google Account, you'll also need a phone handy to verify your new account while you set up your Chromebook.

Turning on your device

Regardless of the brand you choose, the Chromebook is built for speed — and you'll notice this speed the first time you turn on your device! To turn on your device, you may simply need to plug in the power cord and open the laptop. If your Chromebook doesn't turn on automatically, locate the Power button, which may be located on the top-right corner of the keyboard itself. (Figure 1-3 shows the Power button on the Acer C720P.)

Power button

Figure 1-3:
A Chrome-
book Power
button.

When you turn on the device for the first time, a Chrome logo pops up on the screen, and within seconds, the computer powers on and displays the Welcome window.

Selecting a language

When the Welcome window appears, start by selecting your language. (I wish there was an option for Pirate English. *"Select your languaaaarge, matey!"*)

Once you've selected your language, make sure you select the keyboard layout. If you're living in the U.S., you likely want to select the defaults here, which are English (United States) and US Keyboard.

Connecting to the Internet

Next, you need to select a network to connect to the Internet. If no network is available, I suggest holding off on attempting to set up your Chromebook until you can connect to an Internet source.

If you're using a mobile device that can generate an Internet hotspot, it's time to turn on the hotspot.

Follow these steps to connect for the first time:

1. **Click the Open the Network drop-down list and select your network name.**

   Your Chromebook may detect several other nearby home or business networks. You can ignore them.

2. **If your Chromebook requests it, enter your network password.**

   Once you select the network and enter a password, if applicable, the Wi-Fi bars onscreen fluctuate as your computer tries to connect. (Figure 1-5 shows the Wi-Fi signal icon.) After the connection is established, the Continue button at the bottom of the dialog window becomes active.

3. **Click the Continue button.**

Agreeing to the Terms of Service

If you've installed software or activated a device within the last 10 years, you've likely seen a terms-of-service agreement. You can accept it by following these steps:

1. **Review the Terms of Service.**

2. **(Optional) When you're satisfied that you understand and agree to the terms, select or deselect the check box that sends usage stats back to Google.**

   I recommend that you leave this box checked. The data is useful for identifying and fixing bugs, creating new features, and otherwise making the Chromebook better for everyone! (The NSA has all of our information anyway, so why not?)

3. **Click Accept and Continue to move to the next step.**

Logging In for the First Time

To unlock all of the features that your Chromebook has to offer, you must first log in with a Google username and password. You can use your existing Google Account or create a new account at this time.

Logging in using an existing Google Account

You can log in by using your Google Account username and password:

1. **Enter your Google Account username into the Username field.**

2. **Enter your Google Account password into the Password field.**

3. **Click Login.**

   The option to select a profile picture appears.

4. **Select your profile picture.**

   Pick one of the default pictures, use your existing Google profile picture, or take a new picture.

5. **Click OK.**

   This completes the initial login process.

Creating a new Google Account

You can create a Google Account by following these steps:

1. **On the login screen, click the Create a Google Account Now option.**

   The Chrome web browser launches and takes you to a page where you can create your account.

2. **Complete the form and click Next.**

   On this screen, Google wants to verify you are a real human being.

3. **Enter your phone number and whether you'd rather be called or texted, and click Next.**

   Google will contact you in the manner you selected to provide you with a verification code.

4. **Enter the verification code and click Continue.**

5. **Close the browser by clicking the X in the upper-right corner of the browser window.**

   At this point, Google encourages you to set up a Google+ profile, but you don't have to.

6. **On the bottom-right of the screen, click the word Guest.**

   This reveals a pop-up menu with several options.

7. **Select Exit Guest from the list.**

8. **Log in to your Chromebook with your new Google Account.**

Using Chromebook as a guest

Logging in to your Google Account allows you to use all of Chromebook's functionality, but you can still access many of these functions without logging in. Chromebook allows you to use the device as a guest by selecting the Browse as Guest option.

If you select Create a Google Account and then close the browser, you will be logged in as a guest and free to use the device with guest privileges.

If you browse the device as a guest and then later decide to register or log in as a user, you first need to log out of the device. You can log out by clicking the word Guest on the bottom-right of your screen and then selecting Exit Guest from the top of the list. (See Figure 1-4.) This takes you back to the login screen.

The Exit Guest button

Figure 1-4:
The Exit
Guest
button.

Transitioning to a Chromebook

Transitioning from a computer that uses Mac OS X or Windows will require a few different steps that are outlined below. All of the items are covered later in this book:

- ✔ **Get a Google Account.** The section, "Creating a new Google Account," earlier in this chapter, shows you how to get a Google Account. Your Google Account will be the key to nearly everything you do on your Chromebook moving forward.

- ✔ **Move your files.** In Chapter 6, you can find out how to access your Chromebook hard drive, external storage, and Google Drive (which is where the bulk of your files will reside once you make the leap to Chromebook).

- ✔ **Use your Chrome bookmarks.** If you've signed in while using the Chrome web browser on other devices, then your bookmarks, apps, and extensions will come with you to your new Chromebook! I cover bookmarks in Chapter 3.

- ✔ **Find new apps.** Your Chromebook comes with several applications in your App Launcher by default. You can, however, add new apps by navigating to the Chrome Web Store and adding them to your menu. In Chapter 5, you can look at some of the existing apps on your Chromebook, as well as discover ways to locate and add new apps that are useful to you.

Chapter 2

Working with the Desktop

*T*he Chromebook desktop is a visual interface that uses a system of windows to control, organize, and manage files, data, and applications. You can interact by using a mouse, keyboard, touch screen, or your voice. Lastly, your desktop has a launching point where you can manually navigate your computer's file system. Other operating systems have similar launching points: Microsoft Windows uses the *Start button* or the *taskbar,* and Macintosh has the *dock.* On your Chromebook, this launching point is called the *shelf.*

In this chapter, you explore the Chromebook desktop and the shelf. You learn how to find, add, and organize apps, as well as how to modify basic Chromebook settings and navigate the Chromebook window system.

The conquering desktop

With your desktop, you can create, edit, and otherwise manipulate files by dragging, dropping, and clicking filenames or icons. However, this wasn't always the case. Did you know that the first desktop — the graphical user interface (GUI) kind of desktop, not the physical kind — was actually created back in 1970 by Xerox? This version of the desktop never really took off because the device and software were too expensive. Apple and Microsoft took note of the innovation, and in the '80s and '90s, both companies rolled out their own versions — Windows and Mac OS X.

The desktop was a revolutionary approach to interacting with a PC because it simplified things (for most people, anyway) by making things visual. These days, of course, the desktop is a staple of all major operating systems, but in the early days of computing, users could interface with computers only by typing obscure commands in a command line. (Remember DOS?) The desktop was a quantum leap in accessibility, and it made possible the digital future we're all living in today.

Accessing the Chromebook Shelf

The shelf is where all the magic happens on your Chromebook. Your shelf is customized specifically to you. In order to access it, however, you must first log in to your Chromebook with your Google username and password. (Refer to Chapter 1 for instructions on creating an account.)

Signing in takes you out of Guest mode. When you're in Guest mode, you can't install apps or permanently customize your Chromebook, so it's of limited use. However, Guest mode is a great way to give your friends and family access to your Chromebook without fear of them changing or manipulating your settings in any way.

Okay, now that you're logged in, you find a row of icons lined up along the bottom of the screen. This is the *shelf.* The shelf appears by default at the bottom of the screen. You *can* change the location of your shelf — but for now, leave it on the bottom of the screen. A quick tour of the shelf reveals two key groupings of icons — one on the left and one on the right (see Figure 2-1):

✔ The icons on the left include

- **The App Launcher (on the far-left of the screen):** This is similar to the Start button in Windows. Click the App Launcher icon, and a collection of app icons appears arranged in a grid. Click any icon to launch the app.

- **App shortcut icons (immediately to the right of the App Launcher):** Any of the apps you see in the App Launcher can be placed for convenience on your shelf. By default, your Chromebook comes with a few popular app shortcuts already installed on the shelf. You can add or remove any of these as you like.

✔ The group of icons on the right is referred to as the *status area.* These icons include

- Clock

- Wi-Fi signal indicator

- Battery icon (indicates battery charge)

- Google profile picture

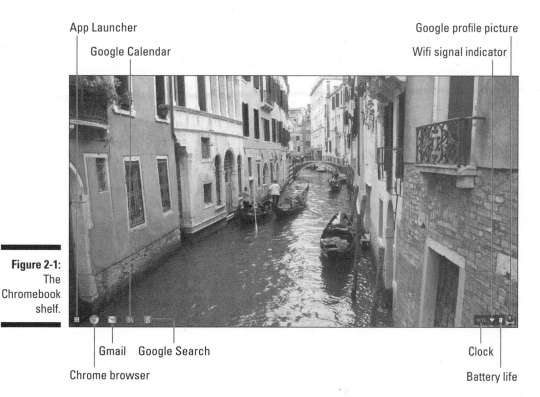

App Launcher

Google Calendar

Google profile picture

Wifi signal indicator

Figure 2-1:
The
Chromebook
shelf.

Gmail   Google Search

Chrome browser

Clock

Battery life

Using the App Launcher: Chromebook's Start Button

Among the icons on the left side of the screen is one icon that looks like a grid of nine boxes. This is your App Launcher icon, comparable to the Start button on Windows. When you click the App Launcher icon, you reveal the *App Launcher,* a pop-up window containing a number of applications. Until you add applications yourself, the only apps that appear here are the default ones that come with your machine and any apps already associated with your Google Account.

Navigating the App Launcher

The App Launcher can contain up to sixteen apps. As you install applications, Chrome OS will add additional windows to contain your applications. When you have more than 16 applications, buttons shaped like horizontal bars will appear at the bottom of the screen. These buttons indicate the presence of additional windows of applications. The color of the button indicates which window is active. You can navigate between windows by clicking these buttons. (See Figure 2-2.)

Figure 2-2:
The
Chromebook
App
Launcher.

Organizing the App Launcher

If you like to keep things in a particular order, you will appreciate being able to organize your App Launcher as you see fit. Simply click on an application and drag it around the window until it is in the order you desire. You can move applications between windows in the app folder by following these steps:

1. **Click and hold the application icon that you wish to move.**

2. **Drag the icon in the direction of the window in which you would like to place your selected application.**

   Wait patiently until the window shifts.

3. **Drop in the desired location.**

When you finish browsing your apps, you can close the App Launcher by clicking outside of it or by clicking the App Launcher icon on your shelf.

Setting Up App Shortcuts

Next to the App Launcher icon, you'll see several additional application icons. These are shortcuts to frequently used applications on your Chromebook. If you find yourself frequently using applications like Gmail, Calendar, Docs, or Drive, adding shortcuts to these apps on your shelf is a great way to streamline your user experience.

Pinning app shortcuts

You can add application icons to your shelf by following these steps:

1. **Click the App Launcher icon.**

   The App Launcher appears.

2. **Navigate to the application that you wish to add directly to your shelf.**

   This may require moving between App Launcher windows.

3. **While holding down the Alt key, click on the application.**

   A menu with several options appears.

4. **Select Pin to Shelf from the top of the list.**

   Your application shortcut has been added to your shelf. (See Figure 2-3.)

Figure 2-3: Pinning application shortcuts to your shelf.

A second option for pinning apps to your shelf is the drag-and-drop method. Simply click and hold the icon for any application you want to pin and drag it down to the shelf. You can easily move the icon to any position you desire. Then, just release to drop it in place.

Don't worry — pinning icons to your shelf doesn't remove the application from the App Launcher. It simply creates an additional shortcut to the application so that you can quickly move between your frequently used applications.

Once you pin an application to your shelf, you can place your icons in the order that you desire simply by clicking and dragging icons left or right along the shelf.

Removing app shortcuts from your shelf

If you want to remove an application shortcut from your shelf, you have a few options. Here's one easy method:

1. **Hold the Alt key and click on the application icon.**

   This reveals a pop-up menu with several options.

2. **Select Unpin to remove the icon from your dock.**

   This won't delete the application from your machine; it merely removes the shortcut from your shelf.

Another easy method: Just click and drag the icon you wish to remove off the shelf. (If you have a touchscreen, you can just tap and drag the icon off the shelf.)

Getting the Scoop in the Status Area

On the right side of your screen is a bunch of icons and your Google profile picture. This is your status area. The leftmost icon in this group is nothing more than a box with a number in it, and your number may be zero. This is the *notification panel*. (See Figure 2-4.) If you click this icon, your notification window will appear. Notifications can be many things, including

✔ Calendar event reminders

✔ Stock tickers

✔ Sports scores

✔ Weather

✔ Email

✔ Application updates

Google selects its notifications by learning from your behavior. Google has a search application for your iPhone or Android device called *Google Now.* By using Google Now for repeated searches, the app starts to learn your common searches and automatically funnels those search results into your notification panel. Additionally, as you use the Google search engine (www. google.com) through the Chrome web browser on your Chromebook, Google tracks and learns your searches in the same manner.

For instance, say you're a huge Indiana Pacers fan and you keep up with the scores by conducting Google searches. Google will learn your search habits and begin sending scores automatically to your notification panel.

The notification icon will disappear if you have no new unread notifications.

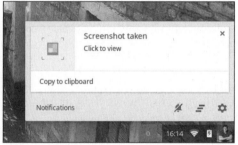

Figure 2-4: The Chromebook notification panel.

Next to your notifications is the Settings area. This area contains the current time, a Wi-Fi signal indicator, and a battery indicator. Click anywhere in this area to reveal your Settings page. In your Settings page, you can make some basic settings tweaks that include

✔ **Wi-Fi:** Click the Wi-Fi option to view available wireless networks. If you're already connected to a network and you want to view information specific to that connection, simply click the network, and a window will pop up revealing additional and advanced information.

✔ **Bluetooth:** In the Bluetooth section, you can enable or disable your Bluetooth signal. This is extremely useful because Bluetooth can quickly drain your battery if left unchecked. In this section, you can browse Bluetooth devices and manage your connections.

✔ **Volume:** Easily control volume levels by dragging the slider to the right to increase and to the left to decrease the volume level.

As you navigate through the different basic settings windows, you always have the option to navigate back to the main Settings page by clicking the left-pointing arrow at the bottom of the window. If you're in the Wi-Fi window, for example, the button at the bottom will look like < Network. If you're in the Bluetooth window, the button will be < Bluetooth. If you want to get into the advanced settings, you can do so by clicking Settings in the settings panel window.

Taking Charge of Window Controls

The other main feature of your Chromebook desktop is the window system. When opened, almost all applications will load into a system of windows, much as they would on a Windows or Apple computer. The difference, though, is that the windows on a Chromebook are all Chrome web browser windows.

By default, a newly opened window appears *maximized,* which means that it fills the screen. You can close a window by clicking the X located in the top-right corner. Next to the X in the top-right corner of the window is a square icon. Clicking this icon will shrink the window enough to be moved and manipulated by clicking and dragging. However, hovering your mouse over the square icon gives you access to a menu with three other options (see Figure 2-5):

- ✔ Clicking the leftmost button shrinks the window so that it occupies only the left half of the screen.

- ✔ Clicking the middle button *minimizes* the window, meaning it will remove the window from the screen, hiding it behind the Chrome icon on your shelf. To restore the window, just click the Chrome icon.

- ✔ Clicking the rightmost button shrinks the window so that it occupies only the right half of the screen.

Figure 2-5:
Hover over the window controls to reveal three options for resizing your window.

Using Tabs to Multi-Task

Sometimes you may want to multi-task. You can multi-task by activating several Chrome windows at once or by opening several tabs within one Chrome window. *Tabs* are simply additional windows that are grouped together, so named because they look like tabs in a filing cabinet at the top of the browser. You can quickly switch between windows by clicking on the desired tab. (See Figure 2-6.)

Tabs

Figure 2-6:
Navigating
between
windows
with tabs.

Each tab can be closed individually by clicking the X located on the right side of the tab.

All tabs behave in the same manner as the window that contains them.

If you would like to make a tab into a stand-alone window, you can do so by following these steps:

✔ **Locate the tab that you wish to break out.**

✔ **Click and hold the desired tab.**

   This brings the tab to the front and makes it active.

✔ **Drag the tab in any direction until it pops out into its own window, as shown in Figure 2-7.**

✔ **Release your click.**

Figure 2-7:
The tab
is now a
window.

Chapter 3

Surveying the Chrome Browser

In This Chapter

▶ Taking an in-depth look at the Chrome web browser

▶ Creating and managing bookmarks

▶ Dealing with your browser history

*I*n late 2008, after a brief beta run, Google released the first consumer-ready version of its Chrome web browser. Google's goal was to create an alternative to popular existing web browsers such as Internet Explorer, Safari, and Firefox. The application was launched globally in 43 languages, and Chrome quickly gained about one percent of the web-browser market.

Chrome's stripped-down approach, and its speed and extensibility, proved to be popular with a wide range of users, from dabblers to the technologically savvy. It was quickly developed for other operating systems like Mac OS X and Linux. Today, Chrome accounts for 43 percent of all web browsing on the Internet.

At their core, web browsers are nothing more than vehicles for surfing the web, but in a Chromebook, your browser does a lot more. Google has done a good job integrating Chrome into their operating system platform, extending its usefulness well beyond the offerings of competing web browsers like Safari, Internet Explorer, and Firefox. In this chapter, you take an in-depth look at the Chrome browser for Chromebook. Learn how to create and manage you bookmarks, manage your browser history, and surf without leaving a record in your browser history.

Navigating the Chrome Browser

Before breaking down the Chrome browser into its different pieces, let me give you a quick tour. Figure 3-1 shows an open Chrome browser window. At the top-left corner is the tab — in this figure, the only tab — featuring the word Google and the lowercase *g* icon; below the tab are the navigation buttons. To the right is the navigation bar, also referred to as the *Omnibox*.

On the far right of the Omnibox is an icon that looks like three dashes — the Settings button. Below the Omnibox is the bookmark bar, and below the bookmark bar is where web pages are loaded.

Navigation buttons   Bookmark bar   Maximize button   Settings button

Tab   Navigation bar (Omnibox)   Star icon (bookmarks)   Close button

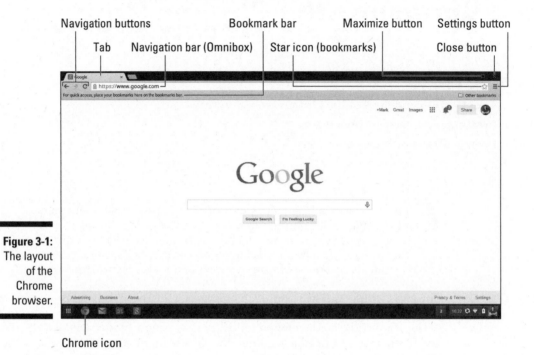

Figure 3-1:
The layout of the Chrome browser.

Chrome icon

Sizing the Chrome window

To launch Google Chrome on your Chromebook, just click the Chrome icon in the bottom-left of your screen. (Refer to Figure 3-1.)

Chrome opens in full-screen mode, also referred to as *maximized*. By default, Chrome opens only one browser window. You can launch additional windows by holding the Ctrl key and clicking the Chrome icon again or by pressing Ctrl+N.

Instead of opening additional windows, consider using multiple tabs within a single window to achieve the same effect. (I introduce tabs in the next section.)

You can close an open Chrome window by clicking the X-shaped Close button in the top-right corner of the browser window or by pressing Ctrl+W.

When a window is maximized, it should take up the entire screen of your Chromebook. If you would like for Chrome to take up only a portion of your screen, however, you have a few options. These include

✓ **Restoring a window to a non-maximized size:** You can de-maximize a window by clicking the box-shaped Maximize icon at the top-right of the browser window or by clicking the header space between the tab and the Maximize button. Either method shrinks your window, allowing you to move it around on the screen.

✓ **Docking a window on half of your screen:** Chrome also gives you the option to reduce the size of a maximized window by half and then dock it on the left or right half of the screen. To do this, hover your cursor over the Maximize button until a drop-down menu of options appears, and then click either the arrow icon on the right (to dock the window on the right) or the arrow icon on the left (to dock the window on the left).

✓ **Minimizing a window:** *Minimizing* shrinks the active window so that it's hidden from the screen but not closed. This is helpful when you want to open a different application or perform some function on your Chromebook without the Chrome window being in the way. To do this, hover your cursor over the Minimize button until a drop-down menu of options appears, and then click the button in the middle.

If you only have one Chrome window open, you can also minimize by clicking the Chrome icon in your shelf.

Working with tabs

More often than not, you will find that using Chrome window tabs is much easier and more efficient than opening and managing multiple windows. The tab system is a lot like tabs on folders in your filing cabinet. Take a look at Figure 3-2 to see what Chrome tabs look like. You can have one website open per tab and almost a limitless number of tabs open in one Chrome window.

Tab close buttons

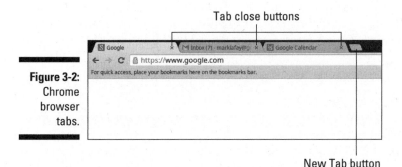

Figure 3-2:
Chrome
browser
tabs.

New Tab button

By default, when you launch Chrome or open a new Chrome window, there is one tab opened. If you would like to open additional tabs, click the New Tab button located to the right of the last tab in your browser window.

Multiple tabs makes it easier to surf the web without losing your place.

You can also open additional tabs by pressing Ctrl+T.

You can close a tab by clicking the X in the right corner of the tab or by pressing Ctrl+W.

Using the Omnibox and the navigation buttons

Chrome's Omnibox and navigation buttons allow you to surf the web. They're located at the top of the Chrome browser window. (Refer to Figure 3-1.)

In non-Chrome web browsers, the Omnibox is known as the address bar. This is where you type the address (or *URL*) for the website you desire. In Chrome, however, you can enter more than just addresses — you can now enter search queries. This is why Google calls this space the Omnibox: Chrome treats any non-URL term entered here as a search query and submits it to your default search engine (which is Google.com, of course, unless you specify otherwise).

From left to right, the navigation buttons found to the left of the Omnibox are

- **Back:** Allows you to navigate to the web page that you were on previous to the current page.
- **Forward:** Takes you forward one page in your browser history. Chrome isn't psychic, however; this button remains grayed-out and inaccessible until you've used the Back button. Go backward one page, and clicking the Forward button returns you to your original page.
- **Refresh:** Reloads your current page. Sometimes you might want to use the Refresh button to load new information that may be in process of launching. Have you ever been waiting on a ticketing site for concert tickets to go on sale? You might hit the Refresh button over and over again until the purchase button is activated.

Saving your place with the bookmark bar

Just as a bookmark helps you remember your place in the book you're reading, Chrome's bookmarks allow you to quickly pick up where you left off. If you find a place on the Internet where you would like to return in the future, you can create a bookmark so that you can get there with a click of the mouse.

To create a bookmark in Chrome, first navigate to the web page you want to save, and then click the star icon on the right side of the Omnibox. This automatically adds the name and address of the site to your list of bookmarks in the Bookmark Manager. If your bookmark bar is enabled, and if you have space available, your new bookmark will also appear there.

You can also bookmark a page simply by pressing Ctrl+D while you're on the page that you wish to bookmark.

Chrome will store almost an unlimited number of bookmarks in your Bookmark Manager. Chrome also gives you the option of saving a small number of bookmarks in the bookmark bar in the browser window. The bookmark bar is located directly under the navigation buttons and Omnibox. As you can see in Figure 3-3, there is limited space in the bookmark bar. Keep your best bookmarks in the bookmark bar, then — the places you visit most frequently.

Figure 3-3: The bookmark bar has limited space.

If you can't see the bookmark bar, it may not be turned on. To turn it on, follow these steps:

1. **Click the Settings button on the right side of the Omnibox.**

   The Settings menu appears.

2. **Hover your cursor over the Bookmarks option in the Settings menu.**

   A sub-menu appears.

   3. Check the Show Bookmarks Bar option.

   The bookmark bar now appears in your browser window.

Now your favorite places on the Internet are only one click away!

Customizing and Controlling Chrome

You can access many of Chrome's functions and advanced settings in the Settings menu. The Settings menu contains quite a bit of general-purpose functionality. Within the Settings menu you can

- ✔ Launch a new tab.
- ✔ Open a new window.
- ✔ Open a new incognito window (more on this in the section "Going incognito," later in the chapter).
- ✔ Access and manage bookmarks.
- ✔ View recent tabs.
- ✔ Copy and paste text.
- ✔ Find text on a page.
- ✔ Zoom in to make web pages appear larger.
- ✔ View browser history and download history.

The Settings menu also has features and settings for advanced users and developers alike. With these options, you can

- ✔ View the HTML source of a web page.
- ✔ Inspect web page elements.
- ✔ Debug JavaScript.

If you're not sure how to go about doing something in the Chrome browser, the Settings menu is a good place to start looking.

You can access the Settings menu by clicking the Settings button on the right side of the Omnibox. The button looks like a vertical stack of three lines. (See Figure 3-4.)

Figure 3-4:
The Settings
menu.

Managing bookmarks

To access the Bookmark Manager, click the Settings button to the right of the Omnibox, then hover your cursor over the Bookmarks option in the menu that appears, and in the resulting sub-menu, select Bookmark Manager. (See Figure 3-5.)

In the Bookmark Manager, you can perform the following actions:

- ✔ Add or edit bookmarks.
- ✔ Delete bookmarks.
- ✔ Organize bookmarks in folders.
- ✔ Add or remove bookmarks to the bookmark bar.
- ✔ Search for saved bookmarks.

The Bookmark Manager window is divided into two main sections: folders for organizing bookmarks on the left and the bookmarks themselves on the right.

You can add new folders to the section on the left by following these steps:

1. Click the Organize button (see Figure 3-5).

The Organize button is located directly above the folder list.

A menu of options appears.

2. Click Add Folder.

A new folder is added to your folder list.

3. Type in the desired name for your folder and press Enter.

Your new folder will be saved in the Bookmark Manager.

The Organize button

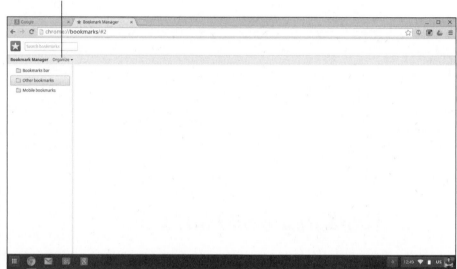

Figure 3-5:
The Chrome
Bookmark
Manager.

On the right side of your Bookmark Manager window is the bookmark folder contents pane. In this pane you'll see bookmarks and sub-folders. You can organize your bookmarks in this pane by dragging the bookmarks to any position you wish. If you want to add a bookmark to one of the folders in the leftmost pane, just click and drag the bookmark to the desired folder.

To delete a bookmark, simply select it and hit the Delete key.

Managing your history and downloads

As you surf the Internet, you create a breadcrumb trail of activity, otherwise known as your Internet history. Chrome stores your history so that you can go back to a page that you may not have bookmarked. Because the sites you visit are stored in your history, in the event your Chrome window closes unexpectedly while you're surfing the web, Chrome will remember all of the websites that were loaded into tabs and windows prior to closing.

In addition to tracking the websites you visit, Chrome's manages the files downloaded with your Chrome browser. The Download Manager keeps track of files downloaded and logs where they reside on your Chromebook. The Download Manager also gives you options for re-downloading lost files and for pausing large downloads for resuming at a later time.

There are advantages to keeping track of your Internet and download history. For one thing, it can improve your web-surfing experience: Sometimes when you go to a website, Chrome will save information about that website on your computer so that it will load faster the next time you visit it. Also, many parents use Internet history to keep track of their children's web-surfing habits in order to keep their kids safe.

If you would like to view your Internet history, click the Settings button. In the Settings menu that appears, select the History option to open the History page. (See Figure 3-6.)

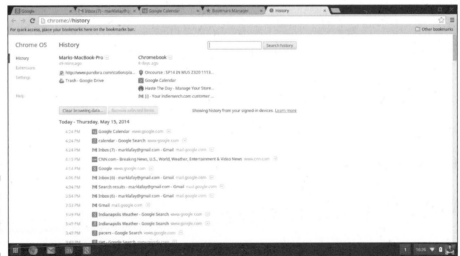

Figure 3-6:
The Chrome History page.

The Chrome History page is broken up into three distinct sections:

- ✔ **The Search History box:** The top of the page contains the search box for quickly searching through your browsing history.

- ✔ **Device-specific history:** The section below the search box contains the recent web history grouped by the browsing device.

   You might recall earlier in the book that when you log in to your Chromebook, all of your browsing data, bookmarks, and plug-ins are imported to your device. If you use the Chrome browser on your smartphone or on another computer, Google tracks your web history and makes it accessible wherever you log in to a Chrome web browser.

✔ **Complete browsing history:** Below the device-specific section of the History page is your complete browsing history from each of your devices, combined into one list and organized by date and time.

On the right side of each history entry is a menu icon that looks like an arrow pointing down. Clicking this icon gives you the option to remove the site from your history or to filter your complete history to include only history entries from that particular site.

Erasing your browsing history

Before you sell your computer (or loan it to someone else), you may want to remove any personal information first. Your browsing history certainly qualifies as personal information. To erase your entire browser history, then, just follow these steps:

1. **In the History page, click the Clear Browsing Data button.**

   A window with several options appears (see Figure 3-7).

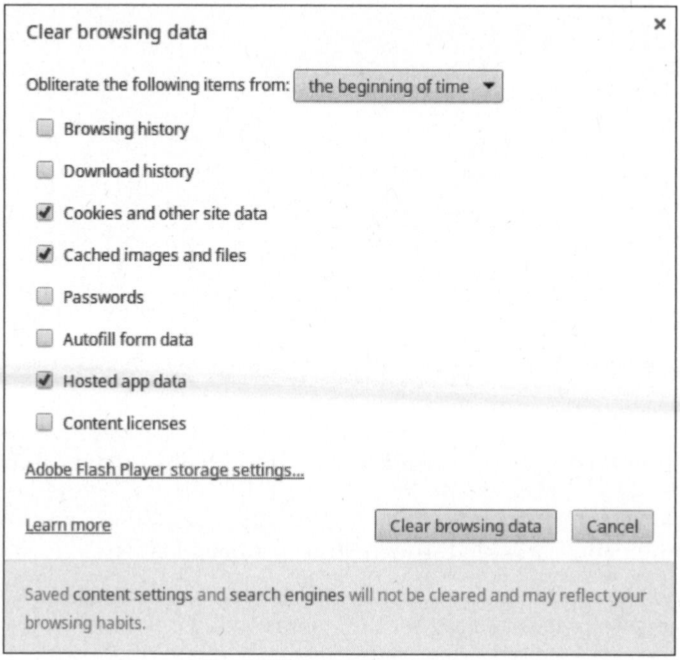

```
Clear browsing data                                          ✕

Obliterate the following items from:  [ the beginning of time  ▼ ]

   ☐ Browsing history

   ☐ Download history

   ☑ Cookies and other site data

   ☑ Cached images and files

   ☐ Passwords

   ☐ Autofill form data

   ☑ Hosted app data

   ☐ Content licenses

Adobe Flash Player storage settings...

Learn more                              [ Clear browsing data ]  [ Cancel ]

Saved content settings and search engines will not be cleared and may reflect your
browsing habits.
```

Figure 3-7:
The Clear
Browsing
Data
window.

2. **(Optional) Use the Obliterate the Following Items From drop-down menu to select a period of time in your history that you would like to delete.**

    The Beginning of Time is typically the default.

3. **Select the Browsing History check box. (Uncheck all remaining boxes, unless you want to remove those items as well.)**

    In addition to clearing your browsing history, you can clear out several other items by checking their associated boxes. These items include

    - Download history

    - Passwords

    - Website *cookies,* which are files associated with websites that remember things specific to you

    - Images and files stored on your Chromebook to decrease the time it takes to load a website

    If you're browsing the web quite a bit, these collections of information can get rather large and begin eating up your available storage space. For this reason, try to periodically clear out that information.

4. **Click Clear Browsing Data.**

Going incognito

Sometimes you may want to browse without worry of creating a trail of crumbs for someone to follow. You may be using a public computer or a computer that's not yours. Or maybe you're planning to surprise someone and you don't want him to stumble across your surprise when he uses the Chrome browser on your computer. Whatever your reason for wanting to not leave a history trail, Chrome gives you the option to go incognito.

For Chrome, going incognito means opening an *incognito browser window.* This window is separate from any other open browser windows, and it functions differently. In an incognito browser, Chrome doesn't keep a record of the sites you visit or any downloads you make, and any cookies sent to an incognito browser are deleted when the browser is closed. This is incognito only up to a point, however. Although Chrome doesn't keep records of your history in an incognito browser, your Internet service provider, employer, or anyone else monitoring web traffic still can. An incognito browser window is simply a good way to surf the web without needing to manually clear the history from your account.

Follow these steps to open an incognito window:

1. **Click the App Launcher icon in the shelf.**

   The App Launcher opens.

2. **Hold Alt and click the Chrome icon.**

   Your incognito browser window opens.

If you're already browsing the web in a Chrome browser that's not incognito, you can open an incognito window by clicking the Settings button to the right of the Omnibox and selecting New Incognito Window in the Settings menu that appears.

You know you're incognito if you see the silhouette of a person wearing a hat and sunglasses in the top-left corner of your Chrome browser window. (See Figure 3-8.)

Figure 3-8:
The Incognito window.

Chapter 4

Getting Your Hands on the Keyboard and Touchpad

In This Chapter

▶ Taking a tour of the keyboard and touchpad

▶ Learning about shortcut keys

▶ Changing your keyboard and touchpad settings

▶ Using an external keyboard and mouse

*I*t's hard telling whether Christopher Latham Sholes thought that his design and letter layout of the keyboard would still be in use well into the 21st century. Regardless of what his original intent was, his legacy is alive and well in the world today. When Sholes devised the layout and functionality of the keyboard that we use today, his intent was to reduce typewriter jams and speed up the typist. (Although some argued that the new arrangement of letters was really to slow down the typist and thus also reduce typewriter jams.)

Over the last 140 years, the keyboard has evolved very little. The basic layout of letters and numbers is the same, the only major additions have been adding multi-purpose keys like the ?/ key or the :; key. Additionally, with the advent of word processors and computers, keys like Caps Lock and Shift, as well as function keys (you know, the F keys located at the top of the keyboard), appeared.

There have also been several modifications as computer manufacturers and software developers like Microsoft and Apple fought to differentiate themselves within the marketplace. For instance, Windows computers have a Start key and rely heavily on the function keys. Apple keyboards ditched the Alt key for the Apple key (now the Command key) and the Fn key.

Each manufacturer created nuances designed to improve the user's experience typing and otherwise operating their machines. The Chromebook is no different! In this chapter, you explore the Chromebook keyboard and touchpad in all of their glory. You learn how to customize the language of your keyboard, adjust the function of some keys, and save time with keyboard shortcuts. You also learn how to add an external mouse or keyboard and how to customize external devices.

The Chromebook Keyboard at a Glance

Google didn't stray too far from the norm when they created the keyboard for the Chromebook. Figure 4-1 shows the keyboard on the Acer C720P. Check out the top row: If you've done much work on a Mac or a PC, you probably remember the function keys (F1 through F12), used as shortcuts for various operating-system-specific functions. On Chromebook, the function keys are gone, replaced by a series of more intuitive keys, called *shortcut keys*.

Figure 4-1:
The
Chromebook
keyboard.

Moving left to right, the shortcut keys are

- **Esc:** Often used to stop a process. In the web browser, it stops a page from loading.

- **Back:** Navigates to the previous web page.

- **Forward:** If you navigated back a page, use forward to navigate forward.

- **Refresh/Reload:** Reloads your current web page.

- **Full Screen:** Makes the current window full-screen, without the menu bar or other ancillary window controls.

- **Reveal All Windows:** If you have multiple windows open, this reveals them all on the screen at once so that you can quickly click and navigate between windows.

- **Dim:** If you're in a dark environment, you may want to reduce the screen's brightness so that the light emitted isn't a disturbance to others.

- **Brighten:** If you're in a bright environment, you may want to brighten your screen because the screen may be too dim to see.

- **Mute:** Quickly eliminates all sound coming from your machine.

- **Volume Down:** Decrease your machine's volume incrementally.

- **Volume Up:** It's time to party, turn up the volume!

- **Power:** Turn your Chromebook on or off by pressing the Power key.

The remaining keys on the keyboard are more or less what you'd expect — with the exception of the Search key, as shown in Figure 4-2.

Figure 4-2:
The
Chromebook
Search key.

Pushing the Search key opens the App Launcher and puts your cursor in the search bar so that you can quickly submit a search query. If you're searching for an application, like Gmail, simply type in **gmail** and your Chromebook will open the Chrome web browser and load your Gmail. Maybe you want to quickly do a Google search. You can do so by entering your query in the search bar and pressing Enter. Chromebook will open a Chrome browser and load Google.com with your search results teed up.

The last thing you should notice about the keyboard is that the bottom row of keys includes no Start key, Fn key, or Command/Apple key. Instead, it simply has a Ctrl and Alt key on both sides of the spacebar. Ctrl and Alt are used quite a bit in shortcut combinations, so you might as well get used to them being there!

Using Shortcut Key Combinations

In addition to shortcut keys, there are several key combinations that will perform a litany of tasks on your Chromebook without making you navigate and click your way through the Chrome OS menu system. Tables 4-1, 4-2, 4-3, and 4-4 show several different shortcut key combinations that will make your experience on a Chromebook more intuitive and efficient!

Table 4-1	Shortcuts for Tabs and Windows
Shortcut	*Function*
Ctrl+N	Open a new window.
Ctrl+Shift+N	Open a new window in incognito mode.
Ctrl+T	Open a new tab.
Ctrl+O	Open a file in the browser.
Ctrl+Shift+Q (twice)	Sign out of your Google Account on Chrome OS.
Ctrl+W	Close the current tab.
Ctrl+Shift+W	Close the current window.
Ctrl+Shift+T	Reopen the last tab you've closed. Google Chrome remembers the last ten tabs you've closed.
Ctrl+1 through Ctrl+8	Go to the tab at the specified position in the window.
Ctrl+9	Go to the last tab in the window.
Alt+1 through Alt+8	Activate App Launcher items 1 through 8.
Search+1 through Search+=	Use F1 to F12.
Alt+9	Go to the last window opened.
Ctrl+Tab	Go to the next tab in the window.
Ctrl+Shift+Tab	Go to the previous tab in the window.

Shortcut	Function
Alt+Tab	Go to the next window you have open.
Alt+Shift+Tab	Go to the previous window you have open.
Click and hold the Back or Forward arrow in the browser toolbar	See your browsing history for the tab.
Backspace or Alt+left arrow	Go to previous page in your browsing history.
Shift+Backspace or Alt+right arrow	Go to the next page in your browsing history.
Ctrl-click a link	Open the link in a new tab in the background.
Ctrl+Shift-click a link	Open the link in a new tab and switch to the newly opened tab.
Shift-click a link	Open the link in a new window.
Drag a link to a tab	Open the link in the tab.
Drag a link to a blank area on the tab strip	Open the link in a new tab.
Type a URL in the address bar, then press Alt+Enter	Open the URL in a new tab.
Hold Esc while dragging a tab	Return the tab to its original position.
Ctrl+Shift+L	Lock your screen.

Table 4-2	Shortcuts for Pages
Shortcut	**Function**
Alt+up arrow	Page up.
Alt+down arrow	Page down.
Spacebar	Scroll down the web page.
Ctrl+Alt+up arrow	Home.
Ctrl+Alt+down arrow	End.
Ctrl+P	Print your current page.
Ctrl+S	Save your current page.
Ctrl+R	Reload your current page.
Ctrl+Shift+R	Reload your current page without using cached content.
Ctrl++ (plus sign)	Zoom in on the page.
Ctrl+- (dash)	Zoom out on the page.

(continued)

Table 4-2 *(continued)*

Shortcut	Function
Ctrl+0	Reset zoom level.
Esc	Stop the loading of your current page.
Alt-click a link	Open the link in a new tab in the background.
Ctrl+D	Save your current webpage as a bookmark.
Ctrl+Shift+D	Save all open pages in your current window as bookmarks in a new folder.
Ctrl+F	Open the find bar to search your current page.
Ctrl+G or Enter	Go to the next match for your input in the find bar.
Ctrl+Shift+G or Shift+Enter	Go to the previous match for your input in the find bar.
Ctrl+K or Ctrl+E	Perform a search. Type a search term after the question mark in the address bar and press Enter.
Ctrl+Enter	Add www. and .com to your input in the address bar and open the resulting URL.
Ctrl+Reveal All Windows	Take a screenshot of your current page.
Ctrl+Shift+Reveal All Windows	Take a partial screenshot.
Ctrl+U	View page source.
Ctrl+Shift+I	Toggle the display of the Developer Tools panel.
Ctrl+Shift+J	Toggle the display of the DOM Inspector.

Table 4-3   Shortcuts for Browser Settings

Shortcut	Function
Ctrl+Shift+B	Toggle the display of the bookmarks bar. Bookmarks appear on the New Tab page if the bar is hidden.
Alt+Shift+M	Open the Files app.
Ctrl+. (period)	Display hidden files in the Files app.
Ctrl+H	Open the History page.
Ctrl+J	Open the Downloads page.
Shift+Esc	Open the Task Manager.
Ctrl+Alt+/	Open the list of available keyboard shortcuts.
Ctrl+?	Go to the Help Center.
Ctrl+Full Screen	Configure monitor display.

Shortcut	*Function*
Shift+Alt+S	Open the status area in the bottom-right corner of the screen.
Shift+Alt+L	Place focus on the App Launcher.
	✔ Press Tab or the right arrow to focus on the next item in the toolbar.
	✔ Press Shift+Tab or the left arrow to focus on the previous item in the toolbar.
	✔ Press the spacebar or Enter to activate buttons, including page actions and browser actions.
	✔ Press Shift+Increase Volume to open the context menu for the button (if available).
	✔ Press Esc to return focus to the page.
Ctrl+Back or Ctrl+Forward	Switch focus to the next keyboard-accessible pane. Panes include:
	✔ Status area, which contains the time, network icon, and battery icon in the bottom-right corner of the screen
	✔ App Launcher
	✔ Address bar
	✔ Bookmarks bar (if visible)
	✔ Web content (including any infobars)
	✔ Downloads bar (if visible)
Alt+Shift+B	Place focus on the bookmarks bar. Use the actions listed for Shift+Alt+T to move the focus.
Alt+E or Alt+F	Open the Chrome menu on the browser toolbar.
Shift+Search+Volume Up	Open right-click menus for focused items.
Ctrl+Alt+Z	Enable or disable accessibility features if you're not signed in with a Google Account. If you are signed in, you can configure the accessibility feature on the Settings page.
Ctrl+Shift++ (plus sign)	Increase screen scale.
Ctrl+Shift+- (dash)	Decrease screen scale.
Ctrl+Shift+) (close parenthesis)	Reset screen scale.
Ctrl+Shift+Refresh	Rotate screen 90 degrees.

Table 4-4	Shortcuts for Text Editing
Shortcut	*Function*
Ctrl+A	Select everything on the page.
Ctrl+L or Alt+D	Select the content in the address bar.
Ctrl+Shift+right arrow	Select next word or letter.
Shift+Search+right arrow	Select text to the end of the line.
Shift+Search+left arrow	Select text to the beginning of the line.
Ctrl+Shift+left arrow	Select previous word or letter.
Ctrl+right arrow	Move to the end of the next word.
Ctrl+left arrow	Move to the start of the previous word.
Alt+up arrow	Page up.
Alt+down arrow	Page down.
Ctrl+Alt+up arrow	Home.
Ctrl+Alt+down arrow	End.
Ctrl+C	Copy selected content to the Clipboard.
Ctrl+V	Paste content from the Clipboard.
Ctrl+Shift+V	Paste content from the Clipboard as plain text.
Ctrl+X	Cut.
Ctrl+Backspace	Delete the previous word.
Alt+Backspace	Delete the next letter (forward delete).
Ctrl+Z	Undo your last action.

The good news is that if you don't have your copy of *Chromebook For Dummies* nearby, Google has a built-in Help tool you can quickly reference. To access the visual helper, follow these steps:

1. **Press Ctrl+Alt+?.**

   The Keyboard Shortcut Help tool appears in an onscreen overlay, as shown in Figure 4-3.

2. **Press Ctrl, Alt, Shift, or any two of these three keys in combination.**

   A keyboard shortcut map specific to the key (or keys) you press appears.

Use the Keyboard Shortcut Help tool for a quick reminder as you use your Chromebook.

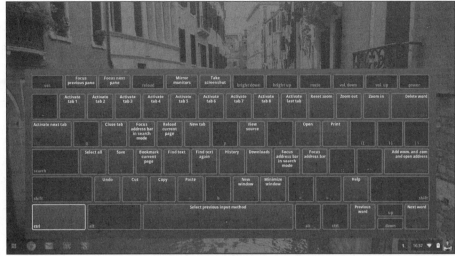

Figure 4-3:
The
Keyboard
Shortcut
Help tool.

Configuring Keyboard Settings

The first time you turn on your Chromebook, you have to complete a basic setup process that includes selecting your language and desired keyboard language layout. This setting, among other keyboard settings, can be edited after the fact. To access your keyboard settings, follow these steps:

1. **Click the status area located in the bottom-right corner of your desktop.**

   You might recall that the status area contains your clock, Wi-Fi indicator, and battery charge level indicator. It is also pictured in Figure 4-4.

   Your settings panel appears.

Figure 4-4:
The status
area.

2. **Select Settings.**

   A window launches and loads your Chromebook Settings page.

3. **Scroll down to the Device section and select Keyboard Settings.**

   A Keyboard Settings dialog box appears, pictured in Figure 4-5.

Figure 4-5:
The
Keyboard
Settings
dialog box.

In the Keyboard Settings dialog box, you can

- ✔ Reconfigure your Search, Alt, and Ctrl keys.
- ✔ Turn your shortcut keys into function keys (F keys).
- ✔ Change your keyboard language configuration.

These options are discussed more fully in the next few sections.

Reconfiguring keyboard keys

By default, the Alt, Ctrl, and Search keys perform their intended tasks: The Alt and Ctrl keys are used in combination with other keys (and clicking) to access additional functionality, and the Search key is used to quickly access the search function in the App Launcher.

However, you can modify these keys so that they serve a different purpose. For instance, you can change your Search key to behave like a Caps Lock or set your Ctrl key to act like the Alt key. To change the function of the Alt, Ctrl, and Search keys, follow these steps:

1. **Click the status area in the bottom-right of your desktop.**

   The settings panel appears.

2. **Click Settings.**

   Your Chromebook Settings page loads in the Chrome browser.

3. **Scroll down to the Device section and select Keyboard Settings.**

   The Keyboard Settings dialog box appears.

   Another way to quickly open the Keyboard Settings dialog box is to press your Search key, type **chrome://settings/keyboard-overlay**, and then press Enter.

4. **Click the corresponding box for the key you wish to reconfigure.**

   A drop-down list appears with options for changing the selected key's function. (See Figure 4-6.)

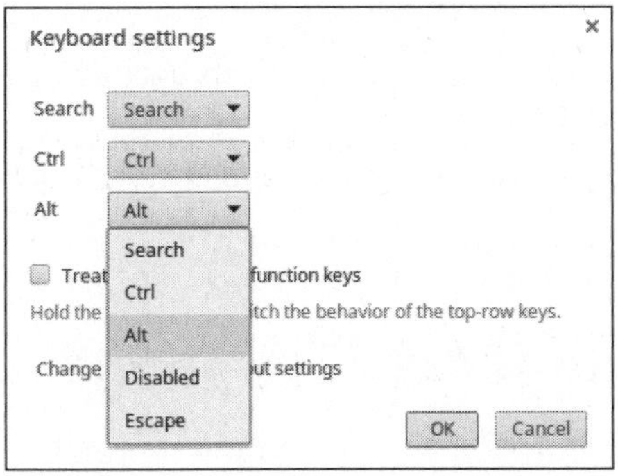

Figure 4-6:
Recon-
figuring the
Alt key.

5. **Make your desired changes and click OK.**

This feature allows you to configure your keyboard in a manner that is convenient to you. You can reconfigure your keys as many times as you like.

Turning shortcut keys into function keys

On most Chromebooks, the function keys (F1 to F10) common to Macs and PCs have been replaced by shortcut keys. Few Chromebook models come with F11 or F12, and depending on your Chromebook model, you may not even have a reference to the function key on each shortcut key.

If you have a need for function keys, don't fret, you can disable the shortcut keys and enable function keys in your keyboard settings by following these steps:

1. **Click the status area in the bottom-right of your desktop.**

   The settings panel opens.

2. **Select Settings.**

   Your Chromebook Settings page appears in the Chrome browser.

3. **Scroll down to the Device section and select Keyboard Settings.**

   The Keyboard Settings dialog box appears.

4. **Select the Treat Top-Row Keys as Function Keys check box.**

5. **Click OK.**

   This disables the shortcut functionality of the shortcut keys and enables their function as function keys.

   To re-enable shortcut keys and disable function keys, simply uncheck the box and click OK.

Changing your keyboard language

Your keyboard language configuration is set the first time you log into your Chromebook. If you're in America, you probably set your language to English (United States) and your keyboard to US Keyboard. If you would like to change your keyboard language, you can do so by following these steps:

1. **Click the status area in the bottom-right of your desktop.**

   The settings panel appears.

2. **Select Settings.**

   Your Chromebook Settings page loads in the Chrome browser.

3. **Scroll down to the Device section and click Keyboard Settings.**

   The Keyboard Settings dialog box appears.

4. **Click the Change Language and Input Settings link at the bottom of the dialog box.**

   The Languages and Input dialog box appears, as shown in Figure 4-7.

   The language you selected when setting up your device appears in the Languages pane on the left side of the dialog box.

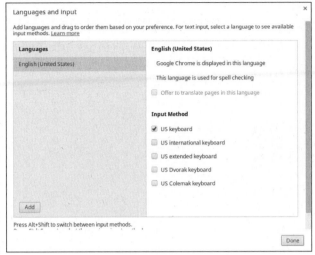

Figure 4-7:
The
Languages
and Input
dialog box.

5. **To change the language, click the Add button at the bottom of that pane.**

   The Add Language dialog box appears. (See Figure 4-8.)

Figure 4-8:
The Add
Language
dialog box.

6. **Select the language you desire from the drop-down list of available languages.**

7. **Click OK.**

   The language you selected is added to the list of languages in the Languages pane.

8. **Click the newly added language to highlight it.**

   A list of options appears in the right pane of the Languages and Input dialog box.

9. **In the Input Method section, check the box for the desired keyboard(s).**

10. **Click Done.**

    You know that you successfully added another keyboard language if a language indicator appears in your status area in the lower-right corner of the screen, as shown in Figure 4-9.

Figure 4-9:
The key-
board
language
indicator.

Keyboard language
indicator

You can activate your newly-added keyboard by following these steps:

1. **Click the status area in the lower-right of your desktop.**

   The settings panel opens.

2. **Click the keyboard option located at the top of the panel.**

   A menu of available keyboards appears.

3. **Click the desired keyboard language.**

After you switch your keyboard, you'll notice as you type that your keys have changed to the standard for the language and country you selected. Change your language by repeating the preceding steps.

Using the Touchpad

Over the years there have been numerous different laptop mouse controllers. The trackball was cool until you got too much of your lunch stuck under the ball. The joystick was nice if you didn't mind that it was the size of a pencil eraser. Then came the touchpad. The touchpad on the Chromebook is a lot like most touchpads that have come before it. Here are some basic gestures to get you going:

✔ To move the cursor across the screen, simply place one finger on the touchpad and move it in any direction.

✔ Click buttons and links by pressing down on the bottom half of the touchpad until you feel or hear a click.

✔ Right-click by pressing down with two fingers.

✔ Scroll vertically by placing two fingers on the touchpad and moving them up and down; moving them left and right scrolls horizontally.

✔ Drag items, scroll, or highlight text by simultaneously pressing (and holding down) with one finger and moving the pointer using another finger.

Finger gestures

Google aimed to make Chromebook the easiest and most intuitive device on the market. Naturally, they have built in several advanced features for the touchpad to make using the Chromebook fluid and intuitive. Some of these features include the following:

✔ You can reveal all available windows by placing three fingers on the touchpad and swiping up simultaneously. You can then click on the desired window to make it active and bring it to the front.

✔ While you are in the Chrome browser, use two fingers to swipe from left to right across the touchpad to go back in your browsing history.

✔ In the Chrome browser, use two fingers to swipe right to left across the touchpad to go forward in your browsing history.

Touchpad and keyboard combinations

Google has implemented several different ways to perform the same function, mainly to accommodate users transitioning from other devices. Some quick ways to use the touchpad and keyboard together are

✔ **Right-click.** Hold down the Alt key and click the touchpad. Right-clicking is useful in revealing common functions without having use a menu or shortcut keys.

✔ **Highlight content:** Click on one side of the content you want to highlight. Then, holding down the Shift key, click on the other side of the content. The text is highlighted. This is particularly useful when you want to copy a body of text. Alt-click on the highlighted text to reveal options like Copy or Cut.

Customizing Touchpad Settings

The touchpad is not without customization. You can make changes to the touchpad settings from within the Chromebook Settings page. To open the touchpad settings, follow these steps:

1. **Click the status area in the bottom-right of your desktop.**

   The settings panel opens.

2. **Select Settings.**

   Your Chromebook Settings page opens in the Chrome browser.

3. **Scroll down to the Device section and select Touchpad Settings.**

   The Touchpad dialog box appears, as shown in Figure 4-10.

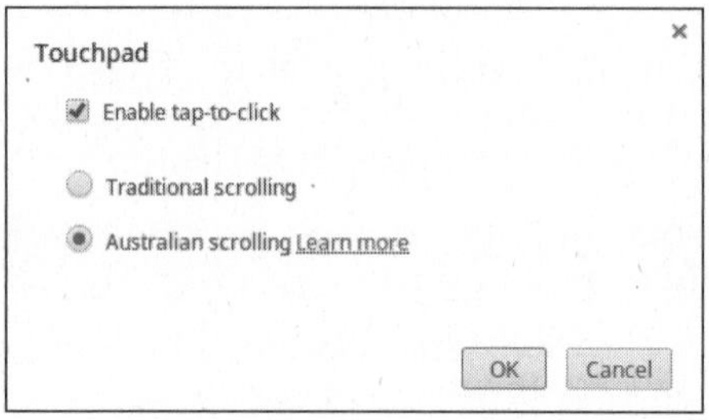

Figure 4-10:
The
Touchpad
dialog box.

> Touchpad ×
>
> ☑ Enable tap-to-click
>
> ○ Traditional scrolling
>
> ⦿ Australian scrolling Learn more
>
> [OK] [Cancel]

In the Touchpad dialog box, you can make the following customizations:

✔ Change the touchpad speed.

✔ Adjust your click settings.

✔ Change scroll directions.

These settings are discussed in the next few sections.

Changing the touchpad speed

In the Device section of your Chromebook Settings page, the Touchpad Speed slider allows you to adjust the speed of your touchpad — that is, the distance your cursor moves onscreen in relation to the distance your finger travels on the touchpad. To move the cursor faster, move the slider to the right. To move it slower, move the slider to the left. (See Figure 4-11.)

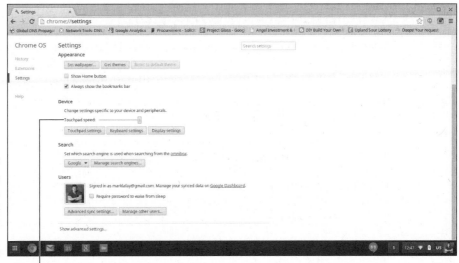

Figure 4-11:
The
Touchpad
Speed
slider.

The Touchpad Speed slider

Adjusting the touchpad click settings

Clicking the touchpad requires you to press down on the bottom half of the touch pad until you hear a *click*. If you wish to use less effort to click, you can also turn on the Tap to Click feature. Once you engage this feature, your touchpad treats any quick tap or touch of the touchpad as a click. To enable this feature, follow these steps:

1. **Click the status area in the bottom-right of your desktop.**

   The settings panel opens.

2. **Select Settings.**

   Your Chromebook Settings page opens in the Chrome browser.

3. **Scroll down to the Device section and select Touchpad Settings.**

   The Touchpad dialog box appears.

4. **Check the Enable Tap-to-Click check box.**

   After you enable this option, you can immediately tap the touchpad to click links, buttons, and so on. You can also double-click by tapping twice.

Changing scroll directions

Scrolling on the Chromebook can be accomplished a few ways:

- ✔ Move your pointer over to the right side or bottom of the screen to reveal available scroll bars. You can then scroll by clicking on the scroll bar and dragging up and down (to scroll vertically) or left and right (to scroll horizontally).

- ✔ Place two fingers on the touchpad and move them up and down to scroll vertically or left and right to scroll horizontally.

By default, the Chromebook is set up to scroll traditionally, meaning that swiping your fingers up on the touchpad makes the window scroll up and swiping your fingers down makes it scroll down.

You may, however, be more familiar with the opposite action. Meaning that when you swipe up, it's as if you're pushing your finger on the screen and pulling more content from the bottom of the screen and vice versa if you swipe down. On Chromebook, this scrolling style is referred to as *Australian scrolling*. You can activate this feature by taking these steps:

1. **Click the status area in the bottom-right of your desktop.**

   The settings panel appears.

2. **Select Settings.**

   Your Chromebook Settings page opens in the Chrome browser.

3. **Scroll down to the Device section and select Touchpad Settings.**

   The Touchpad dialog box appears.

4. **Select the Australian Scrolling radio button.**

5. **Click OK.**

   Your scroll has now been changed!

Connecting a Mouse or Keyboard

Sometimes when duty calls, you have to post up and work on your computer for hours on end. Spending hours upon hours using a smaller keyboard and touchpad may make your mobile-computing experience a bit of a grind. To make things easier, it's sometimes nice to have a separate keyboard or mouse that can be plugged in and used with your laptop. With your Chromebook, this is possible through USB or Bluetooth.

To connect a USB keyboard or mouse to your Chromebook, you just need to locate the USB port on the side of your computer and insert the USB connector for your device in the port. (Your USB connector can only go in one way, so don't force it.) Your Chromebook automatically detects the new keyboard and applies all existing keyboard settings to it.

If your keyboard or mouse and your Chromebook are Bluetooth-enabled, then no cable is necessary! Connect your Bluetooth keyboard or mouse by following these steps:

1. **Click the status area in the bottom-right of the desktop.**

   The settings panel opens.

2. **Select Bluetooth.**

3. **If your Bluetooth is disabled, click to enable it.**

   Chromebook begins searching for available Bluetooth devices.

4. **Ensure your Bluetooth keyboard/mouse is enabled and wait for it to appear in in the Bluetooth list.**

5. **Select your keyboard/mouse from the list and follow any instructions that appear.**

6a. **When connecting a keyboard, enter the randomized pin on the keyboard to ensure it's the correct device.**

   Upon successfully pairing your keyboard with your Chromebook, your Bluetooth keyboard assumes all existing keyboard settings, and you can start typing immediately.

6b. **When connecting a mouse (optional): After your mouse has been plugged in or paired and Chromebook has identified it, you can configure it to be a "left-handed" mouse — that is, to swap the functionality of the left and right mouse buttons — by following these steps:**

   a. *Open the settings panel and choose Settings.*

   b. *Scroll down to the Device section and select Touchpad Settings.*

      The Touchpad dialog box appears. (See Figure 4-12.)

   c. *Select the Swap Primary Mouse check box, then click OK.*

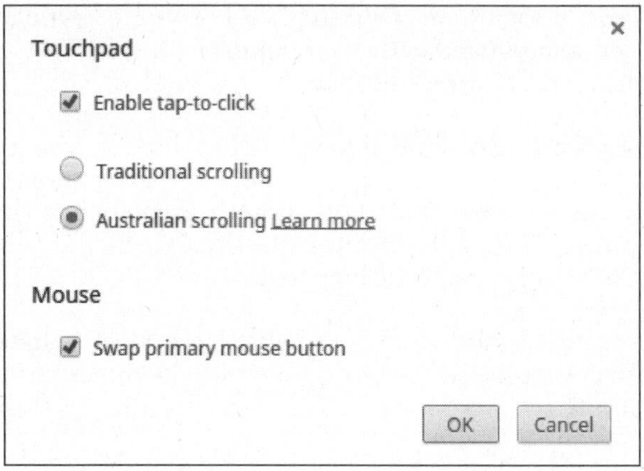

Figure 4-12:
Configuring
a mouse.

Chapter 5

Exploring Chromebook Apps

*B*ecause Google's original vision for Chromebook was to create a computer that did most of its work over the Internet, Chromebook operates almost completely out of the Chrome web browser. Unlike Windows or Mac machines, applications aren't installed on the Chromebook; instead, they're stored on remote computers and accessed over the Internet. Google has numerous web-based applications to help you with work, school, personal development, entertainment, and more. This concept — using online applications and eliminating the need to install software locally — reduces costs for both Google and for the consumer because the Chromebook doesn't require expensive hardware to run the applications.

In this chapter, you get a brief overview of the applications that come with your Chromebook, as well as the lowdown on how to find and add new applications to your App Launcher. Keep in mind that adding apps to your Chromebook requires little more than adding a shortcut to your menu and adjusting a few settings.

Exploring Chromebook's Pre-Installed Apps

On Chromebook, very few applications are actually installed on the hard drive. Instead, the applications shown in your App Launcher are more like links that open web applications in the Chrome web browser. You can view the applications on your computer in a couple different ways:

> ✔ **Press the Search key.** This opens the App Launcher and places a cursor in the search bar. You can then scroll between your windows in the App Launcher by using two fingers to swipe up or down on the touchpad.
>
> ✔ **Click the App Launcher icon.** This icon is located on the bottom-left of your desktop on your Chromebook shelf.

Your Chromebook comes with shortcuts for several applications already in place, this may differ slightly from Chromebook to Chromebook. If we cover an application not already existing on your Chromebook, it can be easily added through the Chrome Web Store. The next few sections give you a quick look at some of the more critical applications.

Storing data on the web with Google Drive

Whether you're creating applications through the Google web-based OfficeSuite or you just want a place to store your important files, Google Drive is your hard drive in the cloud. Save your files to your Google Drive folder, and it will sync to every device you own that has Google Drive installed. You can even access your files through a web browser on any computer with a web connection. Google Drive is a necessity for any Chromebook user.

Word processing with Docs

Docs is Google's word-processing application. If you have done any work with Microsoft Word, then you'll be at home with Google Docs. Create text documents; format your text; add links, images, videos, tables, and more; and save in numerous formats including Microsoft Word, OpenDocument, Rich Text Format (RTF), or Portable Document Format (PDF). Documents created with Google Docs are automatically saved to Google Drive and accessible from any device that can access the Internet. You can even invite others to collaborate on your Docs files without having to email files and worry about duplication of efforts or lost work.

Using spreadsheets with Sheets

Sheets is Google's spreadsheet application. Sheets is a lot like Microsoft Excel and iWork's Numbers. With Sheets, you can build lists, keep track of personal finances, analyze data, and so much more. Build formulas for performing complex calculations and data analysis. Filter, sort, and otherwise organize your data with ease. Just like Docs, all spreadsheets are saved in Google Drive and easily shared with collaborators.

Starting a new business? You should consider using Sheets for your cash-flow projections. You and your business partners can work on it without fear of losing information or overwriting each other's work!

Making presentations with Slides

 Slides is another of Google's web-based OfficeSuite products. With it, you can create beautiful slide presentations with all sorts of pre-built or custom themes. Import images, videos, and other interactive content; link to web content like YouTube videos; and more. Slides is a powerful presentation tool that allows you to present through the web or export to PowerPoint, PDF, and other globally-supported formats. Collaboration is also made easy with Google Drive.

Taking notes with Keep

 Whether you're a student, stay-at-home mom or dad, or in the workforce, note-taking is an important part of life. Google Keep is designed to make note-taking a breeze. Use Keep to take written notes or voice notes. Easily add pictures and videos. Save your notes to Google Drive to share with other users and collaborators. You can even export your notes to services like Dropbox (www.dropbox.com) or Box.com, or you can download them to your computer or storage device. Google Keep's minimalist interface makes it fast and easy-to-use. Take notes more efficiently than paper and pen with Keep.

Organizing and playing music with Google Play

 Google Play Music is the one-stop music utility on your Chromebook! Move your music collection into Google Play and have it be accessible to you anywhere in the world. Organize your songs into playlists, share your playlists, or listen to your friends' playlists. Shop through the Google Play database of songs to purchase and expand your collection. You can even subscribe to get access to stream over 20 million songs at any time. Google Play Music will sync with all of your devices to ensure your music is on all of your devices. (See Figure 5-1.)

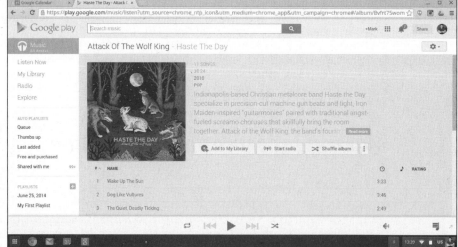

Figure 5-1:
Take your
music col-
lection
with you on
Google Play
Music.

Calling and video chatting with Hangouts

You don't need any fancy hardware or additional software to make calls using your Chromebook! Simply launch Google Hangouts, and you can quickly call any phone number in the world. Domestic calls are usually free, and international calls cost a fee; but you don't need a phone to call your family anywhere in the world! You can even video chat with one, two, three, or more people all at the same time. Chat via text, and take pictures and send them. You can even share your screen or control someone else's desktop from your computer all with Google Hangouts!

Emailing with Gmail

Gmail is Google's powerful and ever-growing free email platform. With Gmail, you can send and receive emails; attach files, pictures, and links; and quickly save attachments to your Google Drive cloud storage. Gmail for Chromebook also has an offline feature so that you can check emails, write emails, and queue them up to send the next time you get online. Google also offers Gmail for businesses so that you can have hosted email that comes from your domain.

Organizing your days with Calendar

Google Calendar is a very powerful calendar system. You can easily create events on your calendar, set them to repeat periodically, set alarms, invite others to attend your events, and more. You can create multiple calendars within your Google Calendar and share the calendar with your family, friends, and co-workers. Organize your calendar and view it by day, week, month, or even agenda. You can also sync your calendar with any modern smartphone, and if you need to access your Google Calendar from a Mac, you can sync it with your Mac's Calendar. You can even bring your Google Calendar into Microsoft Outlook on your PC. (See Figure 5-2.)

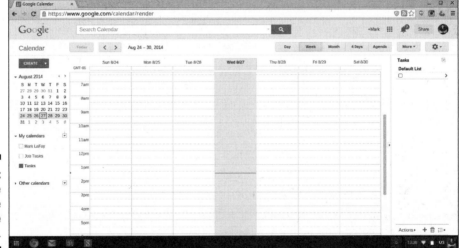

Figure 5-2: Organize your life with Google Calendar.

Remotely accessing with Remote Desktop

Remote Desktop is a powerful tool for accessing your other computers. Install Remote Desktop on your Mac or Windows PC, and you can access them from your Chromebook anywhere in the world. Of course, the computers you want to access must be turned on and connected to the Internet. Other than that, accessing your files, running applications, and otherwise working remotely is a breeze with Remote Desktop.

Reading with Google Play Books

If you've used a Kindle or iBooks, you can probably imagine how easy and awesome Google Play Books is. Shop for books at low costs and store them in your Google Play Books account. Easily sync your books to any device you own that has Google Play Books installed. Then you can read your favorite novel or business book on the beach, in bed, at the office, or on the john — and you can choose: from your phone, your tablet, or your Chromebook! (See Figure 5-3.)

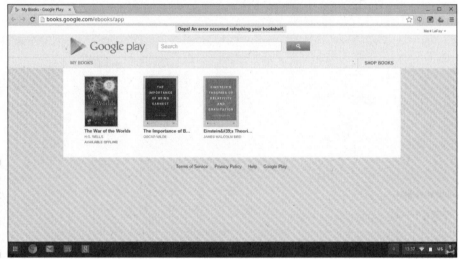

Figure 5-3:
Check out bestsellers at Google Play Books.

Getting directions with Maps

Google Maps is one of the most powerful map programs currently available! Look up point-to-point directions or route a road trip with multiple destinations. Wherever the wind will take you, Google will make sure you're on the right road! Search for businesses, locations, or popular destinations within Google Maps; share maps with friends; and even zoom all the way down to the street view. Switch your views to satellite view and see if you can see the cars parked in your driveway! Google Maps isn't functional, its FUNctional. (See Figure 5-4.)

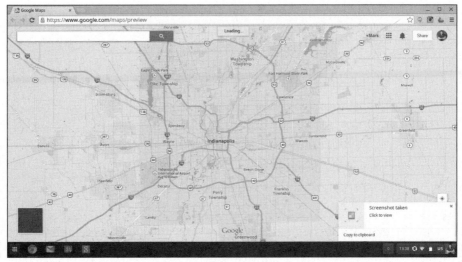

Figure 5-4:
Finding
your way
with Google
Maps.

Finding More Apps with the Chrome Web Store

The Chrome Web Store has many more apps to offer than what appears by
default on your Chromebook. You can search for apps and add them with
great ease by taking these steps:

1. **Click the App Launcher icon located in the bottom-right of your
   screen.**

   The App Launcher, a pop-up window containing your applications,
   appears.

2. **Click the Chrome Web Store icon.**

   A Chrome browser window appears and loads the Chrome Web Store.

3. **Browse applications by category or search by name.**

4. **Click on a desired application.**

   A pop-up window appears that contains information specific to the
   selected application.

5. **To add an application, click the +Free button located in the top-right
   of the pop-up window.**

   The application is added to your App Launcher.

Launching applications that you've added from the Chrome Web Store is the same as apps that come by default with your Chromebook. Just follow these steps:

1. **Click the App Launcher icon located in the bottom-right corner of your screen.**

   The App Launcher opens.

2. **Move between App Launcher windows until you locate the icon of your recently installed application.**

3. **Click the application icon.**

   The application launches.

If you're curious about whether a particular app is useful, or popular, you can go through and read the customer reviews in the Chrome Web Store. These reviews, while they are public opinion, can be helpful in deciding between different apps. The majority of apps in the Web Store are free, so there's actually little risk in simply trying an application. Worst case scenario, you can always uninstall it.

Chapter 6

Finding Your Files

⬤ ⬤

In This Chapter

▶ Working with the Files app

▶ Using external storage on your Chromebook

▶ Setting up and using Google Drive

⬤ ⬤

Chrome OS is a very light operating system, which means that it isn't large in size and doesn't require a lot of power to make it run. This, of course, is by design. Google set out to create a low-cost yet highly useful computer that worked symbiotically with the Google platform. Since your Chromebook uses only web applications, there isn't much need for heaps of storage space. For this reason, the hard drives on Chromebooks are typically less than 32GB.

Although you may not install many applications on the Chromebook itself, you will have a need for some storage. For instance, you might want to download a file attachment from an email, or take a screen shot or capture some video footage or stills with your Chromebook camera. You not only need storage space for these files, but you also need to gain access to them.

If you want to search for files on your Windows PC, you would use Windows Explorer. If you use a Mac, you would turn to the Finder. On Chromebook, you use an app called *Files.* In this chapter, you learn how to navigate your Chromebook file system, how to add and use external storage, and how to set up and use Google Drive.

Finding Files with the Files App

To launch Files, follow these steps:

1. **Click the App Launcher icon in the bottom-left corner of your screen.**

   The App Launcher opens.

2. **Locate the app icon for Files and click it.**

   Files opens in a window that is not a Chrome browser.

Navigating Files

Figure 6-1 shows the open Files app window. On the left side of the window is a listing of storage locations. At first, you'll only have two options here:

- ✔ **Downloads:** Your Downloads folder is your hard drive (also referred to as *local storage*).

- ✔ **Google Drive:** This is Internet-based storage (also referred to as *cloud storage*). I discuss Google Drive in the section "Working with Google Drive," later in this chapter.

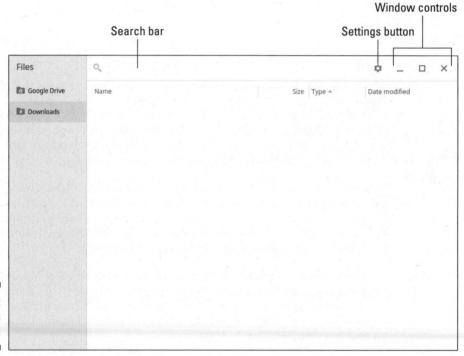

Figure 6-1:
A basic Files
window.

On the right side of the Files app window, you will notice two distinct areas. The top-right of the Files window is your toolbar. In the toolbar, you'll find

- ✔ Search bar
- ✔ Settings button
- ✔ Window controls

On the left side of the toolbar, you'll find the Search bar; and on the right side of the screen, you will see the Settings widget and the window-control buttons that you should be familiar with already. Click the Settings widget to open the File Settings menu, as pictured in Figure 6-2.

Figure 6-2:
The File
Settings
menu.

In this menu, you have the option to launch another Files window, create a new subfolder within the open folder, and change the way files appear in the Files window — either a list (the default) or a grid arrangement.

At the bottom of the Settings menu, a meter shows your available storage. This information is critical because your Chromebook does not offer much storage, so you will want to periodically check to make sure you don't run out. Pictures, screenshots, music, downloads, and the like will add up the more you use your Chromebook, so beware!

Beneath the Files toolbar is the file browser. This is where you will be able to view, edit, move, or otherwise interface with your files.

Creating and navigating folders

Folders are helpful for organizing and sorting your files so that you can easily find them later. Create a new folder by following these steps:

1. **On the left side of the Files window, select the Downloads folder.**

2. **Click the Settings widget in the top-right corner of the window.**

   The File Settings menu appears.

3. **Click New Folder.**

   A new folder appears with the name highlighted to indicate it can be edited.

4. **Type the desired name for the folder and press Enter.**

   The new folder name is saved.

If you would like to open your newly created folder, double-click or double-tap the new folder icon. A window for the folder opens, which at first will be empty.

While you are in your newly created folder, take a look at the bottom of the Files app window. You will see your path, or *breadcrumbs,* as shown in Figure 6-3.

Figure 6-3:
Following
the Files
bread-
crumbs.

On your Chromebook, folders are divided into *parent folders* and *child folders.* A parent folder will contain a child folder or folders. In the path, the parent folder appears to the left of a child folder.

To return to the parent folder, click the parent folder's name in the path. In this case, that would take you back to the Downloads folder, which is the parent folder.

If you need to make several folders, constantly clicking the Settings widget can get tedious. To create a folder quickly, you can press Ctrl+E. You can also rename a folder by following these steps:

1. **Click the desired folder.**

2. **Press Ctrl+Enter.**

   The folder name becomes editable.

3. **Type the newly desired name and press Enter.**

Moving files and folders

Use Files to move and otherwise organize your files. Creating several folders to group your files together and keep things in order is useful as you download and store files on your Chromebook's internal storage. You can move files and folders by following these steps:

1. **Click the App Launcher icon in the bottom-left corner of your screen.**

   The App Launcher appears.

2. **Locate the Files icon and click it.**

   Files opens in a window that is not a Chrome browser.

3. **Click and hold the file that you wish to move, then drag the file to the desired folder. (See Figure 6-4.)**

   When using the touchpad, after clicking and holding the file, use another finger to drag the file to the desired folder.

   Hovering the file over the folder highlights the folder.

4. **Release to drop the file into the target folder.**

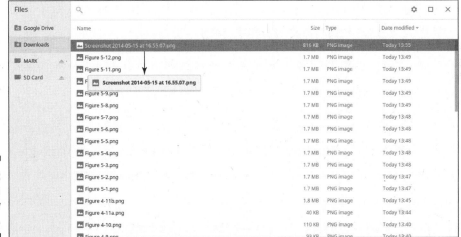

Figure 6-4:
Dragging a
file to a new
location.

If you would like to move multiple files and folders at once, you can do so with the following steps:

1. **From within the Files application window hold the Ctrl key and click the desired files.**

   The files you click are all highlighted.

2. **Click and hold on any part of your selection; without releasing, drag the selection to the desired location.**

   Hovering the files over the destination folder highlights the folder.

3. **Release to drop the files into the target folder.**

If you would like to select an entire collection of files, follow these steps:

1. **Hold down the Shift key, then click with one finger or thumb and move the pointer with another finger to highlight several consecutive files at once.**

2. **Click any part of your selection; without releasing, drag the selection to the desired location.**

   Holding the files over the destination folder will highlight the folder indicating it is okay to release your finger from the touchpad.

3. **Release to drop the files into the target folder.**

Searching for files

If you would like to search for a specific file, you can do so by following these steps:

1. **Click the magnifying glass icon on the far right of your Files toolbar.**

   A cursor appears in the Search bar.

2. **Type in the word or words that are in the name of the file you desire.**

   As you type, Chrome displays all files that fit your search term.

Deleting files and folders

Deleting files and folders can be accomplished with the following steps:

1. **Click the App Launcher icon in the bottom-left corner.**

   The App Launcher appears.

2. **Locate the Files icon and click it.**

   Files opens in a window that is not a Chrome browser.

3. **Select the file that you wish to delete by clicking or tapping the file once.**

4. **Click the trash can icon located in the bottom-right corner of the Files app window.**

   Once you click the trash can icon, your file is gone forever. That's right. There is no trash, no recycle bin, and no opportunity to change your mind. Once you delete an item, it evaporates into the ether.

Make sure you really don't need a file any longer before you delete it!

You can delete multiple files and folders: First, select them by holding down the Ctrl key and clicking the files (or tapping on the files with your touchpad). Then press the trash can icon in the lower-right of the Files app window to delete all the selected files at once. If your files are all in a row, you can select them more easily by pressing the Shift key+click and then moving the cursor to highlight the sequential files.

Adding and Using External Storage

If you have a jump drive, an external hard drive, or an SD card, you can use it without any major problems on a Chromebook. If your jump drive or external hard drive has a USB connection, simply plug it into one of your available USB ports. If your Chromebook has an available SD card slot, simply insert your card. Chromebook automatically detects your storage devices and makes them available to browse within Files, as shown in Figure 6-5.

Eject button

Files				
Google Drive	Name	Size	Type	Date modified ▾
Downloads	▨ MISC	—	Folder	Jul 15, 2012 05:12
MARK	▨ DCIM	—	Folder	Jul 15, 2012 05:12
SD Card				

Figure 6-5: Accessing external storage.

To navigate to your external storage, first select it on the left side of the Files window and then follow the directions outlined in the section "Creating and Navigating folders," earlier in this chapter. Click and drag files or folders to the desired location. If you want to move them to your Chromebook hard drive, just drag them to the Downloads folder that appears under Files on the left side of the Files window. Hover over the Downloads folder long enough to open the folder and then drop the files or folders on the right side of the Files window.

To remove your external storage devices, you must click the Eject button, which is located next to the device name on the left side of the Files window. (Refer to Figure 6-5.) Once you've clicked the Eject button, the device will vanish from your Files window, indicating that it is safe to remove from your Chromebook.

Working with Google Drive

Google Drive (or just Drive) is Google's cloud-based storage solution. *Cloud-based storage* is really just a fancy way of saying "your hard drive on the Internet." Users can create a Drive account at no cost and receive 15GB of storage space. Drive comes with every Chromebook, but you can also install it on your smartphone or on another computer like a Mac or a Windows PC. Anything you put in your Drive folder will then be synced across all of your devices. Pretty awesome, right?!

As a Chromebook owner, Google gives you access to Google Drive at no cost for a limited time. The ASUS C720P, for example, comes with 100GB for free for three years. That's a great value! To take advantage of that discount, you need to first set up your Google Drive account.

Creating a Google Drive account

Account registration is required to use Google Drive. The good news is that Drive access comes with every Google Account. You won't have to actually re-register to gain access to Drive from your Chromebook; however, if you want to take advantage of the free Google Drive upgrade that is made available to Chromebook users, follow these steps:

1. **Click on the App Launcher icon in the bottom-left corner of your screen.**

   The App Launcher opens.

2. **Locate the Chrome web browser icon and click it.**

   The Chrome web browser launches.

3. **In the Omnibox, enter the URL `www.chromebook.com/goodies` and press Enter.**

4. **Scroll down to the Google Drive portion of the website and click the Redeem Offer button.**

   An alert appears, asking you to validate your eligibility.

5. **Click OK to allow Google validate your eligibility.**

Once approved, you will have the bonus amount of Google Drive storage for free! The terms of the Google Drive offer are specific to your particular device. Make sure you understand what the terms are by reading the documentation that came with your Chromebook.

Using Google Drive

There are a few different ways that you can use Google Drive. Google Drive has a web interface that you can access from any Internet-enabled device like a smartphone, tablet, PC, or Mac. To access the Drive web interface from your Chromebook, follow these steps:

1. **Click the App Launcher icon in the lower-left side of your screen.**

   The App Launcher appears.

2. **Locate the Chrome web browser icon and click it.**

   The Chrome web browser launches.

3. **In the Omnibox, enter the web address `http://drive.google.com` and hit Enter.**

   You are directed to your Drive web interface, and you'll already be logged in thanks to Chromebook.

As you can see in Figure 6-6, the Google Drive web interface and Files on your Chromebook are somewhat dissimilar in appearance but similar in function.

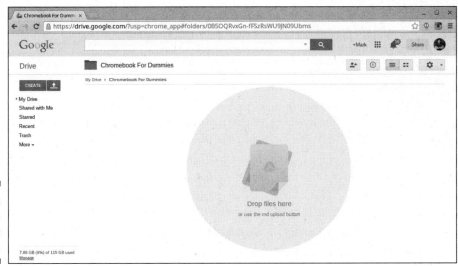

Figure 6-6: The Google Drive web interface.

On the left side of the Drive interface, you have several options:

- ✔ **My Drive:** This is your main Drive folder where you store all of your files.

- ✔ **Shared With Me:** This folder contains all files and folders shared with you by other Drive users. Google Drive is a great tool for collaboration because it simplifies sharing documents and managing versions of documents. When you work on a document, Drive will update the document for everyone that has access to it.

- ✔ **Starred:** You can "star" documents and folders in Drive to indicate them as important. Starred files and folders show up in the Starred folder.

- ✔ **Recent:** Documents that have been created, edited, or otherwise utilized recently appear in this folder. As your Drive gets more and more full, the Recent folder becomes increasingly useful because it allows you to quickly access folders you use frequently thus saving time browsing.

- ✔ **Trash:** Whenever you delete a file (or when a file is deleted automatically), that file is stored in the Trash folder before being annihilated permanently.

The right side of the Google Drive web interface is broken into two key parts. The top portion of the screen contains a Search bar that you can use to search for files by keyword. Next to the Search bar is the Settings area, which contains some buttons for customizing the appearance of your Drive, as well as a widget for accessing your Drive settings.

Directly below the Search bar and Settings area is your main work area. As you add files and folders, they will populate this space.

Uploading files to Google Drive

Transitioning from a Mac or PC to your new Chromebook requires you to migrate your files to Google Drive. Use Google Drive for your file storage so that you can quickly access those files on your Chromebook anywhere you have an Internet connection. There are a few different ways you can upload files to your Google Drive. Follow these steps to upload your files from your Chromebook using the Drive web interface:

1. **Click the App Launcher icon in the bottom-left corner of your screen.**

   The App Launcher opens.

2. **Locate and click the Google Drive icon.**

   A Chrome web browser window opens, displaying your Google Drive.

3. **Click the Upload button on the left of the screen.**

   The Upload button is located next to the Create button.

   A pop-up menu appears, giving you the ability to select files for upload.

   TIP If you are uploading only a few files in the same directory, select file upload. However, if you're uploading a whole directory, select folder upload.

4. **Navigate to your external device and select the files you would like to upload to Drive, and then click Open.**

   Drive begins uploading the files immediately.

Uploading files to Google Drive from a Mac or PC

If you are transitioning to a Chromebook from a Mac or PC, you can migrate your files to Google Drive by following these steps:

1. **Launch your desired web browser on your Mac or PC.**

2. **In the navigation bar, enter the following URL and hit Enter: `https://drive.google.com`.**

   Google Drive's website loads.

3. **Log in using your Google username and password.**

   You will be taken to your Google Drive.

4. **Click the Upload button on the left side of the screen.**

   The Upload button is located next to the Create button.

   A pop-up menu appears, giving you the ability to select files for upload.

5. **Select the files you would like to upload to Drive, and then click Open.**

   Drive begins uploading the files immediately.

Uploading files to Drive from your Mac with the Drive app

If you are transitioning to a Chromebook from a Mac, you can migrate your files to Google Drive by following these steps:

1. **Open your Safari web browser.**

2. **In the navigation bar, enter the following URL and hit Enter:**
   `https://drive.google.com`.

   Google Drive's website loads.

3. **Click Download in the top-right corner of the screen.**

   The Download screen appears.

4. **Click Download Drive.**

   A menu appears.

5. **Click Mac and PC.**

   A window containing Terms of Use loads.

6. **Accept the Terms of Use by clicking Agree and Download.**

   The application downloads.

7. **Click your Download folder, located in your Dock.**

8. **Click the `installgoogledrive.dmg` file.**

   An Install window appears.

9. **In Install window, click and drag the Google Drive logo to the Applications folder.**

10. **Follow the prompts until you are asked to enter your username and password.**

11. **Enter your Google username and password.**

    Google installs and configures your Drive.

12. **Click the Google Drive icon located in the toolbar at the top of your screen.**

    A menu of options opens.

13. **Select Open Google Drive Folder.**

    Your Google Drive directory opens.

14. **Drag and drop your files into your Google Drive directory.**

    Google Drive automatically uploads the files to your Google Drive account.

Uploading files to Drive from your PC with the Drive app

If you are transitioning to a Chromebook from a PC, you can migrate your files to Google Drive by following these steps:

1. **Open your favorite web browser.**

2. **In the navigation bar, enter the following URL and hit Enter:**
   `https://drive.google.com`.

   Google Drive's website loads.

3. **Click Download in the top-right corner of the screen.**

   The Download screen opens.

4. **Click Download Drive.**

   A menu appears.

5. **Click Mac and PC.**

   A window containing Terms of Use loads.

6. **Accept the Terms of Use by clicking Agree and Download.**

   The application downloads and automatically installs on your computer.

7. **Follow the prompts until you are asked to enter your username and password.**

8. **Enter your Google username and password.**

   Google finishes installing and configuring your Drive.

9. **Click the Google Drive icon in the toolbar at the bottom-right of your screen.**

   A menu of options appears.

10. **Select Open Google Drive Folder.**

    Your Google Drive directory opens.

11. **Drag and drop your files into your Google Drive directory.**

    Google Drive automatically uploads the files to your Google Drive account.

Collaborating with Drive

Google Drive makes it easy to share your work with others so that you can collaborate. Drive manages changes and controls versions so that your team is always working on the most current version of the document. Before you can collaborate, you need a document, slide, or spreadsheet in your Drive folder. If you do not have one of these file types in your Drive folder, create a sample Docs file by following these steps:

1. **Click the App Launcher icon in the bottom-left corner of your screen.**

   The App Launcher appears.

2. **Click the Docs icon.**

   Google Docs loads in a Chrome browser window.

3. **Once Docs has finished loading, type a string of text in the document and then close the window.**

   The file now appears in your Drive folder as Untitled Document.

Now you can share your document with others by following these steps:

1. **Click the App Launcher icon in the bottom-left corner of your screen.**

   The App Launcher appears.

2. **Click the Files app icon.**

   Files loads in a window that is not a Chrome web browser.

3. **On the left side of the Files window, click Google Drive.**

4. **Locate the document (in this example, Untitled Document) that you wish to share and click it once to select it.**

   The document is highlighted, indicating it is selected.

5. **Click the Share button at the bottom of the Files window.**

   The Share window opens.

6. **At the bottom of the window in the "Invite people" box, enter the email address for each person you wish to invite for collaboration.**

7. **Click Done.**

   Everyone you invited receives an email with an invitation to collaborate. Upon clicking the link, each collaborator can access your file in his Drive folder. Any changes he makes will be reflected immediately in everyone's Drive folders.

Part II
Harnessing Business Power with Chromebook

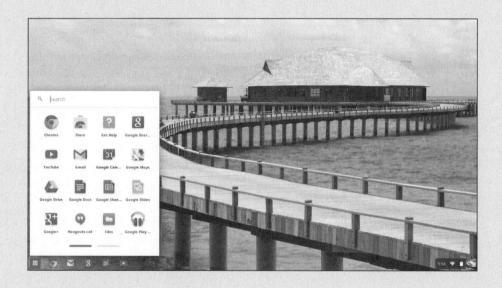

Give your Chrome browser the personal touch that it needs with a design theme. Learn how to find and apply a Chrome theme at www.dummies.com/extras/chromebook.

In this part . . .

✔ Making fantastic documents with Docs, Google's web-based word processor

✔ Accounting and managing data with Google's Sheets

✔ Supercharging your presentation capabilities with Google Presentations

✔ Setting up web-based email with Gmail or using Gmail to manage your non-Gmail email accounts

✔ Keeping your life and the world around you on task with Google Calendar

Chapter 7

Proceeding with Word Processing

. . . .

In This Chapter

▶ Creating new Google Docs documents

▶ Formatting and manipulating text

▶ Saving, exporting, and sharing documents

. . . .

*T*he Chromebook is not just for fun and games. It is a powerful tool for students and business users alike. However, what makes the Chromebook powerful is not the hardware; it's the unrestricted access to — and complete integration with — the Google platform.

One key component to the Google platform is its web-based office tools. The name often used to describe the entire suite of these tools, however informally, is *Google Docs.* However, this can be confusing: *Docs* is also the official name of Google's web-based word processing tool within that suite. For the purposes of this book, then, when I refer to Google Docs, I'll be referring to Google's word processor.

Docs is a powerful word processor that offers an extensive amount of functionality. The goal of this chapter is not to dive into every nook and cranny of the Docs application. Instead, I'll just cover the basics. By the end of this chapter, you should be able to open and create documents; write, format, and otherwise manipulate text; and save, export, and share your documents with anyone across the web for collaboration.

Navigating Google Docs

Docs is Google's answer to Microsoft Word. If you've had any experience working with Word on a Mac or PC, you will find the interface quite similar. If you're using a word processor for the first time, don't worry: Docs is extremely intuitive. To get started, launch Google Docs by clicking the Docs icon in the App Launcher. The Docs application opens in a Chrome browser window and creates a new, untitled document. (See Figure 7-1.)

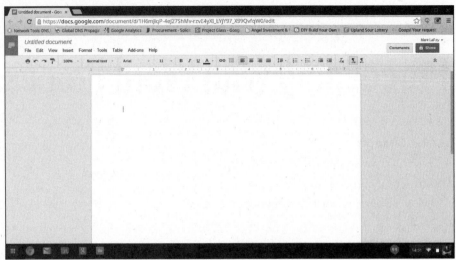

Figure 7-1:
Google
Docs.

Surveying the Docs workspace

The Docs workspace is broken into two main areas: The menu area and the main document area. The menu area, by default, is comprised of the Applications menu and the Edit toolbar, as shown in Figure 7-2.

Applications menu   Edit toolbar

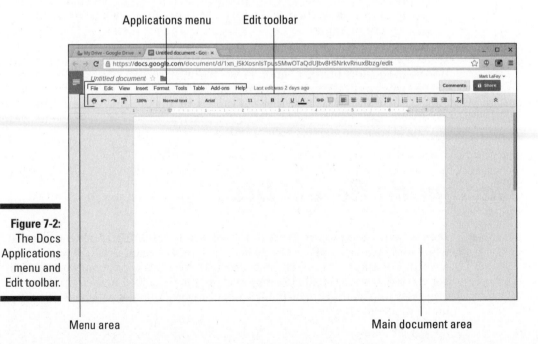

Figure 7-2:
The Docs
Applications
menu and
Edit toolbar.

Menu area   Main document area

The Applications menu contains a standard set of application-specific control options, including

✔ **File:** File-specific options and controls for creating, saving, exporting, printing, and otherwise managing your document on the file level.

✔ **Edit:** Copy, paste, delete, and otherwise move and manipulate text.

✔ **View:** Modify your Docs view by adding and removing toolbars, or change the layout of the main document area.

✔ **Insert:** Add files, images, symbols, headers, footers, and more.

✔ **Format:** Manipulate the appearance of your text.

✔ **Tools:** Spell check, translate text, determine word count, or define specific text.

✔ **Table:** Add tables to your document and manipulate them.

✔ **Add-Ons:** Add software plug-ins to change your Docs experience.

✔ **Help:** Get help with Docs, search for menu options, and more.

The Edit toolbar serves as a shortcut bar to several of the Edit, File, and Format features contained within the Applications menu. With the Edit toolbar, you can quickly

✔ Zoom in or out of your document.

✔ Change the font face of your text.

✔ Change font size.

✔ Bold, italicize, and underline your text.

✔ Add hyperlinks.

✔ Align text.

✔ Add and edit bullets.

✔ Set indentations.

✔ Adjust paragraph styles.

Changing your view

Before you begin to type out your document, you might find it helpful to change your view in Google Docs. One way you can change your view is to hide the Applications menu. Just click View in the Applications menu, and in the View menu that appears, choose Compact Controls. When you do this, the Applications menu will disappear from sight, as shown in Figure 7-3.

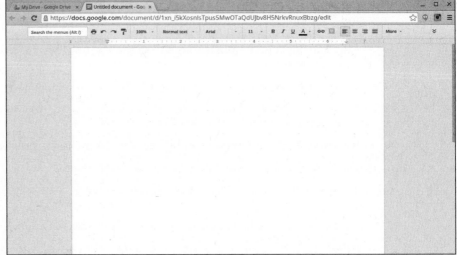

Figure 7-3:
The
Applications
menu is
gone from
sight.

To restore the Applications menu, click the icon that looks like two arrows pointing down located on the right side of the Edit toolbar.

You can also hide the Applications menu by pressing the icon on the far-right of the Edit toolbar that looks like two arrows pointing up, or by using the keyboard shortcut Shift+Ctrl+F to hide and reveal the Applications menu.

If you're the type of person who likes to remove clutter from sight before you begin working, you might find it helpful to hide the ruler, putting Docs into Full-Screen mode. Full-Screen mode hides everything but the main document area. You can turn on Full-Screen mode by following these steps:

1. **Click View in the Applications menu.**

2. **In the View menu that appears, choose Show Ruler.**

   The check mark next to Show Ruler disappears, and the View menu closes.

3. **Again, click View to open the View menu.**

4. **Choose Full Screen.**

   Docs goes into Full-Screen mode.

5. **Exit Full-Screen mode by pressing Esc.**

If you want to eliminate all distractions, put your browser into Full-Screen mode by pressing the Full-Screen shortcut key located four keys to the right of Esc. (See Figure 7-4.)

The Full-Screen shortcut key

Figure 7-4:
The
Full-Screen
shortcut key.

Working with Text

By default, when you open Docs, your cursor will be placed in the main document area. This is helpful if you want to begin typing text immediately because you don't have to click in the workspace to begin. The blinking cursor indicates that you are ready to type. If you do not have a blinking cursor in the main document area, move your pointer anywhere over the main document area and click.

Begin typing a couple sentences or a paragraph of text. As you type, the cursor will move to the right, leaving characters to the left of the cursor. Google Docs is by default *left-justified,* meaning all text is aligned to the left. As you approach the end of a line, the cursor automatically moves to the next line. If you are typing a word that does not fit on the line, Docs will automatically move the word to the next line.

When you are finished typing a paragraph, press Enter to go to a new line. If you are following any sort of paragraph style, you may need to hit Enter twice to space your paragraphs out. This is because Docs does not default to any one particular writing style.

Moving around your document

As you write your document, you may find that there are edits that you want to make to your text. You can move around your document in a number of different ways. To start, take a look at the arrow keys on your keyboard. (See Figure 7-5.)

Figure 7-5:
Arrow keys.

Arrow keys

You can move your cursor by using the arrow keys to navigate to different characters in your text. Press and hold the left arrow key to take you to the left side of your line. Once you've hit the beginning of the line on the left side, keep pressing the left arrow key, and you will notice your cursor will go to the right side of the line above. Conversely, pressing the right arrow key takes you to the right side of the line. As you approach the right end of the line, keep pressing the arrow key to be taken to the left beginning of the next line down. You can also move around the document by using the up and down arrow keys to quickly move to lines above or below the current line, respectively.

You can also navigate your document by using your touchpad or mouse to move the cursor directly to the desired location. Click once to move the cursor and then begin editing using your keyboard. In the event you have several pages of text, you can quickly navigate to various pages by following these steps:

1. **Place two fingers on your touchpad and swipe up or down.**

   If your touch pad is configured to traditionally scroll, swiping up scrolls the document up so you can see previous pages. Swiping down scrolls you down in the document to later pages.

   If your touchpad is configured to Australian scroll, swiping up scrolls your document down to later pages. Conversely, swiping down scrolls your document up to earlier pages.

   Using your touchpad with a two-finger swipe scrolls you to the page that contains the text you would like to edit.

2. **Using one finger on your touchpad, relocate the pointer to the location of the word or words you would like to edit.**

3. **Click your touchpad.**

   Your cursor appears at the location of your pointer.

If you wish to delete text, move your cursor to the right of the text so that you can easily remove it by pressing the Backspace key. If you wish to insert text, position your cursor appropriately and begin typing.

You can also use a feature called *Find and Replace* to find a specific piece of text within your document. To find text using the Find and Replace feature, follow these steps:

1. **Click Edit in the Applications menu.**

2. **In the Edit menu that appears, choose Find and Replace.**

   A pop-up window appears containing multiple inputs:

   - *Find:* Where you enter the text you wish to find.

   - *Replace:* If you wish to replace the text for which you are searching, simply enter the replacement text in this text box.

   - *Match Case:* Select this check box if you wish to search for text that has the same capitalization as you typed in the Find box.

3. **Enter the text you wish to locate in the Find text box.**

   As you type text in the Find text box, Docs highlights words in your document that match your search entry.

Google Docs treats blank spaces as characters. In the event you're looking for a particular word that's not immediately followed by punctuation, place a space after your search term to reduce the number of unneeded results.

4. **Sort through search results by clicking the Next or Previous buttons located in the bottom-right of the Find and Replace pop-up window.**

   As you navigate to the matched words in your document, Docs changes the color of the highlighted word to indicate where you are in the document.

5. **When you successfully locate the word or words in your document, close the Find and Replace pop-up window by clicking the X in the top-right corner.**

   The pop-up window disappears, leaving your desired word highlighted and ready to be deleted or otherwise edited.

Copying and pasting text

As you create documents, you can avoid typing out repetitive text by using the Copy and Paste functions. Copying and pasting can be done in several ways — on the keyboard, with the touchpad, and so on.

Larger documents that contain several thousand words over numerous pages may be too large to effectively navigate with just your keyboard. Your touchpad will come in handy with these documents because you can quickly locate, select, copy, and paste text.

To copy and paste text, follow these instructions:

1. **Using your touchpad, move your cursor to the text you want to copy.**

   You may need to scroll to a different page. To do this you can

   - Place two fingers on your touchpad and swipe up or down to scroll to a different page within your document.

   - Place one finger on the scroll bar and move your pointer to the vertical scroll bar located on the right side of the screen. Click anywhere on the bar to quickly scroll to a different page. Or, on the bar itself, click and drag your cursor up or down to scroll to different pages.

2. **Click and drag your cursor over the section of text you wish to copy. When all the text is selected, release the click.**

   A highlighter follows your pointer as you drag it across the text.

   You can select text using the keyboard by using the arrow keys while holding the Shift key. Go character by character by using the left or right arrow keys. Select entire lines by using the up and right arrow keys at the same time.

3. **In the Applications menu, click Edit⇨Copy.**

   Alternatively, press and hold the Alt key and click on the highlighted text. A pop up menu appears in which you can choose Copy, as shown in Figure 7-6.

   The selected text is copied to your *Clipboard.*

Figure 7-6:
Open a
pop-up
menu by
Alt-clicking.

4. **Using your touchpad, scroll to the location where you would like to place your text and click to place your cursor.**

5. **Open the Edit menu again and select Paste.**

   The copied text will be pasted into the document at the location of your cursor.

   You can paste the contents of your Clipboard as many times as you like. If you need to place the text in numerous locations, simply move to each location and paste the text by following Steps 4 and 5 in the preceding list.

Moving text by cutting and pasting

When you want to replicate text, copying and pasting is the mode of operation you should use. When you want to move text but *not* replicate it, however, instead of using Copy, you should use Cut. To move text in your document using the cut-and-paste method, follow these steps:

1. **Using your touchpad, click and drag your pointer across the text you wish to copy, then release your click.**

   The selected text is highlighted.

2. **Alt-click the highlighted text.**

   A pop-up menu appears, revealing several options.

3. **Select Cut from the menu.**

   The selected text disappears from the screen. Don't worry, it's sitting on your Clipboard waiting to be pasted.

   When you cut text from your document, the text vanishes, perhaps giving you the impression that you have deleted it. You haven't deleted the text, though — it's just been moved to your Clipboard. However, that text *will* be deleted if you cut or copy additional text prior to pasting the already-cut text.

4. **Using the touchpad, navigate to the location where you wish to paste your text.**

5. **Alt-click in the location where you wish to paste your text. In the pop-up menu, select Paste.**

   The copied text is pasted in the location of your cursor.

You can paste text as many times as you like. However, when you copy or cut a new selection of text, the previously cut text will be replaced with the newly cut text.

Formatting Text

Before you can start formatting text, you need to become familiar with a few terms that describe the different characteristics of your text:

- **Font:** Also known in some circles as *font face,* the *font* is the style of type-face. By default, the name of the font used in Docs is Arial.

- **Font size:** The size of your text is often used to indicate hierarchical structure or writing format or style.

- **Font weight:** *Weight* refers to the thickness or boldness of the letters in a font. A *heavy* font weight means the text is bold or very thick and dark.

- **Font slope:** *Slope* indicates the direction and the amount in which your text leans. For example, *italicizing* letters means adding a left-to-right slope.

The formatting of your text is important not only for style but for also adequately communicating your message. Font weight, slope, and size are all used to communicate meaning, emphasis, and more. Font face can also be useful for establishing a personality, tone, and brand. Docs gives you the ability to modify all of these characteristics of your text so that your documents look great and say what you want them to say!

Changing fonts

With Docs, you can change the font of any text contained in your document. Creatively speaking, having many different fonts from different font families in a single document isn't recommended, but Docs does make it possible to change every letter in your document to a different font. Google Docs comes pre-loaded with eight fonts:

- ✔ Arial
- ✔ Comic Sans MS
- ✔ Courier New
- ✔ Georgia
- ✔ Impact
- ✔ Times New Roman
- ✔ Trebuchet MS
- ✔ Verdana

If you would like to change your font, you can do so by following these steps:

1. **Using your touchpad, click and drag your cursor across the text you wish to select.**

   Docs highlights the selected text.

2. **Using the Edit toolbar, click to open the Font menu.**

   The Font menu is located directly to the left of the Font Size menu.

   In the Edit toolbar, the Font menu appears with the name of the font for the selected body of text. By default, all text uses the Arial font.

3. **Select one of the fonts listed.**

   Your highlighted text is changed to the selected font.

If no text was highlighted when you changed the font, the new font will apply only to new text. Any text typed from the current location of the cursor will appear with the font face of the selected font.

Adding fonts

The Google Docs default list of fonts is a brief list of eight. Other word processors like Microsoft Word, Adobe Acrobat, or Apple iWork's Pages have extensive lists of fonts by default. Google provides users with an initial list of the most globally popular fonts to keep things simple at first. You can, however, add additional fonts to your Docs. Follow these steps:

1. **Click the Font menu in the Edit toolbar.**

2. **Select More Fonts to add additional fonts.**

   The Font pop-up window, shown in Figure 7-7, gives you a robust list of new fonts from which to choose. Scroll down through the list to reveal more fonts.

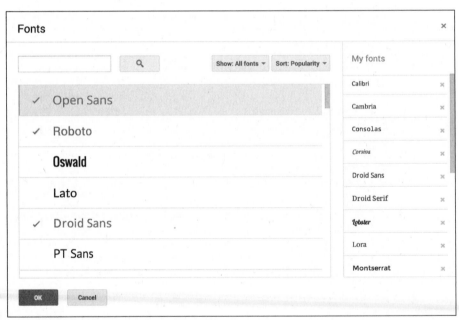

Figure 7-7:
Adding new fonts to Docs.

3. **Select the desired fonts by clicking each.**

   Each selected font is highlighted in blue and given a check mark.

4. **Click OK to finish adding the fonts to your Font menu and exit.**

   When you are ready to change the font of your text, you will be able to choose one of your newly selected fonts from the Font menu.

Removing fonts from the Font menu

The more fonts you add, the more fonts you will have to rifle through when trying to make a decision on changing the font. There will come a time when you will want to remove fonts that you added to your list. To remove fonts from Docs, take these steps:

1. **Open the Font menu in the Edit toolbar.**

2. **Select More Fonts.**

   The Font pop-up window appears. On the left of the window, a list of new fonts appears; on the right, a list of fonts currently in use by your Docs account.

3. **Scroll through the list of fonts currently in use and locate the font or fonts you wish to remove. Then, to remove the font, click the X located to the right of that font's name.**

   The font vanishes from the list of accessible fonts.

4. **Click OK.**

Styling fonts

It is easy to confuse the style of your font with the face of your font. Font face is simply the font itself. Think of a font like a designer pair of jeans. A fashion designer made the jeans to look a particular way. However, no matter how the jeans were made, you can still style the jeans by cuffing the bottoms, cutting the jeans off at the knees, and so on.

You can accentuate a font by applying various styles to the font itself. Those styles include

- **Size:** Makes your text bigger or smaller, depending on where it fits in a hierarchy.

- **Bold:** When you make text bold, the text becomes visibly thicker. This is why a bold font is said to have a *heavy font weight*.

- **Italics:** A slanted font is often referred to as italic.

- **Underline:** Places a line under your text (for example, to indicate importance).

- **Strikethrough:** Places a line through the middle of your text. Useful in communicating a change in your text or simply to illustrate a point.

- **Color:** Track changes, distinguish individual users in collaboration, or simply add style to your text by changing the color of the text itself or by adding a permanent color highlight.

Text size

Changing the size of your text can be done by following these steps:

1. **Using your touchpad, click and drag your cursor across the text you wish to change. When you've selected everything, release your click.**

   The selected text is highlighted.

2. **Open the Font Size menu in the Edit toolbar.**

   It's the number found between the Font menu and the Bold button. (See Figure 7-8.)

   The size of a font is called the *point size*. The *point* is the smallest whole unit of measure in typography. In the industrial era, *typesetting* was the process of manually setting letters into a printing press to print whole sheets of text. The original point varied in actual size between 0.18mm and 0.4mm. In the modern era, the point (abbreviated *pt.*) size doesn't necessarily correspond directly to an actual size on the printed page, rather it is relative.

3. **Select the desired font size.**

   Your selected text becomes the chosen size.

11 ▾	B
8	
9	
10	
11	
12	
14	
18	
24	
30	
36	
48	
60	
72	
96	

Figure 7-8:
Different
text sizes.

Quickly make selected text bold by clicking the Bold button (which displays a capital B) located in the middle of the Edit toolbar. You can also bold your selected text by pressing Ctrl+B.

Applying bold, italics, underline, or strikethrough

To style a specific selection of text with bold, italics, underline, or strike-through, follow these steps:

1. **Using your touchpad, click and drag your cursor across the text you wish to change. When you've selected everything, release your click.**

   The selected text is highlighted.

2. **Open the Format menu in the edit toolbar.**

3. **Select Bold, Italic, Underline, or Strikethrough.**

   Your selected text changes accordingly.

As a quick alternative, you can style selected text just by clicking the appro-priate button in the middle of the Edit toolbar — click the B button for bold, the I button for italic, or the U button for underline. (No button exists for strikethrough on the standard Edit toolbar.) Similarly, you can apply styles by pressing Ctrl+B (bold), Ctrl+I (italic), Ctrl+U (underline), or Alt+Shift+5 (strikethrough).

Coloring your text

Docs gives you the ability to change the color of your text or the color of the background behind your text. Changing the color of your text can be done with these steps:

1. **Using your touchpad, click and drag your cursor across the text you wish to change. When you've selected everything, release your click.**

   The selected text is highlighted.

2. **Open the Text Color menu in the Edit toolbar.**

   It's the A found to the right of the Underline button.

3. **Click the Text button in the Text Color menu.**

   If the Text Color menu was not already active, it appears now with sev-eral options. Otherwise, the list doesn't change.

4. **Select your desired color.**

   Your selected text now appears in the selected color.

If you would like to apply a highlight to your text, you can do so by following these steps:

1. **Using your touchpad, click and drag your cursor across the text you wish to change. When you've selected everything, release your click.**

   The selected text is highlighted.

2. Open the Text Color menu in the Edit toolbar.

It's the A found to the right of the Underline button.

3. Click the Highlight button.

The Highlight Color menu appears with several options.

4. Select your desired color.

Your selected text now appears highlighted in the selected color.

Aligning your text

The *alignment* of your text determines the orientation of the edges of lines, paragraphs, or pages in your document. Google Docs gives you several options for changing the alignment, including:

- ✔ **Left alignment:** This is the default alignment for new documents in Docs. The text is flush with the left margin of your document.

- ✔ **Right alignment:** The text is flush with the right margin of your document.

- ✔ **Center:** The middle of your document is the half-way point between the left and the right margins. With centered alignment, all text is centered on this midway point, regardless of the relation between document margins and document dimensions.

- ✔ **Justified:** *Justifying* your text aligns the text evenly along both the left and right margins. To ensure that the left and right side of your text are flush with the left and right margins, Docs introduces additional spaces between each word.

You can change the alignment of text in your document by the line, paragraph, or page by following these steps:

1. Using your touchpad, select the text you wish to realign.

The selected text is highlighted.

2. Find the alignment buttons in the Edit toolbar.

They're located slightly to the right of middle. They appear in the following order:

- • Left Align
- • Center
- • Right Align
- • Justified

3. Click the desired alignment button.

The selected text is realigned.

Clearing formatting

There comes a time when you need to start with a blank slate. You might be given a document that requires editing or maybe you got a little happy with the formatting tools that Google Docs provides you. Regardless of the reason, Docs makes it incredibly easy to wipe out all formatting in a section of text or a complete document. To clear your formatting follow these steps:

1. **Select the formatted text.**

   The selected text is highlighted.

   To clear the formatting of an entire document, press Ctrl+A instead of selecting a section of text. Pressing Ctrl+A selects the entire document.

2. **Open the Format menu in the Applications menu.**

3. **Select Clear Formatting.**

   The selected text is reset to defaults: left-aligned text with all style elements — including color, underline, strikethrough, italics, bold, and so on — removed.

Saving Documents

One of the many reasons to use Google Docs is the symbiosis between Docs and Google Drive. *Drive* is Google's cloud-based storage solution that allows you to safely store your files and access them from any device with an Internet connection. Every document you create with Docs is saved to your Drive folder so that you can access it at home, on the road, at work, or anywhere else you might need it.

When you create a new document with Docs, Docs automatically saves the document to your Drive. As you edit your document, Docs continuously saves each change to Drive so that you have almost no risk of losing your information. There is actually no manual Save feature in Docs for this very reason: You will forget to save your document, but Docs won't.

Rest assured, your work is safe with Google.

Naming your document

When you open a new document with Docs, the default name for the document will be Untitled Document. However, you won't want to leave your document named this way. Drive doesn't have a problem with storing multiple files with the same name, but it may easily confuse you. It's best, then, if you immediately give your document a more intuitive name. To name your document, follow these steps:

1. **Open a new document.**

   The easiest way to do this is simply to launch Docs from the App Launcher.

   A Chrome web browser opens and loads Docs — and a new document — automatically.

   Once Docs is open, the name of your new document, Untitled Document, appears in the top-left corner, as shown in in Figure 7-9.

2. **Click the name Untitled Document.**

   The Rename Document pop-up window appears in the middle of your screen. The name of the document appears highlighted in a form field.

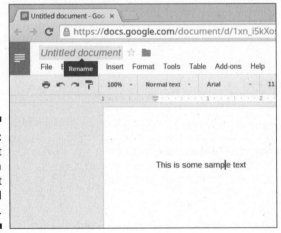

Figure 7-9: The default name for a document is Untitled Document.

3. **Type the new name for your document in the Name field and press OK.**

   The pop-up window disappears, and the name Untitled Document in the top-left corner has been replaced with the new name you entered.

Your document now appears in Google Drive with the new name. As you continue to make edits to the document, those changes will be updated and saved in real-time.

Exporting documents

Unfortunately for you, the entire world does not use the Google platform exclusively. Therefore, you may need to export your documents to formats that others may be comfortable with. Docs presently allows you to export documents to a few standard formats, including

- ✔ Microsoft Word (`.docx`)
- ✔ OpenDocument (`.odt`)
- ✔ Rich Text (`.rtf`)
- ✔ PDF (`.pdf`)
- ✔ Plain Text (`.txt`)
- ✔ Web Page (`.html`, Zipped)

Exporting documents to different file types may change the formatting within your document. Plain Text, for instance, is as the name says: *plain text.* No formatting is carried through. Before sending your exported documents, review them to ensure everything is as it should be!

Exporting your documents can be done by following these steps:

1. **Open the File menu in the Docs Applications menu.**

2. **In the File menu, hover your cursor over Download As.**

   A submenu appears, revealing the document types available for export. (See Figure 7-10.)

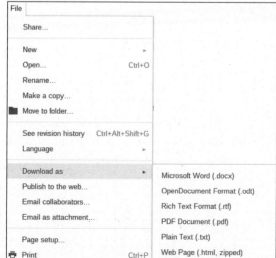

Figure 7-10: The Download As submenu.

3. **Select the desired file type.**

   Your Docs file is exported in the desired file type and is automatically downloaded to your Chromebook.

4. **To view the downloaded file on your computer, click the arrow next to the filename in the bottom of your browser window.**

   A menu revealing several options appears.

5. **Select Show in Folder.**

   Files launches, showing you the file in your folder.

Collaborating in Docs

By default, Docs and Drive make your files inaccessible to anyone other than yourself. You can, however, change the visibility settings on your files and invite specific people, or even the entire world, to comment, view, or edit your documents! To share a document with specific people, follow these steps:

1. **Click the blue Share button in the top-right corner of your Docs window.**

   A pop-up window appears, giving you several options for sharing your document. (See Figure 7-11.)

Sharing settings

Link to share (only accessible by collaborators)

https://docs.google.com/document/d/1xn_i5kXosnlsTpus5MwOTaQdUJbv8H5NrkvRnu

Share link via:

Who has access

🔒 Private - Only you can access   Change...

👤 Mark LaFay (you) marklalay@gmail.com   Is owner

Invite people:

Enter names or email addresses...

Editors will be allowed to add people and change the permissions. [Change]

Done

Figure 7-11:
The Share pop-up window.

2. **In the Invite People text box at the bottom of the pop-up window, enter the email address of each person with whom you wish to share your file.**

   Be sure to separate the addresses with commas.

   If the email address is in your address book, Docs will try to auto-fill their information.

3. **To set the permissions of the collaborators, first click the link directly to the right of the name of the invitee.**

   A drop-down menu with three options appears:

   - *Can Edit:* Allows users to edit the document and change permissions.

   - *Can Comment:* Allows users to comment on the document but not to change any content or security settings.

   - *Can View:* Allows users only to view the document.

4. **Select from the menu the permission setting you want to apply to this collaborator.**

5. **Check the "notify people via email" box directly above the *send* button to notify the specified collaborators, by email, that you have shared a document with them.**

6. **Click Send.**

   Your document is made available to the collaborators immediately.

The collaborators who are invited to view, edit, or comment on your document will have to log into Google Docs using the email address with which you shared the document. If a collaborator doesn't have a Google Account under the email address that you used, you have to invite her by using her Google Account address. She also has the option to create a Google Account using the email address to which you sent the invitation.

Tracking Revisions

Keeping track of revisions is very important when creating documents with multiple collaborators. Luckily, Google Docs handles version control masterfully. The Revision History tool, however, is not intended to be used as a Track Changes tool. As you and your collaborators make changes to your documents, Docs will time-and-date stamp those changes so that you can view previous versions of your document and even revert to an earlier version if you need to.

Revision tracking is a default feature of Docs,. To view your revision history, follow these steps:

1. **Open the File menu in the Docs Applications menu.**

2. **Select See Revision History.**

   A Revision History box appears in the right portion of your screen. (See Figure 7-12.) The box contains the various versions of your document in order from most recent to oldest.

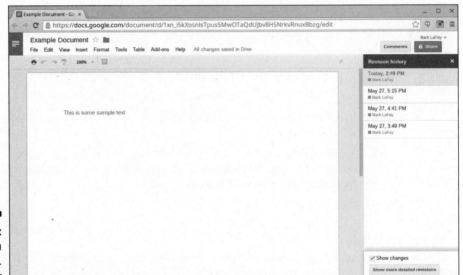

Figure 7-12: The Revision History box.

3. **Click a revision date in the Revision History box.**

   A preview of the revision you chose appears in the main document area. Changes that occurred between versions appear in green.

4. **To change versions, click Restore This Revision.**

   The restored version becomes the current version and the previous version of the application is saved in the Revision History so you can revert back to it if needed.

Using Docs Offline

Google Docs is a web-based word processor, which means that you must have an Internet connection to access all of its features. However, an offline version of Docs is available in the event you find yourself without a connection to the Internet.

To use Google Docs offline, follow these steps:

1. **To use Google Docs offline, you must first enable Google Drive for offline use. To ensure that Google Drive is properly enabled, open the App Launcher and click the Google Drive icon.**

   A Chrome web browser appears and takes you to your Drive.

2. **On the right side of the screen, click the settings icon (it looks like a gear).**

   A menu will appear revealing several options.

3. **Click Settings.**

   A pop-up window will appear giving several general settings options.

4. **Locate the check box to sync your work for offline use and check it.**

5. **Click *Done*.**

   The pop up window will disappear indicating that the changes have been made. Your Docs files will now be synced and available for offline editing.

6. **You can test whether you have properly enabled offline access by turning off your Wi-Fi. To do this, open the settings panel in the bottom-right of your screen and select WIFI.**

   The WIFI menu appears.

7. **At the bottom of the WIFI menu, click the WIFI indicator to turn off your Wi-Fi.**

8. **With your Wi-Fi turned off, switch back to Google Drive, locate your synced documents and click to open one.**

   If your document opens and you are able to edit it, you know you have successfully engaged offline use and synced your documents.

While offline, you won't be able to access some of the features available to Docs users that are connected to the Internet. You will, however, be able to create documents and save them. Later, when you connect to the Internet, Drive uploads the saved documents and enables all Internet-only features.

Chapter 8

Summarizing Sheets

• •

In This Chapter

▶ Creating new spreadsheets

▶ Entering and formatting numbers

▶ Use Sheets to calculate

▶ Save, export, and collaborate with Sheets

• •

*B*efore the era of computers, accounting and other business finance–related mathematical computations were performed with good old paper and pencil. Accounting worksheets provided on-sheet organization with rows and columns that intersected to create *cells*. Each cell would then contain some sort of value, and calculations could then be performed and written into corresponding cells in different rows and columns.

When personal computers came on the scene, they revolutionized the way that businesses and finance professionals conducted business. Digital spreadsheets made it easier to enter data and automatically calculate results. And, of course, editing without needing a pencil eraser or whiteout was a miracle!

Spreadsheets have evolved quite substantially over the years, and while Microsoft Excel and Apple's Numbers have quite a bit of market share, Google Sheets is fast on the rise and has some extremely powerful features just by nature of being a part of the Google ecosystem. In this chapter, you take an introductory look at Sheets: You can explore the Sheets interface and learn how to enter data into a cell, edit data, and perform basic calculations. Collaboration is also important with Sheets, so you learn how to save and export your data and share it with others for collaboration; and in the event you don't have an Internet connection, you will be able to use Sheets offline.

Navigating Google Sheets

Sheets is Google's answer to Excel and Numbers. If you've had any experience working with Excel or Numbers, you'll find the Sheets interface quite similar. If this is your first time using a spreadsheet tool, you'll find that Sheets is extremely intuitive.

To get started, launch Google Sheets by opening the App Launcher and clicking the Sheets icon. The Sheets application will open in a Chrome browser window and create a new, untitled spreadsheet. (See Figure 8-1.)

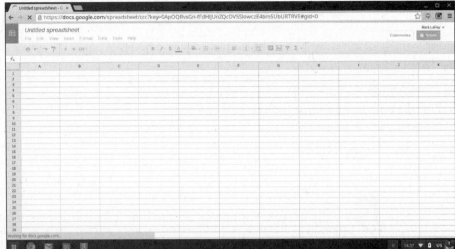

Figure 8-1:
Google
Sheets.

Surveying the Sheets menu area

The Sheets work area is broken into a couple key areas: The menu area and the main document area, which is the actual spreadsheet. The menu area, by default, is comprised of the Applications menu, Edit toolbar, and Formula bar, as shown in Figure 8-2.

The Applications menu is located at the top of the menu area and is home to several application-specific controls and options, including

- ✔ **File:** File-specific options and controls for creating, saving, exporting, printing, and otherwise managing your document on the file level.
- ✔ **Edit:** Copy, paste, delete, and otherwise move and manipulate data.
- ✔ **View:** Modify your view by adding and removing toolbars or change the layout of the spreadsheet by adding or removing gridlines, freezing columns and rows, and more.
- ✔ **Insert:** Insert rows, columns, cells, worksheets, charts, images, and more.
- ✔ **Format:** Manipulate the appearance of your data, auto-format number data, align cell contents, and otherwise edit the appearance of your cells.
- ✔ **Data:** Sort and filter your data.

✔ **Tools:** Spell check, protect the sheet to ensure data isn't overwritten, or create a form to gather data.

✔ **Help:** Get help with Sheets, search for menu options, and more.

Menu area   Application menu   Edit toolbar

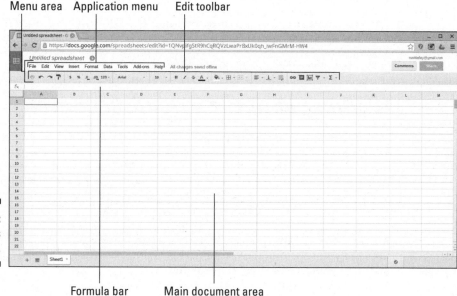

Figure 8-2:
The Sheets
menu area.

Formula bar   Main document area

The Edit toolbar, located directly under the Applications menu, contains several shortcuts to features contained in the Applications menu. The Edit toolbar makes the performance of routine tasks faster and easier. With the Edit toolbar, you can quickly perform these tasks:

✔ Print, undo, or redo edits.

✔ Format number data as currency or percentages.

✔ Change fonts.

✔ Change font size.

✔ Bold, italicize, or strikethrough your text.

✔ Color your text.

✔ Fill a cell or cells with color.

✔ Add, edit, or remove cell borders.

✔ Merge multiple cells together.

✔ Edit the horizontal alignment of the contents of a cell.

✔ Edit the vertical alignment of the contents of a cell.

✔ Allow text in a cell to wrap to multiple lines.

✔ Add comments or charts, and perform common calculations.

The Formula bar is located directly under the Edit toolbar. You will use the Formula bar to insert data into cells and write formulas for performing calculations.

Working with the spreadsheet area

The spreadsheet area of your Sheets workspace is located directly under the Formula bar. The spreadsheet is made up of a grid of columns and rows. The top of the columns is the column header, and the left side of the rows is the row header. Columns are referenced by letters, and rows are referenced by numbers. There are permanent scroll bars located at the right and bottom of your spreadsheet so that you can quickly scroll through your sheet.

At the bottom of the spreadsheet area, a tab labeled Sheet1 appears. The name of your current sheet is Sheet1. You can, however, have multiple spreadsheets in one Sheets document.

Row numbers and column letters are imperative for precisely communicating locations within a spreadsheet. A cell's coordinates are always communicated first with the column letter and then with the row number. For example, A8.

Coordinating a range of cells in a single row or column can be done by specifying the starting cell coordinates and the ending cell coordinates separated by a colon. For example

```
A8:A24
```

This example references a range of cells starting in the A column at row 8 and ending at row 24. Figure 8-3 illustrates what this range would look like.

If you would like to reference a *matrix* of cells (meaning a range of cells, spanning multiple rows and columns), you can do so by specifying the coordinates of the top-left corner and the bottom-right corner of the matrix separated by a colon. For example

```
A8:C24
```

Figure 8-4 illustrates what this range looks like in the spreadsheet when selected.

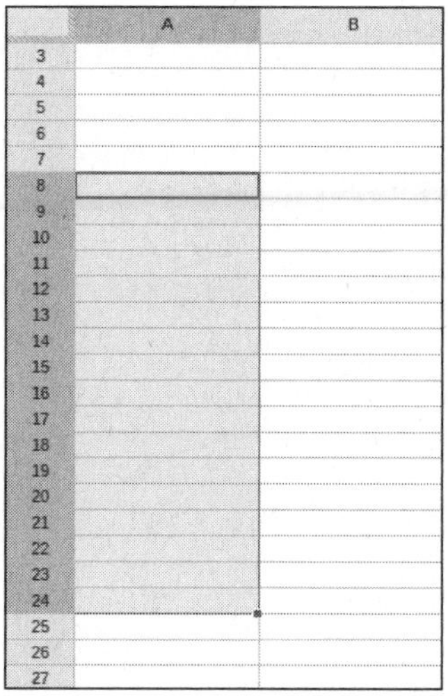

Figure 8-3:
Cells A8
through A24.

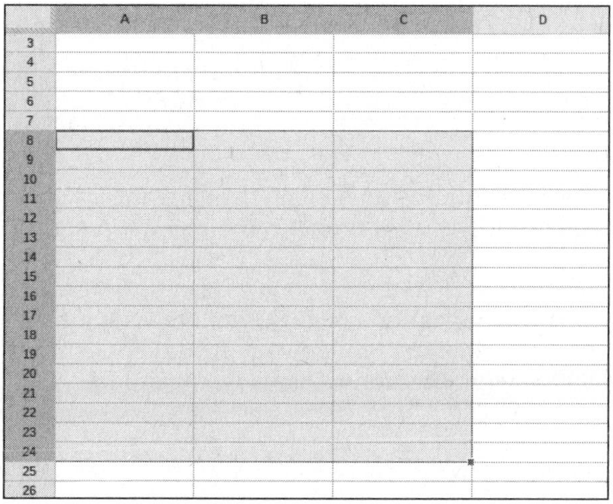

Figure 8-4:
Cells A8
through C24.

Customizing your view

Before you dive into your first spreadsheet, you might find it helpful to
change your view in Google Sheets. You can compact the Applications
menu by opening View in the Applications menu and choosing Compact
Controls. When you compact the Applications menu, the applications menu
is crunched down to create more space. (See Figure 8-5.)

To restore the full Applications menu, just open the View menu and choose Compact Controls again.

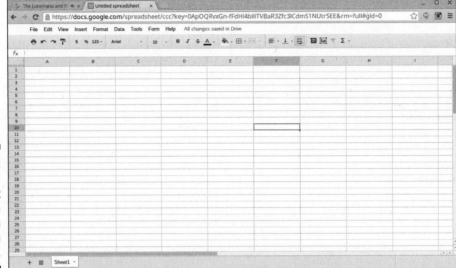

Figure 8-5:
A spread-sheet with the Applications menu compacted.

You can also compact the Applications menu by using the keyboard shortcut Shift+Ctrl+F. You can use this shortcut to either hide or reveal the Applications menu.

If you prefer to hide the Applications menu completely, along with the Edit toolbar, you can do so by opening the View menu and choosing Full Screen. When you select Full Screen, the Applications menu and Edit toolbar vanish. (See Figure 8-6.)

To exit Full Screen mode, simply press the Esc key.

If you prefer to have nothing but cells on your screen, you can remove the Applications menu, Edit toolbar, and Formula bar by following these steps:

1. **Click View in the Applications menu.**

2. **In the resulting View menu, choose Formula Bar.**

   The Formula bar vanishes.

3. **Open the View menu again and choose Full Screen.**

   The Applications menu and Edit toolbar disappear, as shown in Figure 8-7.

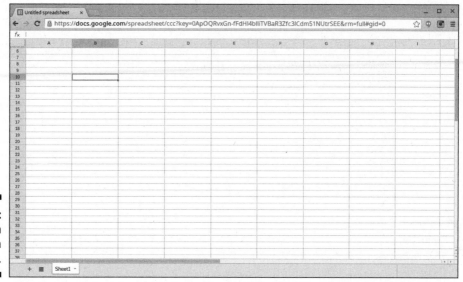

Figure 8-6:
Sheets in
Full Screen
mode.

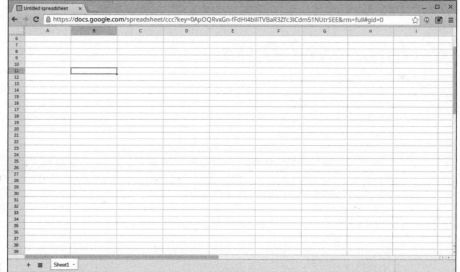

Figure 8-7:
Full Screen
mode with
no Formula
bar.

In your spreadsheet, each cell is outlined with very thin grey lines called *gridlines*. Gridlines are not borders; they are imaginary boundaries, for reference only, and they won't appear when you print. If you would like to work without gridlines, you can hide them by opening the View menu and clicking Gridlines. (Figure 8-8 shows a spreadsheet without gridlines.)

To turn gridlines back on, just open the View menu and choose Gridlines.

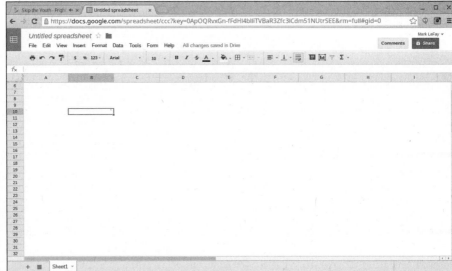

Figure 8-8:
A Sheets
spreadsheet
without
gridlines.

Working with Data

Spreadsheet software was developed to give you the ability to manipulate numeric data with great ease. That doesn't mean, however, that the only data that can go into a spreadsheet is numeric data. You can type text and characters, or even add pictures and graphs.

Open a new Google Sheets spreadsheet. Cell A1 is highlighted with a blue border. This blue border indicates the active cell in your spreadsheet. To enter data into a cell, make sure the blue border is around that cell and begin typing. As you type, your entries appear in the highlighted cell, as well as in the Formula bar, as shown in Figure 8-9.

When you finish typing, press Enter to move the highlight bar to the next cell down. If the text you entered is larger than the cell, your text will hang over into adjacent cells until you resize the column width or row height. (I get into resizing cells in the section "Resizing columns and rows," later in this chapter.)

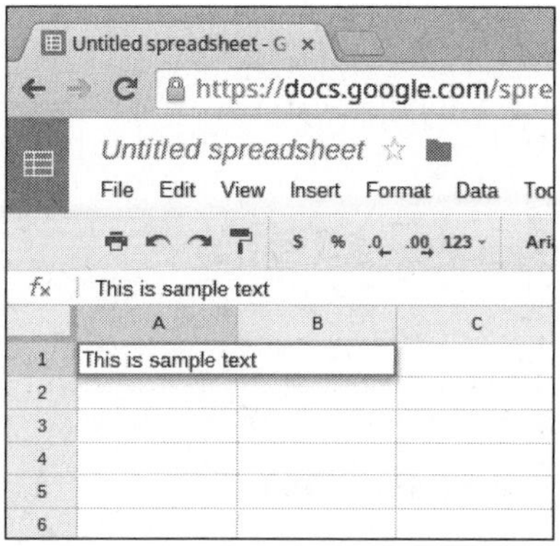

Figure 8-9:
Data entered appears in the selected cell and the Formula bar.

Moving around a spreadsheet

As you enter more and more data into your spreadsheet, you may find a need to hop around to different cells to update your entries. You can do this a number of ways with Sheets. To start, take a look at the arrow keys on your keyboard.

Google Sheets can contain as many as 400,000 cells with a maximum of 256 columns. You don't have to create the cells to be able to use them, you can actually simply navigate to them by using your directional arrows. Move one cell up, down, left, or right by pressing the corresponding directional arrow key once. If you want to quickly move several cells in any particular direction, press and hold the corresponding directional arrow.

You can also navigate your spreadsheet by using your touchpad or mouse. Click once on the desired cell to move the cursor and then begin typing using your keyboard. In the event you need to get to a section of your sheet that is several rows down or columns over, you can quickly navigate there by following these steps:

1. **Place two fingers on your touchpad and move them in the direction you desire.**

   If your touchpad is configured to traditionally scroll, swiping up scrolls up, and swiping down scrolls down. On the other hand, if your touchpad is configured to Australian scroll, swiping up scrolls down, and swiping down scrolls up. Using your touchpad with a two-finger swipe scrolls you to the general area of the cell or cells that you want to edit.

2. **Using one finger on your touchpad, move the pointer to the cell you desire.**

3. **Click your touchpad.**

   The desired cell is now active.

If you wish to overwrite the cell contents, simply start writing. If you wish to delete the cell contents, press Backspace. If you wish to insert additional data in a cell that already contains data, follow these steps:

1. **Click the desired cell once.**

   The selected cell is highlighted with a blue border.

2. **Click the Formula bar.**

   A blinking cursor appears in the Formula bar, indicating you can add, edit, or delete text using your keyboard.

3. **Add or edit text as you like, then press Enter.**

You can also use a feature called Find and Replace to find a specific piece of data within your spreadsheet. To find data using the Find and Replace feature, follow these steps:

1. **Open the Edit menu and choose Find and Replace.**

   A pop-up window appears. In this window, you can specify what you want to search for and what you want the search string replaced with, among other options.

2. **Fill in the information you want to use for your search.**

   You can specify any of the following options:

   - *Find:* The text or data you wish to find.

   - *Replace:* If you wish to replace the data for which you're searching, simply enter new data here.

   - *Search:* In this section, you can specify the scope of the search in a drop down menu — every sheet in your document, the current sheet, or a specific range of cells. You can also check boxes to match case, entire contents of a cell or search formulas and formula expressions.

   - *Match Case:* Check this box if you wish to search for text exactly as you type it in the Find box.

   - *Match Entire Cell Contents:* The complete cell must match your search query.

   - *Search Using Regular Expressions:* Search for a particular character pattern.

   - *Also Search within Formulas:* Search formulas, not just formula calculations.

   Use the provided check boxes to fine-tune your search and reduce potentially inaccurate search results.

3. **Click Find.**

4. **Sort through search results by clicking the Find button in the bottom-right of the Find and Replace pop-up window.**

   As you navigate through the search results in your document, Sheets changes the highlight color on the cell to indicate where you are in the spreadsheet.

5. **When you successfully locate the word or words in your spreadsheet, click the X in the top-right corner of the Find and Replace pop-up window to close that window.**

   The window disappears, but the text you searched for remains highlighted and ready to be deleted or otherwise edited.

Copying and pasting data

As you enter data into your spreadsheet, you can avoid typing out repetitive text by using the Copy and Paste functions. Copying and pasting can be done in a couple ways — on the keyboard, with the touchpad, or a combination of both. To copy and paste a single cell, follow these steps:

1. **Select the cell that you want to copy.**

   If you would like to copy and paste a range of cells, you can do so by selecting the first cell in the range, holding the Shift key, then selecting the last cell in the range.

   The selection area will be highlighted in blue.

2. **Open the Edit menu and choose Copy.**

   The selected cell's contents will now be copied and stored in memory, also referred to as the Clipboard.

   The Clipboard can remember only one thing at a time. If you copy a selection of text and then copy another selection of text without pasting the first selection of text, Sheets forgets the first selection.

3. **Navigate to the cell where you would like to paste the copied data.**

4. **Once again, open the Edit menu. This time, choose Paste.**

   The data copied to the Clipboard is now pasted into the selected cell.

When copying and pasting large areas of data, it's easy to underestimate the amount of space needed for the paste and inadvertently overwrite meaningful data. You can undo any past action by clicking the Undo button in the Edit toolbar. The Undo button looks like an arrow in the shape of a half circle pointing to the left.

If you need to paste the contents of one cell in a cell that's several rows or columns away, you may find that the keyboard is too slow a means of navigating through your spreadsheet. Your touchpad offers a fast and convenient option to quickly copy and paste. To copy and paste a cell by using your touchpad, use the following steps:

1. **Using your touchpad, move your cursor to the cell you wish to copy.**

2. **Click the desired cell once to select it.**

   If you want to select a range of cells, click the first cell in the range and, without releasing your click, move to the other end of the range you wish to copy, and then release.

3. **Open the Edit menu and select Copy.**

   The selected cell is copied to the Clipboard.

4. **Using your touchpad, scroll to the desired location and click on the desired cell.**

   If you want to paste a range of cells, select the cell you wish to be the top-left corner of your pasted range.

5. **Open the Edit menu and choose Paste.**

   The copied selection is pasted in.

To save time, you can use shortcut keys to copy and paste cells. Press Ctrl+C to copy a cell or cells, and press Ctrl+V to paste the copied cells. You can also quickly undo a paste (or many other actions) by pressing Ctrl+Z.

Alt-click your selection to reveal a menu of options, including Copy and Paste.

Moving data with cut and paste

When you want to replicate data, Copy and Paste is the mode of operation you should use. When you want to move data but not replicate it, however, use Cut. To move data in your sheet using the Cut and Paste method, follow these steps:

1. **Using your touchpad, click to select the cell you wish to move (or click and drag your cursor across all the cells you wish to move, then release).**

   The cell(s) are highlighted.

2. **Alt-click on the highlighted cell(s).**

   A pop-up menu appears, revealing several options.

3. **Select Cut from the menu.**

   A dashed border surrounds your selection, indicating that the enclosed data has been cut.

4. **Using the touchpad, navigate to the location where you wish to paste your data.**

5. **Alt-click in the cell where you wish to paste your data.**

   A pop-up menu appears.

6. **Select Paste.**

   The data is moved accordingly.

You can paste data that you've cut as many times as you like. However, when you copy or cut a new selection of text, the previously cut text will be replaced with the newly cut text.

Using Autofill to save time

The Autofill feature in Sheets makes it easy for you to copy and paste a particular pattern of data or to expand a series of data without having to manually enter the data or use the Copy and Paste feature repeatedly. To use Autofill to expand a series of data, follow these steps:

1. **In cell A1, type the word** Monday.

2. **In cell A2, type the word** Tuesday.

3. **In cell A3, type the word** Wednesday.

4. **Click on cell A1 and select these cells by dragging your cursor down to cell A3.**

   Notice that a blue square appears in the bottom-right corner of your selection, as pictured in Figure 8-10.

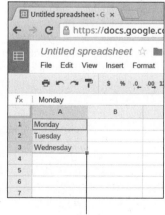

Figure 8-10:
The Autofill square.

The autofill square

5. **Click the blue Autofill square and drag your selection down to Cell A10.**

6. **Release your click.**

   Sheets automatically fills your selection with the identified sequence, as shown in Figure 8-11.

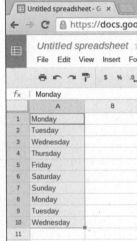

Figure 8-11:
Sheets completes our sequence of days of the week.

You can use Autofill to complete most sequences as long as you give Autofill enough information to guess what your sequence is. If Autofill can't identify your sequence, it simply replicates your data as a pattern.

Formatting Data

Google Sheets gives you great control over the appearance of the content in your spreadsheet. You can change the formatting of a complete spreadsheet, rows, columns, or single cells. You cannot, however, apply multiple style changes to the contents within a cell. Any formatting tweaks you make in a cell get applied to the entire contents of the cell.

Google Sheets allows you to style your sheet in many different ways, including the following:

✔ **Font formatting:** *Font* is another way to say *style of typeface*. With Sheets, you can change fonts, change the size or color of a font, or apply to a font new styles like bold, italics, underline, or strikethrough.

✔ **Cell formatting:** You can put borders around a cell or group of cells, or apply a background color. You can also auto-format numbers in a cell so that they take on a particular format like currencies, percentages, dates, and times, to name a few.

✔ **Alignment:** You can change the horizontal alignment of the text within a cell to be left-, center- or right-aligned, or change the vertical alignment so that your text appears at the top, middle, or bottom of the cell. You can even style text so that it wraps to another line in your cell.

Working with fonts

With Sheets, you can change the font of any data contained in your spreadsheet. The options are potentially limitless, but for clarity, it's better to limit the number of fonts that appear in one spreadsheet. Google Sheets comes preloaded with six fonts, and as of recently, Google has removed the capability to add additional fonts to Sheets. For now, your font options are

✔ Arial

✔ Courier New

✔ Georgia

✔ Times New Roman

✔ Trebuchet MS

✔ Verdana

If you would like to change your font, follow these steps:

1. **Using your touchpad, select the cells you want to change by clicking and dragging your cursor.**

   Sheets highlights the selected cells.

2. **Open the Format menu, and then open the Font submenu.**

   The Font submenu reveals the default font choices.

   The Font submenu is titled with the name of the font for the selected body of text. By default, all text appears in the Arial font.

3. **Select any one of the fonts listed.**

   The contents of the highlighted cells are changed to the selected font.

   If the selected cells contain no data, the new font will apply only to new text. Any data entered afterwards will appear in the selected font.

Styling your data

You can accentuate a font by applying various styles to the font itself, including

- ✔ **Size:** You can make your data bigger or smaller as you see fit.
- ✔ **Bold:** You can make data bold, which makes the text visibly thicker. Bold font is sometimes referred to as having a *heavy weight*.
- ✔ **Italics:** A slanted font is often referred to as italicized.
- ✔ **Underline:** Place a line under your data to indicate importance.
- ✔ **Strikethrough:** Place a line through the middle of your data. This is useful in communicating a change in your text or to illustrate a point.
- ✔ **Color:** Track changes, distinguish individual users in collaboration, or simply add style to your data by changing the color.

Changing font size

Changing the size of your data can be done with these steps:

1. **Using your touchpad, select the cells you wish to change by clicking and dragging your cursor.**

   The selected text is highlighted.

2. **Open the Font Size menu in the Edit toolbar.**

   It's the number found to the left of the Bold button in the Edit toolbar. When you click it, a menu appears, revealing several font sizes (in points) to choose from, as shown in Figure 8-12.

3. **Select the desired font size.**

   Your selected data is now the chosen size.

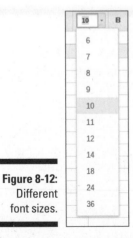

Figure 8-12:
Different
font sizes.

Applying bold, italics, underline, or strikethrough to your data

To apply formatting to a specific selection of cells, follow these steps:

1. **Using your touchpad, select the cells you wish to change by clicking and dragging your cursor.**

   The selected cells are highlighted.

2. **Apply bold, italics, underline, or strikethrough, as needed.**

   To do this, use either of the following methods:

   - *To add bold, italics, or strikethrough:* Click the appropriate button in the middle of the Edit toolbar — the B button for bold, the I button for italic, or the S button for strikethrough. (No button exists for underline on the standard Edit toolbar.)

   - *To add an underline:* Open the Format menu in the application menu and select Underline.

   Your selection changes appropriately.

You can quickly apply styles to your data by using hotkeys. Just press Ctrl+B (for bold), Ctrl+I (italic), Ctrl+U (underline), or Alt+Shift+5 (strikethrough).

Coloring your data

Sheets gives you the ability to change the color of your data so that you can visually group your data, indicate important information, or just give your spreadsheet a little pizzazz! To change the color of your data, follow these steps:

1. **Using your touchpad, select the cells you wish to change by clicking and dragging your cursor.**

   The selected cells are highlighted.

2. **Open the Color menu in the Edit toolbar.**

   It's the A found to the right of the Underline button.

   A Color menu appears, revealing several color options.

3. **Select your desired color.**

   The data in the selected cells now appears in the selected color.

Changing alignment

Google Sheets gives you several options for changing the horizontal and vertical alignment of your data. Horizontal alignment options include

✔ Left

✔ Right

✔ Center

Vertical alignment options include

✔ Top

✔ Middle

✔ Bottom

To adjust the alignment of your data, follow these steps:

1. **Using your touchpad, select the cells you wish to realign by clicking and dragging your cursor.**

   The selected cells are highlighted.

2. **In the Edit toolbar, find and click the appropriate Alignment button.**

   The Vertical Alignment button is located seven buttons from the end of the right side. The Horizontal Alignment button is next to it, eight buttons from the end of the right side.

   A menu with the alignment options appears.

3. **Click the desired alignment.**

   The selected cells of data will be realigned accordingly.

Wrapping text in a cell

By default, when you enter text into a cell, the text appears on a single line. That means that in order to show all of the entered text, the width of your cell may have to be adjusted. However, Sheets has a feature that causes text to go to the next line once it hits the maximum width of your cell — *wrap text*. With this feature, you can set text to wrap in one cell or in every cell in a sheet. To activate text wrapping, follow these steps:

1. **Using your touchpad, select the desired cells by clicking and dragging your cursor.**

   The selected cells are highlighted.

2. **Open the Format menu.**

3. **Choose Wrap Text.**

   Text that extends beyond the boundaries of your cell walls will be wrapped to another line, as shown in Figure 8-13.

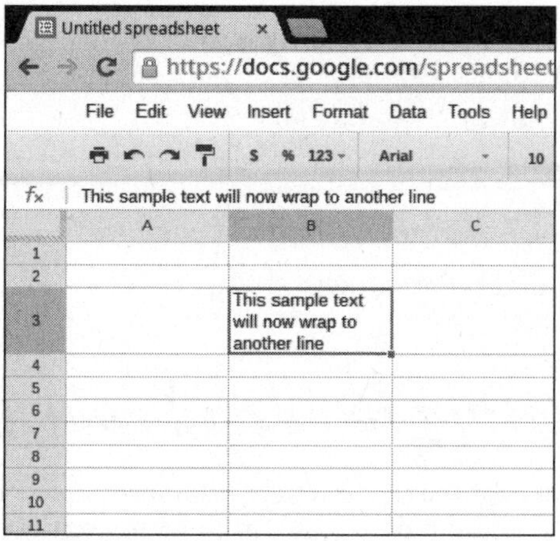

Figure 8-13:
Text
wrapping
in action.

Clearing formatting

Sometimes you just need to start over. The good news is that Sheets makes it incredibly easy to wipe out all formatting in a section of cells or your complete spreadsheet. To clear your formatting, follow these steps:

1. **Select the formatted cells you want to clear.**

   The selected cells are highlighted.

   To clear the formatting of an entire document, press Ctrl+A instead of selecting cells. Pressing Ctrl+A selects the entire document.

2. **Open the Format menu in the Applications menu.**

3. **Select Clear Formatting.**

   The selected data is reset to defaults: left-aligned, with all style elements — including color, underline, strikethrough, italics, bold, and so on — removed.

Customizing Your Spreadsheet

When you open Sheets for the first time, you're presented with a blank canvas of empty, uniform cells organized in a neat grid pattern. Sheets allows you to customize this grid of information so that it looks and works exactly how you like. You can

✔ Change the height of rows and the width of columns.

✔ Add and remove columns and rows.

✔ Merge multiple cells together into one cell.

✔ Hide rows and columns.

✔ Add borders to individual cells and groups of cells.

✔ Customize the background color of cells.

Adding and deleting rows and columns

Adding rows or columns makes it easier to insert data into areas that are already populated with data. Instead of cutting and pasting data to make room, you can simply add an empty row or column.

The same goes for removing rows or columns. Deleting a column or row is a fast way to remove extraneous cells from your spreadsheet. When we get into formulas (see the section "Making Calculations with Formulas," later in this chapter), you will also find that adding and deleting rows and columns will keep your formulas intact.

Adding a new row or column

Adding a new row or column can be done by following these steps:

1. **Using your touchpad, move your cursor to the row or column header of the row or column next to which you would like to insert a new row or column. Column headers are indicated with a letter. Row headers are indicated by a number. Alt-click the row or column header.**

   A menu appears, revealing several options. (The menu for rows is shown in Figure 8-14.)

2. **Insert a new row by choosing Insert 1 Above or Insert 1 Below, or insert a new column by choosing Insert 1 Left or Insert 1 Right.**

   A new row or column is inserted accordingly.

Don't worry about making your spreadsheet too big. Size is never a problem. The largest spreadsheet you can make with Sheets would have 400,000 cells and 256 columns!

Figure 8-14:
The Alt-click
menu for
rows.

Deleting a row or column

You can delete a row or column by following these steps:

1. **Using your touchpad, move your cursor to the header of the row or column you wish to delete.**

2. **Alt-click on the row number or column letter.**

   A menu appears, revealing several options.

3. **Click Delete Row or Delete Column.**

   The row or column is deleted. The remaining rows or columns move together to fill the gap.

Resizing columns and rows

The row and column sizes in Sheets are set by default to an arbitrary size. You can build a perfectly functional spreadsheet and never resize the columns or rows. However, resizing is a great way to ensure that your data is viewable. If a string of text is too big for the current column width or row height, Sheets lets you quickly change the width or height to accommodate your needs.

To resize your column or row, follow these steps:

1. **Using your touchpad, move your pointer to the column or row header you want to resize.**

   Make sure your pointer is over the line on the right side of the column or bottom side of the row that you would like to resize.

   Your pointer will turn into a set of arrows.

2. **Click and drag to change the size of the column or row.**

3. **When you are satisfied with the new size, release your click.**

You can also change the size of multiple rows or columns at the same time. To do so, the columns or rows must be sequential. For example, you can resize columns 1, 2, and 3 at the same time, but you can't resize columns 1, 2, and 5 at the same time. To resize multiple columns or rows, follow these steps:

1. **Using your touchpad, click the header for the first column or row in the series you wish to resize.**

   The selected row or column is highlighted.

2. **Shift-click the header for the last of the columns or rows in the series you wish to resize.**

   Every row or column in the series is selected.

3. **Relocate your pointer so that it rests over the line dividing two rows or columns in your selection.**

   The pointer turns into a set of arrows.

4. **Click and drag the column or row to resize.**

5. **When you're satisfied, release your click.**

   Each row or column in the series is resized.

Hiding columns and rows

Hiding rows and columns is handy when you're presenting a spreadsheet and want to hide a row or column of notes, or when some of your data is necessary for calculations but not relevant enough to be shown. Hiding is a great way to keep data in its place but out of sight. To hide a row or column, follow these steps:

1. **Using your touchpad, move your pointer over the header of the row or column you wish to hide.**

2. **Alt-click the row or column header.**

   A menu appears, revealing several options.

3. **Select Hide Column or Hide Row, whichever is appropriate.**

   The associated row or column vanishes, leaving only a set of arrows over the column or row dividing line.

   To restore your hidden column or row, click these arrows.

Merging cells

There are times when you will want or even need to have a heading over several columns or rows. To do this, you will need to merge multiple cells together so that they form a single cell spanning multiple columns or rows. To merge cells together, follow these steps:

1. **Shift-click the contiguous cells you wish to merge.**

   The selected cells become highlighted.

2. **Click the Merge Cells button in the Edit toolbar, located nine buttons from the right.**

   The highlighted cells merge.

   Any data in merged cells may be lost. Be sure to have a copy of the cell's contents prior to merging.

3. **To unmerge the cells, select the newly merged cell and click the Merge Cells button again.**

   The cells that you merged are restored.

Formatting numbers

Spreadsheets are used primarily to organize and calculate numeric data. With Sheets, you can auto-format your cells to accommodate several numeric data types, including

- Currency
- Percentages
- Decimals
- Financial notation
- Scientific notation
- Date
- Time

Formatting cells for these numeric types can be done by following these steps:

1. **Using your touchpad, select the cell or cells you wish to format.**

2. **Open the Format menu.**

3. **Move your pointer over Number in the menu.**

   A submenu appears, revealing several formatting options.

4. **Select the desired formatting style.**

   The selected cells now auto-format numeric entries to match the selected style.

Grouping cells with colors and borders

When working with spreadsheets containing large amounts of data, the numbers and letters can begin to blend together. You can distinguish groups of cells with borders or colors to make navigating your spreadsheet easier. Borders and cell shading can also add a nice touch of style to your spreadsheets. You can add borders to your spreadsheet by following these steps:

1. **Using your touchpad, select the cells you want to style by clicking and dragging your cursor.**

   The selected cells are highlighted.

2. **Click the Border button in the Edit toolbar.**

   The Border button is located ten buttons from the right.

   A menu appears, giving you several options.

3. **To simply place a border around your cells, locate the image that shows a border outline and click it.**

   The images in the Border menu, as shown in Figure 8-15, illustrate precisely where the border will go if selected. You can also change the border style to dotted or dashed by selecting the line option in the Border Style menu or change the color of your border by using the Border Color option.

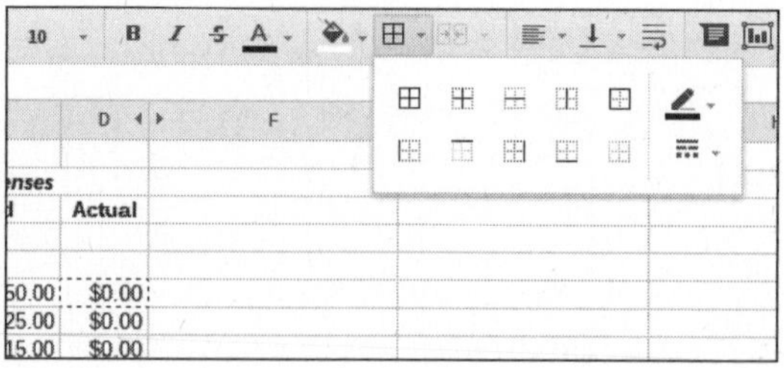

Figure 8-15:
Adding a
border.

You can also create visual separation in your spreadsheet by incorporating color into your cells. To apply a color background to a cell or group of cells, follow these steps:

1. **Using your touchpad, select the cells you want to color by clicking and dragging your cursor.**

   The selected cells are highlighted.

2. **Click the Background Color button in the Edit toolbar.**

   This button is located eleven buttons from the right and looks like a paint can.

   A menu appears, giving you several options.

3. **Select a color from the menu.**

   The background of the selected cells is changed to the chosen color.

Making Calculations with Formulas

Google Sheets is an extremely powerful spreadsheet tool. With Sheets, you can perform analysis on text and numeric values alike, and incorporate financial, mathematical, and statistical analysis. The following sections serve as an intro to Sheets's basic functions and formulas.

Adding basic mathematical formulas

Sheets can perform mathematical calculations for you. All you have to do is tell Sheets that you want it to perform a calculation on the information you enter in the cell. To do this, you must start your equation with an equals sign (=). Make sheets do basic addition by following these steps:

1. **With Sheets open, select a cell.**

2. **Type the following string of characters precisely:**

   ```
   =50+50
   ```

3. **Press Enter.**

   Sheets solves the equation and displays the answer, 100.

There are several mathematical operators that you can use to perform calculations with Sheets. They include:

- ✔ Addition: +
- ✔ Subtraction: –
- ✔ Division: /
- ✔ Multiplication: *

Sheets interprets the order of operations according to simple rules: It performs calculations within parentheses first, then multiplication or division (from left to right), and finally, addition or subtraction (from left to right).

To ensure Sheets always follows the mathematical order of operations you intended, use parentheses to group operations together. For example, in another cell, enter the following equation:

```
=((5+5)*8)/2
```

You get the answer 40. When more than one set of parentheses exists, Sheets performs the instructions within the innermost set first, then works its way outward. Without parentheses, the equation becomes

```
=5+5*8/2
```

This returns the answer 25. Use parentheses to ensure your operations are performed in the order you intended.

Building formulas can become complex very quickly. To edit a formula, select the cell that contains the formula, and then click in the Formula bar at the top of your Sheets window to edit the formula. Typing in the cell itself overwrites the contents, leaving you to start again!

Adding Formulas to calculate values in cells

Sheets was designed for use beyond just standard calculator functions. You can also use Sheets to perform calculations using data in multiple cells within your spreadsheet. Instead of entering numbers into your equations, you enter cell coordinates. Use Sheets to add three cells together with the following steps:

1. **With Sheets open, enter the number** 25 **into cell A2.**

2. **Enter the number** 50 **into cell A3.**

3. **Enter the number** 75 **into cell A4.**

4. **In cell B5, enter the following equation:**

   ```
   =A2+A3+A4
   ```

5. **Press Enter.**

   Sheets adds cell A2, A3, and A4 together, then displays the answer —
   150 — in cell B5.

You can also use Sheets to calculate values in cells along with fixed values
that you enter yourself. Try it yourself with these steps:

1. **With Sheets open, enter the number** 25 **into cell A2.**

2. **Enter the number** 50 **into cell A3.**

3. **Enter the number** 75 **into cell A4.**

4. **In cell B5, enter the following equation:**

   ```
   =(A2+A3+A4)*10
   ```

5. **Press Enter.**

   Sheets adds cells A2, A3, and A4 together and then multiplies the total
   by 10. The resulting answer is 1500, which it displays in cell B5.

Working with spreadsheet functions

Sheets has an extensive library of functions that perform a vast array of computations. However, the most widely used functions in Sheets are

- **SUM:** Adds all the numbers in a range of cells.
- **AVERAGE:** Outputs the average of the values in a specific set of cells or
  in a range.
- **COUNT:** Count how many numbers are in a list of cells. You can specify
  cells or enter a range.
- **MAX:** Outputs the largest number in a specific set of cells or a range.
- **MIN:** Outputs the smallest number in a specific set of cells or a range.

Functions simplify the process of writing complex formulas and reduce the
amount of typing needed to get a desired result. To use the SUM function,
follow these steps:

1. **With Sheets open, enter the number** 25 **into cell A2.**

2. **Enter the number** 50 **into cell A3.**

3. **Enter the number** 75 **into cell A4.**

4. **In cell B5, enter the following equation:**

```
=SUM(A2:A4)
```

5. **Press Enter.**

   The formula tells Sheets that you want to add the values in cells A2 through A4. The output value is 150, which Sheets displays in cell B5.

6. **To use parentheses to set the order in which functions are used in the equation, in cell B5, enter the following equation:**

```
=(SUM(A2:A4)*10)
```

7. **Press Enter.**

   Sheets first calculates the sum of the values in cells A2 through A4 and then multiplies the total by 10, displaying 1500 in cell B5.

Saving Documents

As you work in Google Sheets, Google will save almost every change in real-time to your Google Drive account. (Drive is Google's cloud-based storage solution that allows you to safely store your files and access them from any device with an Internet connection.) Every file you create with Sheets is saved to your Drive folder so that you can access it at home, on the road, at work, or anywhere else you might need to. As is the case with Docs, there is no manual Save feature in Sheets.

Naming your document

When you open a new spreadsheet with Sheets, the default name for the spreadsheet will be Untitled Spreadsheet. You don't, however, want to leave your spreadsheet untitled. Drive doesn't have a problem with storing multiple files with the same name, but it's best if you name your spreadsheet immediately so that you save yourself a little confusion. To name your spreadsheet, follow these steps:

1. **Open a new spreadsheet.**

   The easiest way to do this is by launching Sheets from the App Launcher.

   A Chrome web browser opens and loads Sheets — and a new spreadsheet — automatically.

   Once Sheets is open, the name of your new document, Untitled Spreadsheet, appears in the top-left corner, as shown in Figure 8-16.

2. **Click Untitled Spreadsheet in the top-left corner of your spreadsheet.**

   The Rename Document pop-up window appears in the middle of your screen. The name of the spreadsheet appears highlighted in the Enter a New Spreadsheet Name text box.

3. **Type a new name for your spreadsheet in the Enter a New Spreadsheet Name text box, and then click OK.**

   The pop-up window disappears, and the name Untitled Spreadsheet is now replaced with your new name.

   Your newly named spreadsheet now appears in Google Drive. As you continue to make edits, the spreadsheet document will be updated and saved in real-time.

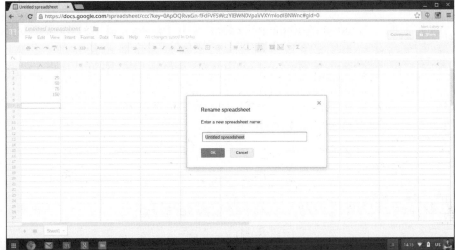

Figure 8-16:
You can change the spreadsheet's name.

Exporting documents

From time to time, you may need to export your spreadsheets to formats that others may be comfortable with. Sheets allows you to export spreadsheets to a few standard formats, including

- ✔ Microsoft Excel (`.xlsx`)
- ✔ OpenDocument (`.ods`)
- ✔ PDF (`.pdf`)

✔ Comma-separated values (.csv)

✔ Tab-separated values (.tsv)

✔ Web page (.html)

Exporting documents to different file types may change the formatting within your document. CSV and TSV will strip out all formatting. Before sending along your spreadsheets after an export, you should review them to ensure everything is as it should be!

You can export your documents by following these steps:

1. **Open the File menu and hover your cursor over Download As.**

   A submenu appears, revealing the file types available for export.

2. **Select the desired file type.**

   Your spreadsheet is exported in the desired file type and is automatically downloaded to your Chromebook.

3. **To view the downloaded file on your computer, click the arrow next to the filename in the bottom of your browser window.**

   A menu revealing several options appears.

4. **Select Show in Folder.**

   Files launches, showing you the file in your folder.

Collaboration with Sheets

By default, Sheets and Drive make your files inaccessible to everyone other than you. You can, however, change the visibility settings on your files and invite specific people, or even the entire world, to comment, view, or edit your document! To share your Spreadsheet with specific people, follow these steps:

1. **Click the blue Share button in the top-right corner of your Sheets window.**

   A pop-up window appears, giving you several options for sharing your spreadsheet.

2. **Enter the email address of each person with whom you wish to share your file in the Invite People field at the bottom of the pop-up window.**

   Be sure to separate the addresses with commas.

   If the email address is in your address book, Sheets tries to autofill the information.

3. **To set the permissions of the collaborators, first click the link directly to the right of the Invite People field.**

   A menu with three options appears:

   - *Can Edit:* Allows users to edit the spreadsheet and change permissions
   - *Can Comment:* Allows users to comment on the spreadsheet but not to change any content or security settings
   - *Can View:* Allows users only to view the spreadsheet

4. **Select the appropriate permission setting from the menu.**

5. **Check the Notify People Via Email box to notify the specified users, by email, that you have shared a document with them.**

6. **Click Send.**

   Your document is made available to the users immediately.

 The users who are invited to view, edit, or comment on your spreadsheet have to log into Google Docs using the email addresses with which you shared the spreadsheet. If a user doesn't have a Google Account under the email address you used, you have to invite him with the address he uses for his Google Account. He also has the option to create a Google Account using the same email address.

Tracking Revisions

Keeping track of revisions is very important when creating documents with multiple collaborators. Luckily, Google Sheets handles version control masterfully. The Revision History tool, however, is not intended to be used as a Track Changes tool. As you and your collaborators make changes to your spreadsheets, Sheets will time-and-date stamp those changes so that you can view previous versions of your spreadsheet and even revert to an earlier version if you need to.

Revision tracking is a default feature of Sheets, so you need to do nothing to take advantage of it. To view your revision history, follow these steps:

1. **Open the File menu and select See Revision History.**

   A Revision History box appears in the right portion of your screen. The box contains the various versions of your spreadsheet in order from most recent to oldest.

2. **Click a revision date in the Revision History box.**

   A preview of the revision you chose appears in the main document area. Changes that occurred between versions appear in green.

3. **To change versions, click Restore This Revision.**

   The restored version becomes the current version, and the previous version of the application is saved in the Revision History, so you can revert back to it if needed.

Using Sheets Offline

Google Sheets is a web-based spreadsheet tool, which means that you must have an Internet connection to access all of its features. However, an offline version of Sheets is available in the event you find yourself without a connection to the Internet.

While offline, you won't be able to access some of the features available to Sheets users who are connected to the Internet. You will, however, be able to create documents and save them. Later, when you connect to the Internet, Drive will upload the saved spreadsheets and enable all Internet-only features.

To use Google Sheets offline, follow these steps:

1. **To use Google Sheets offline, you must first enable Google Drive for offline use. To ensure that Google Drive is properly enabled, open the App Launcher and click the Google Drive icon.**

   A Chrome web browser appears and takes you to your drive.

2. **On the right side of the screen, click the Settings icon (it looks like a gear).**

3. **In the resulting menu, click Settings.**

   A pop-up window appears.

4. **Select the check box to sync your work for offline use.**

5. **Click Done.**

   Your Sheets files is now synced and available for offline editing.

6. **You can test whether you have properly enabled offline access by turning off your Wi-Fi. To do this, open the Settings panel in the bottom-right of your screen and select WIFI.**

   The WIFI menu appears.

7. **At the bottom of this menu, click the WIFI indicator to turn off your Wi-Fi.**

8. **With your Wi-Fi turned off, switch back to Google Drive and open one of your synced spreadsheets.**

   If your spreadsheet opens and you are able to edit it, you know you have successfully engaged offline use and synced your documents.

Chapter 9

Preparing Presentations

• •

In This Chapter

▶ Navigating Google Slides

▶ Creating presentations

▶ Using Presentation mode

▶ Saving, exporting, and collaborating

▶ Taking Google Slides offline

• •

*P*resentations have come a long way in the past 30 years. You might recall family picture night used to be a slide projector with 50+ pictures loaded into a circular carousel that Mom or Dad would click through while the kids sat in misery. Through your school years, there was the overhead projector with transparencies. Now we have interactive presentations that involve text, images, audio, and video. There are several presentation suites available today, and you can probably guess the gold standard in corporate America: Microsoft PowerPoint.

PowerPoint has become so entrenched in business and education that the name is almost used interchangeably to mean "presentation." This is not unlike how people refer to tissues as Kleenex and lip balm as ChapStick. But the cultural penetration of PowerPoint didn't keep Google from creating a free presentation software that could rival it.

Google Slides is a free, web-based, presentation software that gives you the ability to make high-powered, engaging presentations you can access anywhere in the world thanks to the vast nature of the Google platform.

In this chapter, you learn how to create beautiful presentations with Google Slides. Use existing templates or create your own; add, edit, and style images and text; collaborate with teams around the globe; and export your presentations to multiple formats so that you can share your presentations with colleagues, coworkers, classmates, and more. Google Slides is a powerful tool for communication in any setting.

Navigating Google Slides

Slides is Google's presentation software and their option for those looking for an alternative to Microsoft's PowerPoint, which is arguably the industry leader in presentation software. Like the rest of the Google office suite, Slides is easy to use for beginners and experienced presentation makers alike. If you have any experience with PowerPoint, the transition will feel very easy to you.

 To launch Google Slides from your Chromebook, open the App Launcher and click the Slides icon. The Slides application will open in a Chrome browser window and create a new untitled document. (See Figure 9-1.)

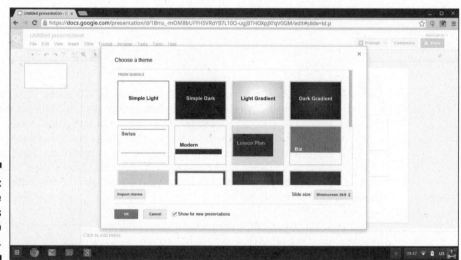

Figure 9-1:
The Google
Slides
startup
screen.

Creating your presentation

The Choose a Theme pop-up window opens automatically when you first open Slides. Presentations can be styled with basic, preexisting themes or with custom themes that you download from the Internet or create yourself. To select an existing theme, follow these steps:

1. **In the Choose a Theme pop-up window, scroll to view the available options.**

2. **Locate a theme you would like to use and click it once.**

   The selected theme is highlighted.

3. Select the shape (Slide Size).

Before you click OK to create your new presentation, you need to be sure you've selected the right shape for your presentation. Slides gives you three options for screen shapes with respect to the aspect ratio of your screen:

- *Standard 4:3:* This was the standard shape of all video captured from the early days of motion pictures. Often referred to as the video format of the 20th century.

- *Widescreen 16:9:* This is the shape of video shown in cinemas and the standard for widescreen HD televisions.

- *Widescreen 16:10:* Also referred to as 8:5, this format is largely the format of computer screens.

If you don't pick the desired aspect ratio for your presentation at this point, Slides defaults to 4:3.

To select your aspect ratio, follow these steps:

a. In the bottom-right corner of the Choose a Theme pop-up window, click to the right of Slide Size.

A drop-down list appears, revealing the three aspect ratio options, as shown in Figure 9-2.

b. Choose an option.

The shape and size of your presentation is set as selected.

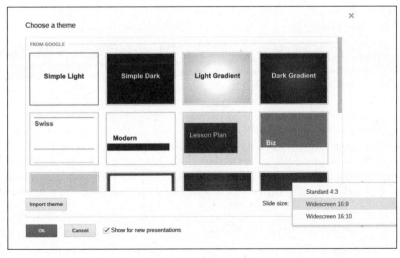

Figure 9-2:
Selecting an aspect ratio for your presentation.

4. **With your theme selected and your aspect ratio set, click OK.**

Google applies the theme to your new presentation.

Surveying the Slides menu area

Slides is divided into three main areas: the menu area, the slide navigator, and the slide editor. The menu area itself can be broken up into two parts: the Applications menu and the Edit toolbar. (See Figure 9-3.)

Menu area   Application menu

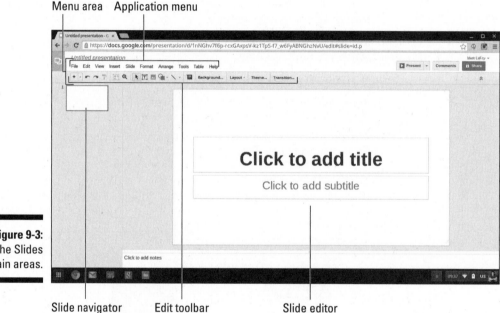

Figure 9-3:
The Slides
main areas.

Slide navigator   Edit toolbar   Slide editor

The Applications menu

The Applications menu features several options:

- ✓ **File:** File-specific options and controls for creating, saving, exporting, printing, and otherwise managing your presentation on the file level.

- ✓ **Edit:** Copy, paste, delete, and otherwise move and manipulate the contents of your presentation.

- ✓ **View:** Modify your view by adding and removing toolbars, zooming in, showing Notes, and going into Presentation mode.

- ✔ **Insert:** Add images, text boxes, video, lines, shapes, tables, comments, and other objects.

- ✔ **Slide:** Add, edit, duplicate, or delete slides, layouts, themes, or transitions — basically, any function that pertains to the slide.

- ✔ **Format:** Manipulate the appearance of your text, apply styles, edit paragraph formats, crop images, and so on.

- ✔ **Arrange:** Arrange objects like text boxes, images, videos, and so on.

- ✔ **Tools:** Spell check, research information, or define words.

- ✔ **Table:** Insert tables and add, edit, or delete rows and columns.

- ✔ **Help:** Get help with slides or search for menu options.

The Edit toolbar

The Edit toolbar, located directly under the Applications menu, contains several shortcuts to features contained in the Applications menu. The Edit toolbar makes the performance of routine tasks faster and easier. With the Edit toolbar, you can quickly perform these tasks:

- ✔ Add slides.
- ✔ Undo/redo changes.
- ✔ Zoom into and out of your presentation.
- ✔ Set your pointer to select objects.
- ✔ Draw text boxes.
- ✔ Add images.
- ✔ Add/draw shapes.
- ✔ Add/draw lines.
- ✔ Add comments.
- ✔ Change slide backgrounds.
- ✔ Edit layouts.
- ✔ Change themes.
- ✔ Add transitions.

The slide navigator

The slide navigator is located directly under the Applications menu and to the left of the slide editor. Slides you add to your presentation appear in the slide navigator. Use the slide navigator to rearrange slides, delete slides, hide slides from presentations, and copy and paste slides within the navigator.

Any selected slide has a blue border. When selected, a slide appears in the slide editor to the right of the slide navigator. By default, you have one slide in your slide navigator. You can add more slides to your presentation by following these steps:

1. **Click the arrow beside the Add Slide button in the Edit toolbar.**

   It's the first button on the left side of the toolbar.

   A menu appears with six layout options for your new slide. (See Figure 9-4.)

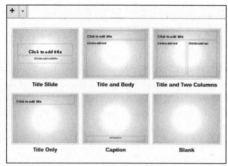

Figure 9-4:
Adding a
slide and
choosing a
layout.

2. **Click any slide layout in the menu to select it.**

   Your new slide appears in the slide navigator directly following the active slide.

   You can quickly add slides by using the keyboard shortcut Ctrl+M.

If you add a slide in the wrong place in your presentation, you can rearrange your slides by following these steps:

1. **In the slide navigator, locate the slide you wish to move.**

2. **Click and drag the slide up or down your slide navigator to the desired location.**

   A location indicator, like the one pictured in Figure 9-5, moves with your selection as you scroll through the slide navigator.

3. **Place the location indicator between the two slides where you would like to relocate your select slide, and then release your click.**

   The slide is moved to the new location.

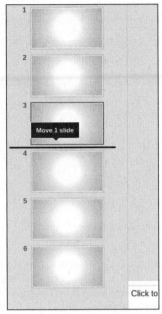

Figure 9-5:
Moving
slides.

To delete a slide from your presentation, use the following steps:

1. **Click the slide you wish to delete in the slide navigator.**

   The selected slide is highlighted with a blue border.

   You can select multiple slides by Ctrl-clicking each slide.

2. **Alt-click the selected slide.**

   A pop-up menu with several options appears.

3. **Select Delete Slide.**

   The selected slide is deleted immediately.

You can also delete a slide by selecting the slide and pressing the Backspace or Delete key.

The slide editor

The slide editor (see Figure 9-6) is the work area located directly below the menu area and directly to the right of the slide navigator. In the slide editor, you can add text, images, video, and other elements to your slide. The selected slide in the slide navigator will appear in the slide editor area, thus making it available to be edited.

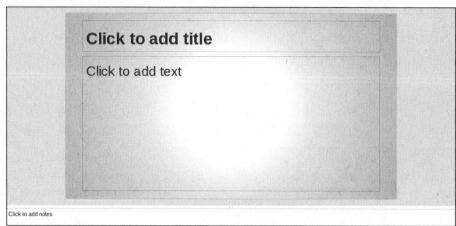

Click to add title

Click to add text

Click to add notes

Figure 9-6:
The slide
editor.

At the bottom of the slide editor is a Speaker Notes bar, in which you can add notes about the current slide. The notes aren't visible to the audience when you make your presentation, but they can serve as talking points for you so that you aren't simply reading the contents of your slides.

Customizing your view

Before you dive into your first presentation, you might find it helpful to change your view in Google Slides. You can compact the Applications menu area by opening the View menu and choosing Compact Controls. When you do this, the Applications menu compacts and disappears from sight, as shown in Figure 9-7.

To restore the menu, click the Show Menus button at the far-right of the Edit toolbar.

You can also use the keyboard shortcut Shift+Ctrl+F to toggle whether the Applications menu is displayed or compacted.

If you prefer to completely hide the Applications menu and the Edit toolbar, you can do so by opening the View menu and choosing Full Screen. (Figure 9-8 shows Slides with the menu and toolbar hidden.) To exit Full Screen mode, simply press the Esc key.

To hide the Speaker Notes bar at the bottom of the slide editor, open the View menu and choose Show Speaker Notes.

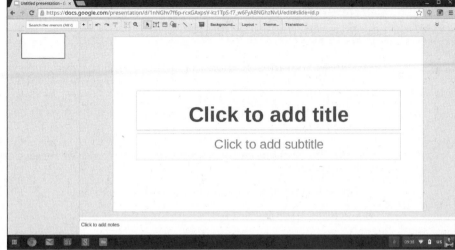

Figure 9-7:
Slides
with the
Applications
menu
compacted.

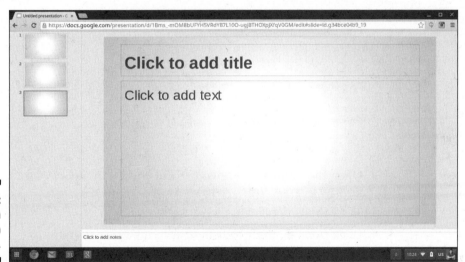

Figure 9-8:
Sheets in
Full Screen
mode.

Styling Your Presentation

Google Slides allows you to customize your presentation to have the look and feel you need. You can use prebuilt themes to apply a predetermined look and feel to your presentation. You can also customize your own theme with background colors, textures, or images, and apply different styles to the text in your presentation.

Changing background color or background image

Each slide in your presentation will have a default background specific to the theme you selected when you created your presentation. If you selected the Light theme, for example, then your background will simply be a solid white. You can, however, change the color of the background of your slide by following these steps:

1. **Using the slide navigator, select the slide that will receive the new background.**

   The selected slide appears in the slide editor.

2. **Click the Background button in the Edit toolbar.**

   The Background pop-up window appears, as shown in Figure 9-9.

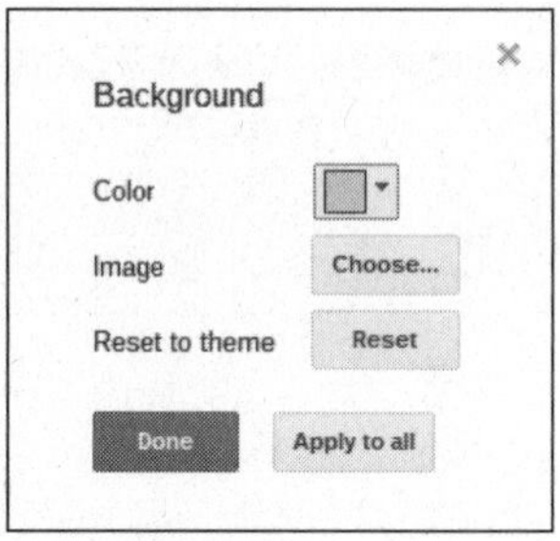

Figure 9-9:
The
Background
pop-up
window.

3. **Open the Color drop-down list and choose the new color for the background of your slide.**

   The color is applied to the background of the current slide.

4. **Click Done to apply the changes to the current slide.**

   Alternatively, you can click Apply to All to apply the changes to every slide in your presentation.

In the event that you want to add a background texture or an image to the background of your slide or slides, you can do so with the following steps:

1. **Using the slide navigator, select the slide that will receive the new background.**

   The selected slide appears in the slide editor.

2. Click the Background button in the Edit toolbar.

The Background pop-up window appears.

3. Click the Choose button located next to the word Image.

The Insert Background Image pop-up window appears, as shown in Figure 9-10, giving you the ability to browse for a photo or to take a snapshot using your device's camera.

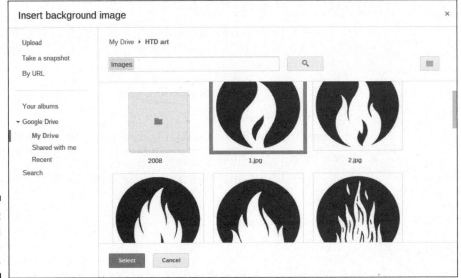

Figure 9-10:
Browsing
for a
background.

4. Select an image and click Select.

The image is applied as a background to the current slide.

5. Click Done to apply the changes to the current slide.

Or you can click Apply to All to apply the changes to every slide in your presentation.

If you decide that you want to clear the color or the image out of a slide, you can easily reset a single slide or every slide in your presentation to your theme's default with these steps:

1. Using the slide navigator, select the slide you want to reset.

The slide appears in the slide editor.

2. Click the Background button in the Edit toolbar.

The Background pop-up window appears.

3. **Click Reset.**

   The background for the selected slide is reset to the theme default.

4. **Click Done to apply the changes to the current slide.**

   Alternatively, click Apply to All to apply the changes to every slide in your presentation.

Applying a different theme

The good news is that if you change your mind about a theme, you can change it, even long after you've begun building your presentation. To change your theme, follow these steps:

1. **Click the Theme button in the Edit toolbar.**

   The Theme Gallery pop-up window appears.

2. **Scroll through the list of available themes to view available options.**

3. **Click a theme's thumbnail to select it.**

   The theme is highlighted, indicating your selection.

4. **Click OK.**

   The selected theme is applied to your presentation.

Importing a presentation theme

Google Slides provides you with a small assortment of themes to get you going with your Slides presentations. However, endless numbers of themes are available for you online that can be imported into your theme gallery. To import a new theme, follow these steps:

1. **Click the Theme button in the Edit toolbar.**

   The Theme Gallery pop-up window appears.

2. **Click Import Theme.**

   The Import Theme pop-up window appears.

3. **Choose a theme that's already available in your Drive account — these are shown under Presentations — or choose one from your Chromebook by clicking Upload.**

4. **After you select a theme, click Select.**

   The theme is uploaded and applied to your presentation.

Working with Text

In Google Slides, all content that you add to a slide is treated as an object, including images, tables, charts, videos, and even text. Objects can then be arranged and organized on the slides to fit the desired look and feel of each slide. To simplify things and provide some continuity within your presentation, your theme comes with several predefined slide layouts. These are particularly useful in ensuring that text boxes like titles are found in the same location from slide to slide. You don't have to use layouts, however; you can make every slide appear as you wish by adding and deleting objects at will. The benefit to this approach is that it gives you a blank canvas on which you can create the exact look you like. Using default slide layouts ensures your text is in the same place from slide to slide, however, so avoiding layouts can produce slides that appear sloppy or out of sync. To apply a default layout to a slide, follow these steps:

1. **Create a new slide by using the keyboard shortcut Ctrl+M.**

   A new slide appears in the slide navigator with a default layout applied.

2. **Using the slide navigator, select the newly created slide.**

   A blue highlight appears on the selected slide.

3. **Click the Layout button on the Edit toolbar.**

   A menu appears, revealing multiple options.

4. **Select the layout you wish to apply to your selected slide.**

   The layout is applied to the slide.

Adding and deleting text boxes

New layouts primarily involve the placement of *text boxes,* which are containers for the text on your slides. When you want to add text to a slide, you must first add a text box, and then you can begin adding text within the text box.

You can add a text box to any slide, regardless of that slide's layout. The following steps show you how. (To minimize confusion, in this example, you add a text box to a blank slide.) Follow these steps to add a text box:

1. **Create a new slide by using the keyboard shortcut Ctrl+M.**

   A new slide appears in the slide navigator with a default layout applied.

2. **Using the slide navigator, select the newly created slide.**

   A blue highlight appears on the selected slide.

3. **Click the Layout button in the Edit toolbar.**

   A menu appears, revealing multiple options.

4. **Select the Blank layout.**

5. **Click the Text Box button in the Edit toolbar.**

   The Text Box button is located eight buttons from the left.

   Upon clicking the Text Box button, your pointer turns into crosshairs.

6. **In the slide editor, move your pointer to where you would like to draw your text box.**

7. **Click and drag your pointer across the slide.**

   A rectangular box appears that can be resized depending on the movement of your pointer. (See Figure 9-11.)

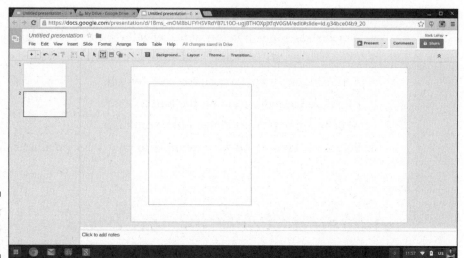

Figure 9-11:
Drawing a text box.

8. **When you're satisfied with the shape and size of your text box, release the click.**

   Your text box is created and made active. (See Figure 9-12.)

You can delete a text box almost as easily as you created it by following these steps:

1. **Ensure that you have your pointer tool selected by clicking the select button located in your Edit toolbar or by pressing Esc.**

   Your pointer should look like an arrow.

2. **Click the edge of the text box that you want to delete.**

   The text box becomes highlighted with a blue border.

3. **Using your keyboard, press the Backspace or Delete key to delete your text box.**

   The text box vanishes.

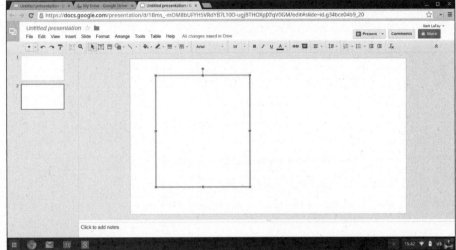

Figure 9-12:
A newly
created text
box.

Resizing, moving, and rotating a text box

Once you create a text box, you may need to adjust its placement on your slide by moving the text box, resizing the box to adjust its shape and size, or rotating the text box (which rotates the contents accordingly). This section shows you how to make these adjustments.

To resize a text box, follow these steps:

1. **Ensure that you have your pointer tool selected by clicking the arrow button located in your Edit toolbar.**

   Your pointer should look like an arrow.

2. **Click on your text box.**

   If your text box doesn't have any text in it, click in the general area of the text box.

   The text box becomes highlighted, and resize points appear in the corners and in the middle of each side of the box.

3. **Move your pointer over one of the resize points on your text box.**

   Your mouse pointer changes shape to a double-sided arrow.

4. **Click and drag the resizing point to shrink or enlarge the text box.**

   The box resizes with the movement of your pointer.

5. **Release your click when you are satisfied with the new shape of your text box.**

You can also move your text box by following these steps:

1. **Ensure that you have your pointer tool selected by clicking the arrow button located in your Edit toolbar.**

   Your pointer should look like an arrow.

2. **Click on your text box.**

   If your text box doesn't have any text in it, click in the general area of the text box.

   The text box becomes highlighted.

3. **Move your pointer over the text box.**

   Your mouse pointer changes into four arrows, one pointing in each cardinal direction.

4. **Click and drag the text box to a new location on the slide.**

   The box moves with the movement of your pointer.

5. **Release your click when you are satisfied with the new location of your text box.**

Google Slides also gives you the ability to rotate your text box at will. This comes in handy when you want to create a vertical text label or add styling to your slide. To rotate your text box, follow these steps:

1. **Ensure that you have your pointer tool selected by clicking the arrow button located in your Edit toolbar.**

   Your pointer should look like an arrow.

2. **Click on your text box.**

   If your text box doesn't have any text in it, click in the general area of the text box.

   The text box becomes highlighted, indicating your selection.

3. **Move your pointer over the circular dot that extends above the top of your text box.**

   Your mouse pointer changes into crosshairs.

4. **Click and drag the crosshairs left to rotate the box counter clockwise or to the right to rotate the box clockwise.**

   The box rotates in the direction and angle of your pointer movement. Your pointer indicates the degree of the angle as you rotate.

5. **Release your click when you're satisfied with the new angle of your text box.**

Copying and pasting text boxes

As you create presentations, you can easily add additional text boxes by using the Copy and Paste functions. To do so, just follow these steps:

1. **Ensure that you have your pointer tool selected by clicking the arrow button located in your Edit toolbar.**

   Your pointer should look like an arrow.

2. **Click the text box you wish to copy.**

   If your text box doesn't have any text in it, click in the general area of the text box.

   The text box becomes highlighted, indicating your selection.

3. **Press Ctrl+C.**

   The text box and its contents are copied into memory.

4. **Use the slide navigator to set the slide where you wish to paste your text box.**

5. **Press Ctrl+V.**

   The text box is pasted to the new slide. Move and adjust it, as needed.

Formatting text

With Slides, you can change the font of any text contained in your presentation. The options are potentially limitless, but for clarity, it's better to limit the number of fonts that appear in one presentation. Google Slides comes preloaded with only a handful of fonts.

If you would like to change your font, you can do so by following these steps:

1. **Using your touchpad, click the text box containing the text that you wish to format.**

   The text box is highlighted in blue.

To change only a section of the text in a text box, make your selection by double-clicking the text box and then dragging your pointer over the text. (See Figure 9-13.)

2. Open the Font menu on the Edit toolbar.

The Font menu is located directly to the left of the Font Size menu.

The Font menu displays the name of the font for the selected body of text. By default, all text is written with the Arial font.

3. Select one of the fonts listed.

All of the selected text is formatted with your newly selected font.

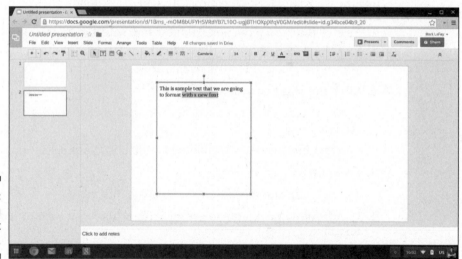

Figure 9-13:
Selecting
text in a text
box.

Adding and removing new fonts

The Google Slides default list of fonts is brief. Google provides users with an initial list of the most globally popular fonts to keep things simple at first. You can, however, add additional fonts to your Slides font list. Follow these steps:

1. Open the Font menu in the Edit toolbar.

2. Choose More Fonts.

The Fonts pop-up window (as shown in Figure 9-14) appears, giving you a robust list of new fonts. Scroll down through the list to reveal more fonts.

3. Select the desired fonts by clicking on each.

Each selected font is highlighted in blue and given a check mark.

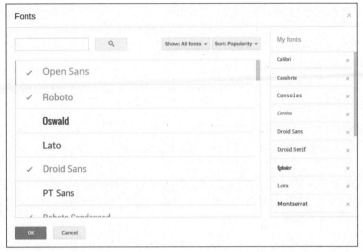

Figure 9-14:
Adding fonts
to Slides.

4. **Click OK to finish adding the fonts to your Font menu and close the Fonts pop-up window.**

When you're ready to change the font of your text, you can choose one of your newly selected fonts from the Font menu.

The more fonts you add, the more fonts you have to rifle through when trying to make a decision on changing. To remove fonts that you added to your list, take these steps:

1. **Open the Font menu in the Edit toolbar.**
2. **Click More Fonts.**

   The Fonts pop-up window appears, displaying a list of fonts. On the right, the My Fonts list displays the fonts currently in use by your Slides account.

3. **Scroll through the My Fonts list to locate the font or fonts you wish to remove. To remove fonts, click the X located to the right of each font.**

   The selected fonts vanish from the list of accessible fonts.

4. **Click OK.**

Text size

Changing the size of your text can be done by following these steps:

1. **Using your touchpad, double-click the text box that contains the text you wish to format.**

   The text box is highlighted in blue. A blinking cursor appears.

2. **Click and drag your pointer across the text whose size you wish to change.**

   The selected text is highlighted.

3. **Click the Font Size menu.**

   It's the number located to the left of the B (Bold) button in the Edit toolbar.

4. **Select any desired font size.**

   Your selected text becomes the chosen size.

Applying boldface, italics, underline, or strikethrough

To make a specific selection of text bold, italic, underlined, or strikethrough, follow these steps:

1. **Using your touchpad, double-click the text box that contains the text you wish to format.**

   The text box is highlighted in blue. A blinking cursor appears.

2. **Select the text you want to change by clicking and dragging.**

   The selected text is highlighted.

3. **Apply boldface, italics, underline, or strikethrough, as needed.**

   To apply a formatting, use one of the following methods:

   • *To add boldface, italics, or strikethrough:* Click the appropriate button in the middle of the Edit toolbar — the B button for bold, the I button for italic, or the U button for underline. (No button exists for strikethrough on the standard Edit toolbar.)

   • *To add strikethrough:* Open the Format menu and select Strikethrough.

   Your selection changes appropriately.

You can quickly apply styles to your data by using hotkeys. Just press Ctrl+B (for bold), Ctrl+I (italic), Ctrl+U (underline), or Alt+Shift+5 (strikethrough).

Coloring your text

Slides gives you the ability to change the color of your text or the color of the background behind your text (that is, adding a highlight). Changing the color of your text can be done with these steps:

1. **Using your touchpad, double-click the text box that contains the text you wish to color.**

2. **Select text by clicking and dragging.**

   The selected text is highlighted.

3. **Open the Text Color menu in the Edit toolbar.**

   It's the A found to the right of the Underline button.

4. **Click the Text button to ensure you are changing the text color and not applying a text highlight.**

   If the Text Color menu was not already active, it appears now with several options. Otherwise, the menu appears unchanged.

5. **Select your desired color.**

   Your selected text now appears in the selected color.

If you would like to apply a highlight to your text, you can do so by following these steps:

1. **Using your touchpad, double-click the text box that contains the text you want to format.**

2. **Select text by clicking and dragging.**

   The selected text is highlighted.

3. **Open the Text Color menu in the Edit toolbar.**

   It's the A found to the right of the Underline button.

4. **Click the Highlight button.**

   The Highlight Color menu appears with several options.

5. **Select your desired color.**

   Your selected text now appears highlighted in the selected color.

Aligning your text

The *alignment* of your text determines the orientation of the edges of lines or paragraphs in a text box. Slides gives you several options for changing the alignment. Horizontal alignment choices include

- **Left:** This is the default alignment for new text boxes in Slides. The text is flush with the left side of the text box.
- **Right:** The text is flush with the right side of the text box.
- **Center:** The middle of your text box is the half-way point between the left and the right sides. With centered alignment, all text is centered on this midway point.
- **Justified:** *Justifying* your text aligns the text evenly along both the left and right sides. To ensure that the left and right sides of your text are flush with the left and right sides of the text box, Slides introduces additional spaces between each word.

Vertical alignment options include

- ✔ Top
- ✔ Middle
- ✔ Bottom

You can change the alignment of text in a text box by the line, paragraph, or page by following these steps:

1. **Using your touchpad, double-click the text box that contains the text you want to realign.**

2. **Select the text you wish to realign by clicking and dragging.**

   The selected text is highlighted.

3. **Click the appropriate alignment button in the Edit toolbar.**

   The vertical alignment button is located six buttons from the end of the right side. The horizontal alignment button is next to it, seven buttons from the end of the right side.

   A menu with the alignment options appears.

4. **Click the desired alignment.**

   The selected text is realigned.

Clearing formatting

Google Slides makes it incredibly easy to clear out the formatting that you applied to a body of text. This can save you quite a bit of time if you intend to clear the formatting from several text boxes. To clear formatting, follow these steps:

1. **Using your touchpad, click once on the text box you wish to select.**

   The selected text box is highlighted.

2. **Click the Clear Formatting button in the Edit toolbar.**

   This button is located at the far-right of the toolbar.

   The alignment of the selected text will be reset to left, and all style elements will be removed, including color, underline, strikethrough, italics, bold, and so on.

Working with Images

Presentations need more than just some text boxes and a colored background to make them interesting. The good news is that you can add images of all types to your presentation. Slides also gives you the ability to apply basic tweaks to your images so that you can make them look just right. With Slides, you can add images from files or use your device's camera to take pictures. You can then rotate, resize, relocate, add borders, and even apply shapes to your pictures.

Adding images to your presentation

Adding an image to your presentation can be done in a few quick steps:

1. **Click the Image button, located nine buttons from the left on the Edit toolbar.**

   The Insert Image pop-up window appears, as shown in Figure 9-15.

2. **Click the Choose an Image to Upload button located in the center of the pop-up window.**

   Files launches, giving you the ability to browse your Chromebook or Google Drive for the image file that you wish to add to your presentation.

3. **Select the image file you wish to add and click Open.**

   Slides uploads the image and embeds it in your document.

You can also add an image from the Internet by following these steps:

1. **Click the Image button, located nine buttons from the left on the Edit toolbar.**

   The Insert Image pop-up window appears.

2. **Click the By URL link located on the left side of the pop-up window.**

   A text box appears in which you can paste the URL to the image you wish to add from the Internet.

3. **Type or paste the URL to the image you wish to add to your slide.**

   If the URL works, Slides shows you a preview of the image, as shown in Figure 9-16.

4. **Click Select.**

Figure 9-16:
Adding an
image from
the Internet
using a URL.

Resizing, rotating, and relocating images

Once you add an image, you may need to adjust its placement on your slide. You can do this by moving the image, resizing the image, or rotating the image. This section shows you how to do each of these actions.

To resize an image, follow these steps:

1. **Ensure that you have your pointer tool selected by clicking the arrow button located in your Edit toolbar.**

   Your pointer should look like an arrow.

2. **Click your image to select it.**

   The selected image is highlighted. Resize points appear in the corners and in the middle of each side of the image.

3. **Move your pointer over one of the corners of the image.**

   Your mouse pointer changes shape to a double-sided arrow.

4. **Click and drag the corner to shrink or enlarge the image.**

   The image resizes proportionately.

   Resizing your image using the points located in the middle of the sides of your image stretches the image without respect for proportion.

5. **When you're satisfied with the new size, release your click.**

You can also move your image by following these steps:

1. **Ensure that you have your pointer tool selected by clicking the arrow button located in your Edit toolbar.**

   Your pointer should look like an arrow.

2. **Click your image to select it.**

   The selected image is highlighted.

3. **Move your pointer over the middle of the image.**

   Your mouse pointer changes into four arrows, one pointing in each cardinal direction.

4. **Click and drag the image to a new location on the slide.**

   The image moves with the movement of your pointer.

5. **When you're satisfied with the new location of your image, release your click.**

Google Slides also gives you the ability to rotate your images. This comes in handy if you need to reorient an image to be in line with your slide. To rotate your image, follow these steps:

1. **Ensure that you have your pointer tool selected by clicking the arrow button located in your Edit toolbar.**

   Your pointer should look like an arrow.

2. **Click your image to select it.**

   The selected image is highlighted.

3. **Move your pointer over the circular dot that extends above the top of your image.**

   Your mouse pointer changes into crosshairs.

4. **Click and drag the image left or right toward the angle you desire.**

   The image rotates in the direction and angle of your pointer movement. Your pointer will indicate the degree of the angle as you rotate, as shown in Figure 9-17.

5. **When you're satisfied with the new angle of your image, release your click.**

Figure 9-17:
Rotating an image.

Cropping images

In Google Slides, you can crop your images. *Cropping* means cutting off portions of an image to retain only the desired area. You may be familiar with cropping images if you have a smartphone and have taken pictures using fun applications like Instagram. Figure 9-18 illustrates what the Slides Crop tool looks like.

To crop an image, follow these steps:

1. **Select the image you want to crop.**

   The selected image is highlighted.

2. **Click the Crop Image button at the far-right of the Edit toolbar.**

   Crop marks appear on your image, indicating you've enabled cropping.

3. **Using your touchpad, move your pointer over one of the black crop marks.**

   Your pointer changes to arrows pointing in two directions, indicating where to drag the crop mark.

4. **Click and drag the crop marks to the desired size.**

   The portion of your image that falls outside of the crop margins appears grayed out.

5. **Click the Crop Image button in the Edit toolbar once again.**

   Your crop settings are applied to the image.

Figure 9-18:
Cropping an image.

Google Slides also comes with an image masking option. *Masking* essentially places your image into a shaped container. The only parts of the image that are shown are the portions not *masked* by the mask filter. Figure 9-19 shows an image with a shape mask applied.

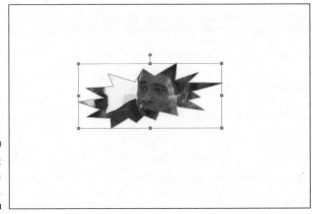

Figure 9-19:
Masking an image.

To mask an image, follow these steps:

1. **Select the image you want to mask.**

   The selected image is highlighted.

2. **Click the Mask Image button at the far-right of the Edit toolbar.**

   The Mask Image button is the down-pointing arrow located on the right portion of the Crop Image button.

   A menu appears, revealing several masking options.

3. **Using your touchpad, navigate through the menu and select the shape you would like to apply to your image.**

   The mask appears on your image; to change the placement and size of the mask, click the crop button. This reveals crop marks on the sides and corners of the mask.

4. **Using your touchpad, move your pointer over one of the black crop marks on your image.**

   Your pointer changes to arrows pointing in two directions, indicating where to drag the crop mark.

5. **Click and drag the crop marks to the desired size.**

   The portion of your image that falls outside of the crop margins appears grayed out.

6. **Click the Crop Image button in the Edit toolbar.**

   Your mask settings are applied to the image.

If you decide that you do not like the crop or image mask that you applied to your image, you can remove it by following these steps:

1. **Double-click the image.**

   The original image is revealed, along with the cropping indicators.

2. **Using your touchpad, click and drag the crop marks so they are flush with the edges of your image.**

3. **Click the Mask Image button in the Edit toolbar.**

   A menu appears, revealing several options.

4. **Hover over Shapes to open the Shapes submenu.**

5. **Click the rectangle shape (the first option).**

   The image mask is changed to the shape of your image.

6. **Click the Crop Image button located in your Edit toolbar.**

   The crop marks are removed from the image.

Making Presentations in Presentation Mode

When you're ready to make a presentation with Google Slides, you need to launch Presentation mode. Presentation mode shows nothing but your finished slides so that you can navigate through them while you present. To launch Presentation mode, follow these steps:

1. **Using your slide navigator, click the first slide in your presentation.**

   Slide 1 becomes highlighted. When you launch Presentation mode, the presentation commences at the active slide in your navigator. If you want to start from the beginning, ensure you've selected your first slide.

2. **Click the Present button in the top-right portion of your screen.**

   The Present button is three buttons from the right.

   Your presentation launches into full-screen Presentation mode, as shown in Figure 9-20.

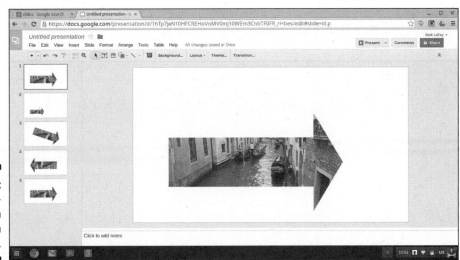

Figure 9-20:
Giving a presentation in Presentation mode.

3. **To exit Presentation mode, press the Esc key.**

   Your presentation closes, and the slide editor reappears.

While in Presentation mode, you can navigate between slides a number of different ways. To move forward in your presentation, press the down or right arrow key, or the spacebar. To move backward in your presentation, press the left or up arrow keys.

Presenting on additional displays

Running Presentation mode on your Chromebook is a great way to test your presentation before you actually give it. When you're ready to present, you'll likely be presenting by using a projector or flat-screen television. To launch your presentations using an additional display device, you first need to connect the projector or TV to your Chromebook. (If you don't know how to connect an additional display to your Chromebook, flip to Chapter 16.) Once your additional display is connected to and recognized by your Chromebook, launch your presentation using these steps:

1. **Using your slide navigator, click the first slide in your presentation.**

   Slide 1 is highlighted.

2. **Click the arrow on the right side of the Present button in the top-right portion of your screen.**

   A menu with three options appears:

   • Present from the Beginning

   • Present with Speaker Notes

   • Present in a New Window

3. **Select Present with Speaker Notes.**

   Presentation mode commences without going into Full Screen mode, and the Speaker Notes window opens, as shown in Figure 9-21.

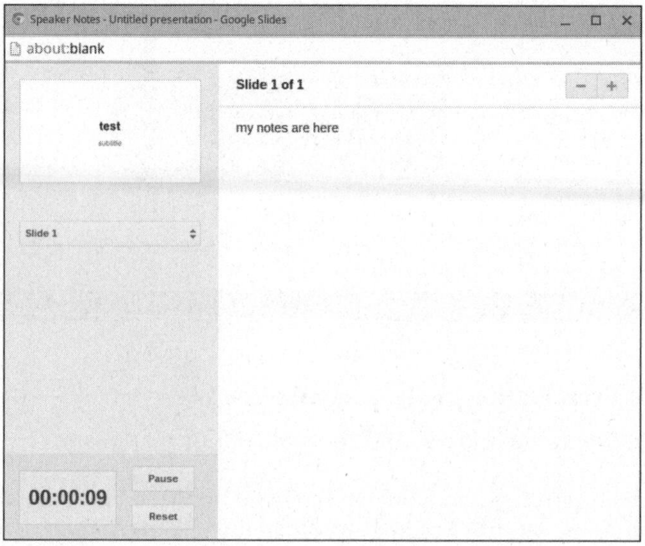

Figure 9-21:
Presentation
mode with
Speaker
Notes.

4. **Click and drag the presentation window to the display you're using to present and leave the Speaker Notes window on the display your audience won't see.**

5. **In your presentation window, click the Full Screen Mode button in the Presenter toolbar in the bottom-left corner of the window, as shown in Figure 9-22.**

   Your presentation goes into Full Screen mode, ready for you to present.

Full-screen mode button

Figure 9-22:
The
Presenter
toolbar.

Speaker Notes window

When you launch a presentation that has Speaker Notes, a window launches that contains all your slide notes, as well as some navigation tools and a timer so that you can keep track of how much time you're using in your presentation. The Speaker Notes window is pictured in Figure 9-23.

The window is broken into two main areas. The left side of the window contains your presentation controls. The right side of the window contains any and all notes written for the current slide. Navigate through your presentation by clicking the slide subtitled Next. Navigate backwards by clicking the slide subtitled Previous. You can also skip to slides by clicking Slide # and selecting a slide from the drop-down list that appears.

Don't read your notes aloud, use them as talking points or cues for presenting. Present to your audience and let the slides merely be props that support your presentation.

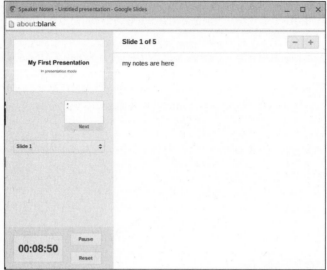

Figure 9-23:
Speaker
Notes
window.

Saving Presentations

As you work in Google Slides, Google saves almost every change in real-time to your Google Drive account. Drive is Google's cloud-based storage solution that allows you to safely store your files and access them from any device with an Internet connection. Every file you create with Presentation is saved to your Drive folder so that you can access it at home, on the road, at work, or anywhere else you might need to. As is the case with Docs and Sheets, there is no manual Save feature in Slides.

Naming your presentation

When you open a new presentation with Slides, the default name for the presentation is Untitled Presentation. You don't, however, want to leave your presentation untitled. Drive doesn't have a problem with storing multiple files with the same name, so it's best if you name your presentation immediately so that you save yourself a little confusion. To name your presentation, follow these steps:

1. **Open a new presentation.**

   The easiest way to open a presentation is simply to launch Slides from the App Launcher.

A Chrome web browser opens and loads Slides — and automatically opens a new presentation.

Once Slides is open, the top-left corner of the screen displays your presentation's name: Untitled Presentation, as shown in Figure 9-24.

2. **Click Untitled Presentation.**

The Rename Document pop-up window appears in the middle of your screen. The name of the presentation appears highlighted in a text box.

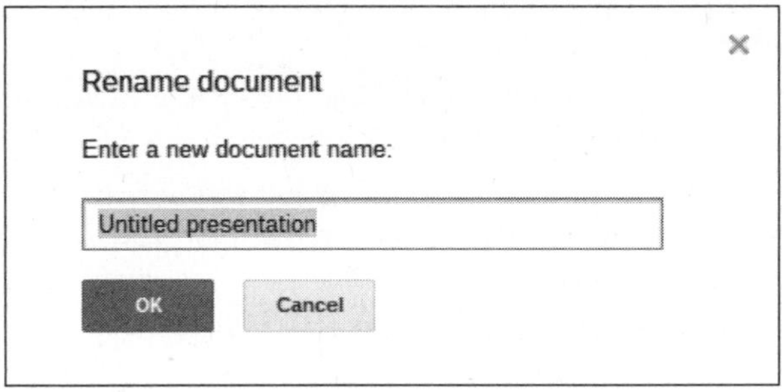

Figure 9-24:
The presentation name.

3. **Type a new name for your presentation in the Name text box and press OK.**

The pop-up window disappears, and what was once Untitled Presentation now bears the name you just entered.

Your newly named presentation now appears in Google Drive with the new name. As you continue to make edits to the presentation, the file will be updated and saved in real-time.

Exporting your presentation

From time to time, you may need to export your presentation to formats that others may be comfortable with. Slides presently allows you to export to a few standard formats:

- ✔ Microsoft PowerPoint (.pptx)
- ✔ PDF Document (.pdf)
- ✔ Scalable Vector Graphics (.svg)
- ✔ PNG image (.png)
- ✔ JPEG image (.jpg)
- ✔ Plain Text (.txt)

Exporting documents to different file types may change the formatting within your document or possibly strip formatting out completely. Before sending along your presentation after an export, you should review it to ensure everything is as it should be!

Exporting your presentation can be done by following these steps:

1. **Open the Files menu in the Applications menu within Slides.**

2. **Hover over Download As to reveal a submenu containing file types available for export.**

3. **Select the desired file type.**

   Your Slides file is exported to the desired file type and automatically downloaded to your Chromebook.

4. **To view the file on your Chromebook, click the arrow next to the filename in the bottom of your browser window and select Show in Folder.**

   Files launches, showing you the file in your folder.

Collaborating in Slides

By default, Slides and Drive make your files inaccessible to everyone other than you. You can, however, change the visibility settings on your files and invite specific people, or even the entire world, to comment, view, or edit your presentation! To share your presentation with specific people, follow these steps:

1. **With Slides open, click the Share button in the top-right corner of the screen.**

   The Sharing pop-up window appears, giving you several options for sharing your presentation.

2. **At the bottom of the Sharing pop-up window, in the Invite People text box, enter the email address of each person you wish to invite to access your file.**

   Be sure to separate the addresses with commas.

   If the email address is in your address book, Slides tries to auto-fill the contact's information.

3. **Set the permissions of the collaborators by clicking the link directly to the right of the Invite People text box.**

A drop-down list with three options appears:

- *Can Edit:* Allows users to edit the presentation and change permissions

- *Can Comment:* Allows users to comment on the presentation but not to change any content or security settings

- *Can View:* Allows users only to view the presentation

4. **Select the appropriate permission setting from the list.**

5. **Check the Notify People via Email box to notify the specified users, by email, that you have shared a presentation with them.**

6. **Click Send.**

   Your Slides presentation is immediately made available to the users you invited.

 A user who is invited to view, edit, or comment on your presentation has to log into Google using the email address with which you shared the presentation. If she doesn't have a Google Account under that email address, you have to invite her with the address she uses for her Google Account. She also has the option to create a Google Account using the email address with which you invited her.

Tracking Revisions

Keeping track of revisions is very important when creating documents with multiple collaborators. Luckily, Google Slides handles version control masterfully. The Revision History tool, however, is not intended to be used as a Track Changes tool. As you and your collaborators create changes to your presentation, Slides will time-and-date stamp those changes so that you can view previous versions of your document and even revert to an earlier version if you need to.

Revision tracking is a default feature of Slides, so to view your revision history, follow these steps:

1. **Open the File menu in the Applications menu within Slides.**

2. **Choose See Revision History.**

   A Revision History box appears in the right portion of your screen. The box contains the various versions of your presentation in order of most recent to oldest.

3. **Click on a revision date in the Revision History box.**

   A preview of the revision appears in the presentation area. Changes appear in green.

4. **To change the current version to the version you're viewing, click Restore This Revision.**

   The restored version becomes the current version, and the previous version of the application is saved in the revision history so that you can revert to it at any point, if needed.

Using Slides Offline

Google Slides is a web-based presentation tool, which means that you must have an Internet connection to access it and all of its features. However, an offline version of Slides is available in the event you find yourself without a connection to the Internet.

To use Google Slides to work on your presentations offline, follow these steps:

1. **To use Google Slides offline, you must first enable Google Drive for offline use. To ensure that Google Drive is properly enabled, open the App Launcher and click the Google Drive icon.**

   A Chrome web browser appears and takes you to your Drive.

2. **On the right side of the screen, click the settings icon (it looks like a gear) and in the resulting menu, click Settings.**

3. **Check the check box to sync your work for offline use.**

4. **Click Done.**

   Your Slides files are now synced and available for offline editing.

5. **You can test whether you have properly enabled offline access by turning off your Wi-Fi. To do this, open the settings panel in the bottom-right of your screen and select WIFI.**

   The WIFI menu appears.

6. **At the bottom of the WIFI menu, click the WIFI indicator to turn off your Wi-Fi.**

7. **With your Wi-Fi turned off, switch back to Google Drive, locate your synced spreadsheets and click to open one.**

   If your Slides file opens and you are able to edit it, you know you have successfully engaged offline use and synced your documents.

Offline, you can't access some of the features available to Slides users that are connected to the Internet. You can, however, create presentations and save them. When you connect to the Internet, Drive uploads the presentations and enables all Internet-accessible features.

Chapter 10

Email with Gmail

*I*n the beginning, Google was a search engine. Over time, however, Google has created or acquired hundreds, if not thousands, of software tools and platforms and connected them together to make up what is commonly referred to as the Google ecosystem. Gmail was an early innovation that quickly took root and gained international appeal. At first, Gmail was nothing more than a free email platform that offered users 1GB of email storage. However, Inbox size, coupled with Gmail's easy-to-use interface, made the perfect recipe for growing a user base. Over the past ten years, Gmail has acquired 425 million users, and it is still free!

In this chapter, you learn how to launch Gmail on your Chromebook, read emails, and sort your emails with labels. You can explore how to write emails, add multiple recipients who are seen and unseen, and attach files to email messages. You learn how to use Gmail to access other email accounts! Navigate your sent mail and save messages in your Drafts folder for editing at a later time. Write emails, even when you don't have Internet access, and send them when you're connected at a later time with Gmail Offline.

Gmail for Chromebook

Before you can access your Chromebook, you must log in using your Google Account username and password. Your Google Account gives you access to almost all of the Google platform, which includes Gmail. This can get confusing very quickly, so you should pay close attention. Your Google Account is created with an email address. The email address doesn't have to be a Gmail address.

There was a time when you would access your Gmail using your Gmail address and password. However, now you access your Gmail using your Google Account email and password. Where this could get a little confusing is if you created a Google Account before you created a Gmail account.

Launching Gmail

Regardless of whether you have a Gmail account, if you want to access any email on your Chromebook, you have to use Gmail as your client, which will require you to create an account.

To launch Gmail, just open the App Launcher and click the Gmail icon. When you do so, Gmail launches in a Chrome browser window.

If you haven't created a Gmail account, you're prompted to create an account, thus adding it to your Google Account. Gmail is free and perhaps always will be. Even if you don't intend to use Gmail as your preferred email application, you still need a Gmail account to send and receive message from other email apps on your Chromebook. To create your Gmail account, follow these steps:

1. **On the Add Gmail to Your Google Account page, shown in Figure 10-1, complete all the fields in the sign-up form on the right side of the screen.**

Figure 10-1:
The Gmail account creation page.

If you intend to use your Gmail account to send and receive email, make sure you select an email address that's easy to remember to avoid awkward conversations down the road.

2. When you complete the form, click Submit.

The Verify Your Account page appears, where you're requested to verify your identity.

3. Enter your phone number, or any phone number at which you can be reached.

Google will call this number to give you a verification number.

4. Using the radio buttons, select to receive a text message or a phone call.

5. Click Continue.

The Verification page appears, on which you're prompted to enter the verification code that you received.

6. Enter the verification code you received by phone call or text.

7. Click Continue.

Once verified, you're logged into your new Gmail account.

Navigating Gmail

When you're logged into Gmail, you'll be looking at Gmail's minimalist interface. (See Figure 10-2.) The Gmail interface is broken up into two main areas. On the left is a list of folders, including your Inbox. In Gmail, these folders are called *labels*. Directly to the right of your list of labels is the email area. Above the email area is the Gmail toolbar, and above the toolbar is the Search bar.

Gmail gives you a default set of labels for categorizing your email, as shown in Figure 10-3. Labels are a lot like folders, except messages, unlike files, can have multiple labels. (More on categorization in the section "Organizing your Inbox," later in this chapter.)

Figure 10-2:
Gmail's
interface.

Figure 10-3:
Email labels.

The basic labels in Gmail are the following:

- ✔ **Inbox:** Your Inbox is the location where your new mail is delivered. The Inbox doesn't include spam, trash, or sent mail.

- ✔ **Starred:** Give your messages a special status by using a star so that you can more easily find them.

- ✔ **Sent Mail:** Any email you send is labeled Sent Mail.

- ✔ **Drafts:** Emails that you write but don't send are labeled Drafts.

- ✔ **Important:** Emails labeled Important.

- ✔ **Chats:** Gmail comes with a chat tool called GChat. Conversations are marked with the Chat label.

- ✔ **All Mail:** Just like it sounds, this label contains every message created, sent, and received, regardless of status.

- ✔ **Spam:** Junk mail that Google automatically identifies as spam.

- ✔ **Trash:** Email that you delete is labeled Trash and can be erased from existence.

Your Gmail view defaults to the Inbox label. When you have unread emails in your Inbox, a number appears directly to the right of the label. Both read and unread emails appear in the main email message area. Unread emails show up in bold, as shown in Figure 10-4. Directly above your email messages, by default, are three tabs — Primary, Social, and Promotions. Gmail automatically sorts the emails in your Inbox based on what it believes the incoming email to be. Emails from social outlets are placed in the Social tab, emails judged to be advertisements are placed into your Promotions tab, and the remainder go in your Primary tab.

Figure 10-4:
The email area.

Customizing your view

There are several ways that you can customize the look and feel of your Gmail application. By default, Gmail leaves a good deal of space between lines, emails, and so on. However, if you prefer, you can condense this space to make room for more information on your screen. To compact the space, follow these steps:

1. **Click the Settings icon on the right side of the toolbar.**

   The Settings icon looks like a gear or widget.

   The Settings menu opens, as shown in Figure 10-5. The first three to four options pertain to your Gmail display. If you have a touchscreen, Touch-Enabled will be the first option, followed by Comfortable, Cozy, and Compact.

2. **Select any display mode from the menu.**

   Your Gmail display automatically reconfigures itself and refreshes the page.

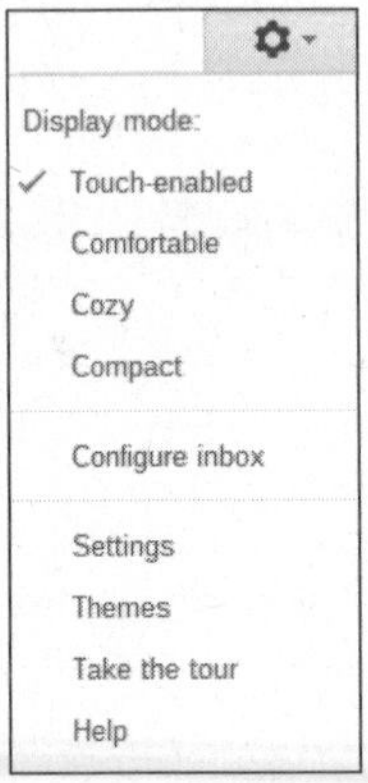

Figure 10-5:
Customizing your Gmail view.

You can also change the way your Gmail account handles the messages in your Inbox. By default, messages are grouped in the order they are received, whether they're read or not, and filtered based on the tab settings you're using. You can, however, change your Inbox view to assign different priorities to the messages you receive. Configuring your Inbox to keep all unread messages at the top can help you avoid missing a message. You can reconfigure your Inbox by following these steps:

1. **Move your pointer over the Inbox label on the left side of your window and click the down-pointing arrow that appears.**

   A menu appears, as shown in Figure 10-6, revealing several options for configuring your Inbox.

2. **Mouse over each option to reveal a description of what the option will do to your Inbox.**

3. **Choose Unread First.**

   Your Inbox is reconfigured to keep all unread emails at the top. All read emails are sorted by date, as shown in Figure 10-7.

Figure 10-6: Configuring your Inbox view.

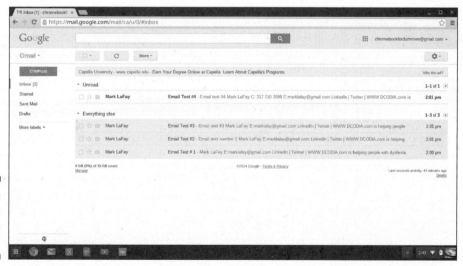

Figure 10-7: Unread emails appear first.

Adding a theme

Gmail also comes with several different themes for adding color and images to your account screen. Add flavor to your Gmail with a theme by following these steps:

1. **Click the Settings icon on the right side of the toolbar.**

   The Settings menu opens.

2. **Choose Themes.**

   Gmail loads the Themes page.

3. **Browse the selection of color themes and HD themes. Select a theme by clicking the option.**

   Gmail automatically applies the theme to your Gmail.

4. **When you're satisfied with the theme you select, click Inbox to be taken back to your Inbox.**

Sending Email with Gmail

All email consists of the same core elements — it must have a sender, a receiver, and a message — and email sent using Gmail is no different. The message is typically comprised of a subject line and a body of text. Nowadays, you can have multiple recipients and, in addition to text, your message can include documents, music, videos, archives, and more.

Navigating Gmail email

The Gmail email window has three main parts. The header of the email window is located at the top of the email message. The header contains the window controls for your email. The footer contains the editing tools for formatting and styling your email, and the middle portion is the email itself. Figure 10-8 is a picture of an email message in Gmail. The email message is made up of the following parts:

✔ **To:** Specify the recipient(s) by entering an email address (or email addresses) here. You can add recipients using the carbon copy feature. Carbon copy is used to send a message to someone that isn't the primary intended recipient. *Carbon copy* (or *Cc,* as it's commonly referred to), is used to start dialogues between multiple people over email. *Blind carbon copy,* or *Bcc,* is used to send an email to one or many recipients without other recipients knowing.

✔ **Subject:** Add a subject line to your email. Subjects are usually 50 characters or fewer.

✔ **Body:** The meat of your message is contained here in the message body.

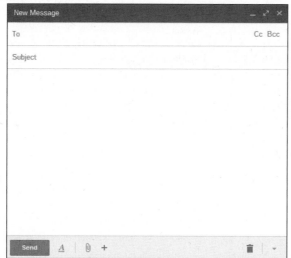

Figure 10-8:
An email
message in
Gmail.

Writing an email

Writing an email with Gmail is very similar to writing a letter using Google Docs or any other word processor. To write an email in Gmail, take the following steps:

1. **Click the Compose button at the top-left of your Gmail window.**

   The Email Editor pops up on the bottom-right of the window.

2. **Click the Recipients field at the top of the Email Editor and enter the email address of the person to whom you want to send your email.**

   Email addresses follow the format of *name@domain.something*; for instance, my email address is chromebookfordummies@gmail.com.

3. **Click in the Subject field and enter a subject line for the message.**

   It's always good advice to keep your subject line short and to the point.

4. **Click in the Body of the email and type your message.**

5. **When you finish writing your email, click Send.**

   The Email Editor vanishes, indicating the email has been sent.

Styling text

Gmail provides you with several advanced features for spicing up your emails, such as word-processor features to style your text. You can make your text bold or italicized by using the formatting palette located in your Email Editor, as shown in Figure 10-9.

Figure 10-9:
The formatting palette in an email message.

To apply boldface, italics, or underline to the text in your email, follow these steps:

1. **Select the text you wish to format by clicking and dragging your pointer.**

2. **Click the A button next to the Send button in the footer of the Email Editor.**

3. **Select the B button (to make the selected text bold), the I button (to make it italic), or the U button (to add an underline).**

   The selected text changes appropriately.

You can use keyboard shortcuts to apply formatting to text in your emails. While your text is selected, use the following shortcuts to apply the associated style:

- ✓ **Bold:** Ctrl+B
- ✓ **Italics:** Ctrl+I
- ✓ **Underline:** Ctrl+U

To change the color of the text in your email, follow these steps:

1. **Select the text whose color you wish to change by clicking and dragging your pointer.**

2. **Click the A button on left side of the formatting toolbar.**

   A menu appears, giving you the option to select a color to apply to your text or to apply as a highlight on your text.

3. **Select your desired color from the available options.**

   Your text changes to the selected color.

Attaching files to an email

Email has come a long way since the early days of the Internet. Now you can send more than just a digital letter; you can also send files with your emails. Want to send pictures of your kids to Mom and Dad? Maybe you need to submit your homework to your teacher? Or maybe you're just swapping files with your friends. Email is a great way to do it.

Most email service providers limit the file size of attachments that can be sent or received to 10MB (megabytes) or less. If you need to send a larger file, you may be forced to find a different way to send it.

Attaching a file to your email can be done by taking the following steps:

1. **Click the Attach Files icon (the paperclip) in the footer of your email.**

   Files launches.

2. **Using Files, navigate to the location of the file you wish to attach. Select the file.**

3. **Click Open.**

   The file uploads and appears at the bottom of your email, as shown in Figure 10-10.

You can also attach files from your Chromebook by dragging and dropping the files directly into the Email Editor.

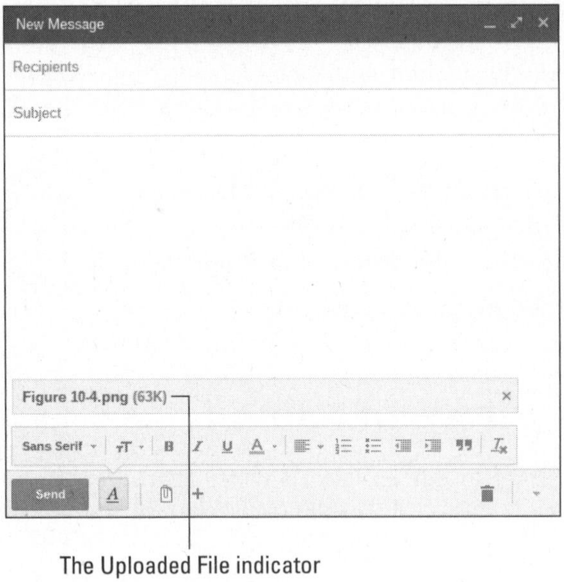

Figure 10-10:
The
Uploaded
File indicator
in an email.

The Uploaded File indicator

Customizing your email view

By default, your email appears as a pop-up window on the bottom-right of your Chrome browser while you're in Gmail. You can, however, change the view so that the Email Editor is full screen (actually it's really only three-quarters full screen, but close enough). The full-screen Editor is helpful for writing emails that are longer in content. You can write emails in Full Screen mode by clicking the arrow icon in the top-right corner of your Email Editor window. To take your Email Editor out of Full Screen mode, click the same arrow icon located in the top-right corner of the full-screen Email Editor.

If you would like Gmail to default to Full Screen mode, you can configure it by following these steps:

1. **Click the Compose button on the top-left of the Gmail window.**

   A new Email Editor window appears in the bottom-right corner of your window.

2. **Locate the down-arrow button in the bottom-right corner of the Email Editor window and click it.**

   A menu appears, revealing several options.

3. **Click Default to Full-Screen.**

   The menu disappears, and the Email Editor window remains the same size. New emails created from this point forward will automatically appear in Full Screen mode.

You can also set the default view of your Email Editor to partial-screen by following the steps outlined above.

Creating an email signature

Every good letter deserves a great closing. As you write emails, you may find that your sign-off is the same for each email. Or you may find that it's helpful to include some contact details in the bottom of each your emails. With Gmail, you can create a standard email *signature* so that every email you write contains a standardized closing. To create an email signature, follow these steps:

1. **With Gmail open, click the Settings icon in the top-right of your screen (which looks like a cog or widget).**

   The Settings menu appears, revealing several options. (Refer to Figure 10-5.).

2. **Choose Settings.**

   The Gmail Settings Editor appears.

3. **To ensure you're in the General tab, click General at the top of the Settings Editor.**

4. **Scroll down to the Signature section and click the radio button located directly below the No Signature radio button.**

5. **Click in the text box, as shown in Figure 10-11, and begin typing your signature.**

6. **When you finish typing your signature, scroll to the bottom of the Settings Editor and click Save Changes.**

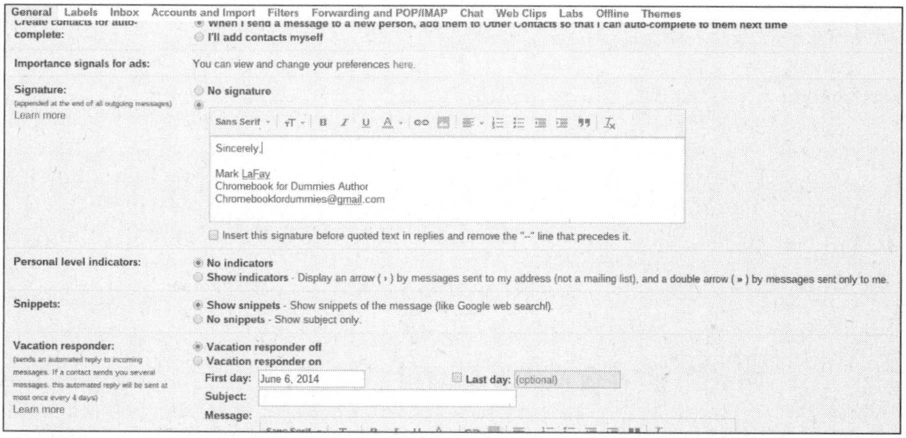

Figure 10-11: Adding an email signature.

Place a line or two of blank space at the top of your email signature to ensure you have enough space separating your signature from the body of your email. You can test your spacing by composing a new email to view your newly created, or edited, signature.

Reading Email

All of your incoming email will be delivered to your Gmail Inbox. By default, the most current emails appear on top unless you changed your view to keep all unread emails on the top regardless of date. Your Inbox gives you just enough information about the email for you to decide whether you want to read it. Each line starts with the name or address of the sender of the email, followed by the subject of the email. Gmail then previews the contents of the email with the remaining available space.

Unread emails appear with the sender's name and subject line in bold. After you read an email, the message appears un-bolded in your Inbox, indicating that it has been viewed. To view an email, place your pointer over the email line and click. Gmail opens the email and loads it in the main email area, as shown in Figure 10-12.

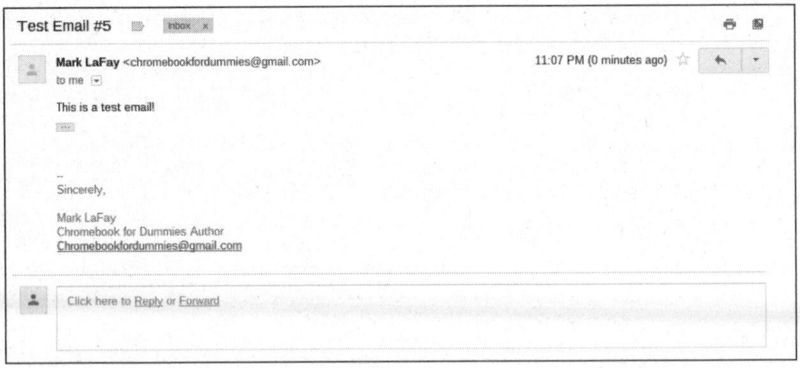

Test Email #5 ▷▷   Inbox   x   🖨 ▢

Mark LaFay <chromebookfordummies@gmail.com>   11:07 PM (0 minutes ago)   ☆   ↰   ▾
to me ▾

This is a test email!

--
Sincerely,

Mark LaFay
Chromebook for Dummies Author
Chromebookfordummies@gmail.com

Click here to Reply or Forward

Figure 10-12:
Reading an
email.

When you finish reading the email, you can click the Inbox link in your labels list on the left side of the Gmail window. You can also click the Older and Newer email buttons located next to the Settings icon in the top-right corner of the Gmail window.

Replying to email

After you read an email, you may want to send a reply message to the sender immediately. You can write a reply email by following these steps:

1. **While viewing an email in your Inbox, click the text box at the bottom of the email message.**

   The text box transforms into an Email Editor containing a flashing cursor, which indicates you can write an email.

   If you're replying to an email that was sent to multiple recipients including yourself, you may want to send your reply to every person on the original email. This action is called Reply All. To reply to everyone, click Reply All in the text box.

2. **Write your reply email.**

   Gmail automatically includes the original email message, so you have a history of your email dialogue in one place.

3. **When you're satisfied with your reply, click Send.**

   Your email is sent.

Organizing your Inbox

Every email you receive is delivered to your Inbox. You can, however, make your Gmail more manageable by placing your emails into groups. Gmail allows you to organize your emails by applying labels.

Gmail uses the term *labels* instead of *folders*. Labels act a lot like folders. However, you can apply multiple labels to an email, thus categorizing it in multiple locations.

By applying labels to your emails, you can quickly locate emails at a later date. Maybe you want to group all emails from your family members with a label you call Family. Or maybe you want to group all emails pertaining to work with the label Work. Whatever the case may be, labels are a helpful way to create order in your Inbox. Add a label to an email by following these steps:

1. **With Gmail open, click the Inbox link in the list of labels to ensure that you're in your Inbox.**

   Your Inbox loads into the main email area.

2. **Locate the email you wish to label and click the check box to the left of the email.**

   The selected email is highlighted.

3. **Click the Label icon (which looks like a tag) directly above the main email area.**

   The Label menu appears, as shown in Figure 10-13.

Figure 10-13:
Placing a
label on an
email.

4. **You can either select the desired labels from the available options or click Create New to create a completely new label.**

   Clicking Create New opens the New Label pop-up window.

   You can also type the name of a label in the Search bar at the top of the Label menu and then click Create New.

5. **Enter the name of the new label.**

6. **(Optional) If you would like to make your label a subcategory of another label, click Nest Label Under and, from the drop-down list, select the label under which you want to create a subcategory.**

7. **Click Create.**

   After you apply a label to your email, that email appears in the associated group in the label list on the left side of the screen.

Setting up a vacation responder

When you're ready to go on that monster vacation that you've been planning, you may want to totally unplug from technology. You don't have to worry about offending your family and coworkers by leaving them waiting for a reply. You can use the auto responder to write a message that Gmail sends to every email you receive. When you come home from your vacation, you can then get to the business of replying to the emails that you received while you were away, without needing to explain the delay to everyone who emailed you. To set up your auto responder, follow these steps:

1. **With Gmail open, click the Settings icon in the top-right corner of the window.**

   The Settings menu appears.

2. **Click Settings.**

   The Settings Editor appears in the main email area.

3. **Scroll to the bottom of the Settings Editor, to the Vacation Responder section. Click Vacation Responder On.**

4. **Enter the first day you want your responder to start in the First Day field.**

   If you know the last day you want your vacation responder on, enter it as well.

   If you don't set a last day for your vacation responder, you need to turn your vacation responder off manually. Otherwise, Gmail will continue to automatically send your message to each email you receive.

5. **Enter the subject in the subject field and body in the body field for your vacation responder email.**

6. **Click Save Changes.**

   Anyone who sends you an email will receive an auto response at least once while you're away.

Use Gmail to Access Non-Gmail Accounts

If you already have an email address and it happens to not be a Gmail account, you may not want to create and use a new email address. That's understandable! Your contacts are likely quite familiar with your current contact info, and changing your details could prove to be frustrating. Gmail can work as an email client for up to five other email accounts.

Gmail can access your other email account, pulling in all of your received emails and categorizing the messages by applying labels to them. You can then use Gmail to compose new email messages but have them appear to be sent from your other email account.

Setting up Gmail to send and receive mail for a different account requires that you provide answers to several highly technical questions. Be prepared to enter your email address, password, POP3 Server address, and security settings. If you don't have this information, don't proceed.

Access your non-Gmail accounts through Gmail by following these steps:

1. **Launch Gmail by opening the App Launcher and clicking the Gmail icon.**

   Gmail loads in a Chrome web browser.

2. **Click the Settings icon in the top-right of the window.**

   The Settings menu appears.

3. **Click Settings.**

   The Settings Editor loads into the main email area.

4. **Open the Accounts and Import tab in the Settings menu at the top of the Settings Editor.**

   The Accounts and Import settings load.

5. **Scroll down and click Add a POP3 Mail Account You Own.**

   A pop-up window appears.

6. **Enter the full email address of your other account and then click Next Step.**

   Another screen appears, displaying several text boxes and options.

7. **Complete the text boxes as indicated and click Add Account.**

   After your account has been added, you're asked if you want to be able to send email as this address.

8. **Follow the prompts accordingly.**

Using Gmail Offline

To send and receive email, you must be connected to the Internet. Gmail, however, has an Offline mode that allows you to write emails, even if you don't have an Internet connection, and will send those emails when you get online next. To use Gmail offline, follow these steps:

1. **Open the App Store by clicking the App Store icon in the App Launcher.**

   The Chrome Web Store loads in a Chrome web browser.

2. **In the Search bar, type** Gmail Offline **and press Enter.**

3. **Click the Gmail Offline App in the search results.**

4. **Click the Free button.**

   Gmail Offline installs on your Chromebook.

5. **Select the option to Allow Offline Mail, as shown in Figure 10-14, and click Continue.**

   Gmail Offline loads.

Figure 10-14:
Enable
Gmail
Offline.

The Gmail Offline interface is far simpler to navigate than the traditional Gmail interface. The left side of the Gmail Offline screen contains offline versions of emails from your Gmail account. The right side of the Gmail Offline screen contains the complete message content of the selected email. Use Gmail Offline to draft messages that will be sent when you acquire an Internet connection. To write an email, follow these steps:

1. **In the Gmail Offline app, click the New Email icon (which looks like a red, square pencil) at the top of the window.**

   An Email Editor window appears.

2. **Enter the recipient's address, a subject line, and the body of your email.**

3. **Click Send.**

   After you click Send, your email is stored in your Outbox.

4. **Connect to the Internet and open Google Offline to send all stored messages.**

Chapter 11

Organizing with Google Calendar

In This Chapter

▶ Exploring Google Calendar

▶ Organizing your life with multiple calendars

▶ Creating and sharing calendar events

▶ Sharing one of your calendars

▶ Using Google Calendar Offline

*R*egardless of whether you're a busy parent trying to keep your social calendar and kids' events organized, or an executive bouncing from meeting to meeting and deadline to deadline; Google Calendar is a robust calendar platform designed to keep your entire life organized. Google Calendar is your daddy's day planner on steroids. With your Chromebook and Google Calendar, you can keep your schedule straight regardless of where you are in the world.

In this chapter, you dive into the Google Calendar system on your Chromebook and learn how to navigate through the various features. You create calendar entries, set alerts to remind you when those entries draw near, and invite others to the calendar events. Add additional calendars to keep work events on one calendar, personal events on another calendar, and so forth. Lastly, you learn how to share your calendar with other users for viewing, editing, and updating. Collaboration is key!

Navigating Google Calendar

 To get started with Google Calendar, make sure you're logged into your Chromebook. Then, open the App Launcher and click the Google Calendar icon.

If this is your first time launching Google Calendar, you're greeted with the Welcome to Google Calendar pop-up window, shown in Figure 11-1, which offers some quick tips on how to get started. Click Next to navigate through the different quick-tip screens until the pop-up window disappears.

Figure 11-1: Welcome tips.

With the Welcome pop-up window closed, take a look at the Google Calendar workspace, as pictured in Figure 11-2. Your Calendar workspace is broken into a few key areas: the left sidebar is your main menu, the right area is your calendar, and directly above the calendar and left sidebar is your Settings bar.

Settings bar

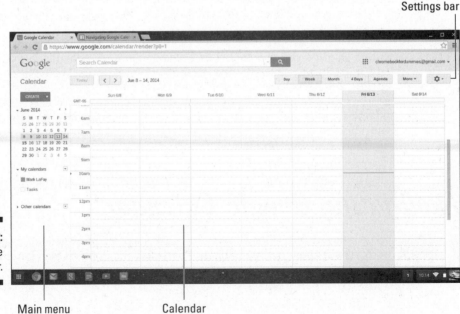

Figure 11-2: Google Calendar.

Main menu

Calendar

The left sidebar contains a mini-calendar that defaults to the current month. Below the mini-calendar is a collapsible list of all your calendars. Below your calendars is another collapsible list of calendars that have been shared with you. The top Settings bar contains buttons for changing your view, navigating through your calendar in the current view, and a Settings icon that can display several options for customizing and controlling your calendar.

The main calendar area is a grid of days and hours. The columns are the days of the week or month, and the rows are the hours of the day. Each cell in your calendar grid is a moment in time that can contain one event or multiple events.

Customizing your view

By default, your calendar shows a complete seven-day week from Sunday to Saturday. Your calendar lets you know the day of the week by highlighting the day in your calendar with a light gray background, as shown in Figure 11-3.

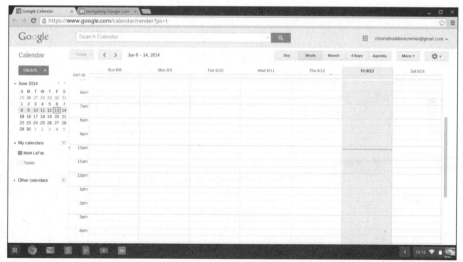

Figure 11-3: The current day is highlighted.

Calendar gives you the option to customize the number of days you view. In the Settings toolbar, located above the calendar area, you can change the view by clicking one of the buttons, as follows:

✔ **Day:** Your view shows the current day's calendar from midnight to midnight. Day view is pictured in Figure 11-4.

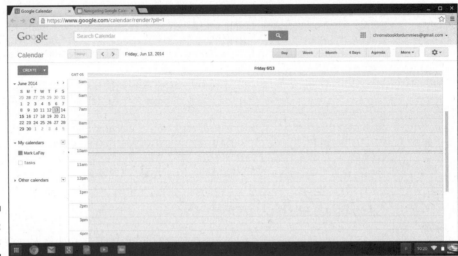

Figure 11-4:
Day view.

✔ **Week:** This is the default view for calendar. Sunday to Saturday is shown.

✔ **Month:** The full month view looks like a traditional calendar. Events are indicated but, due to space limitations, little additional information is provided. Month view is shown in Figure 11-5.

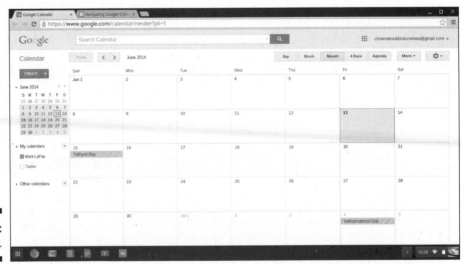

Figure 11-5:
Month view.

✔ **4 Days:** This view shows you four days of events, starting with the current date. 4 Days view is shown in Figure 11-6.

✔ **Agenda:** The Agenda view gives you a list of events across all days in your calendar. Find events by scrolling. (See Figure 11-7.)

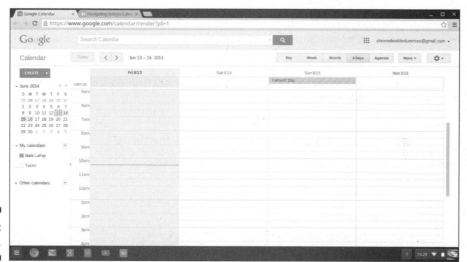

Figure 11-6:
4 Days view.

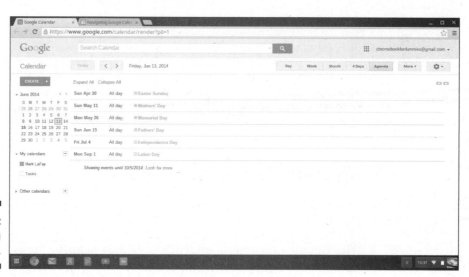

Figure 11-7:
Agenda
view.

Changing your default view

By default, your calendar is in Week view. You can, however, change this to default to a different view. To change the default view, follow these steps:

1. **With Calendar open, click the Settings icon on the right side of the Settings bar to open the Settings menu.**

2. **Choose Settings.**

   Your calendar settings load.

3. **Scroll down to the Default View section and click the drop down box located there.**

   A drop-down list of options appears.

4. **Select the view you desire from the list of available options.**

5. **When you're satisfied with your change, scroll to the bottom of the Settings window and click Save.**

   You're returned to your calendar in the newly defaulted view.

Creating Additional Calendars

Google Calendar gives you the option to have multiple calendars within your Calendar account so that you can organize your events into groups. Use multiple calendars to keep your work and play activities separate. If you're a parent trying to manage the activity schedules for each of your children, create a calendar for your kids or a calendar for each individual kid. You may want to keep the birthdays of your friends and family organized on a calendar so that those reminders don't clutter up your other calendars. With Google Calendar, you can organize the minutia of life any way you see fit.

Adding and configuring calendars

You can add another calendar into your Google Calendar account by following these steps:

1. **With Google Calendar open, click the down-pointing arrow on the right side of the collapsible My Calendars menu in the left sidebar.**

   A menu of options appears, as shown in Figure 11-8.

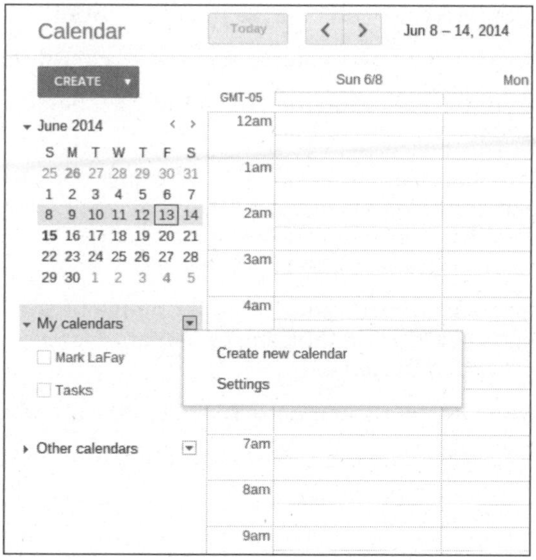

Figure 11-8:
Adding a calendar.

2. Choose Create New Calendar.

The Create New Calendar page, pictured in Figure 11-9, opens.

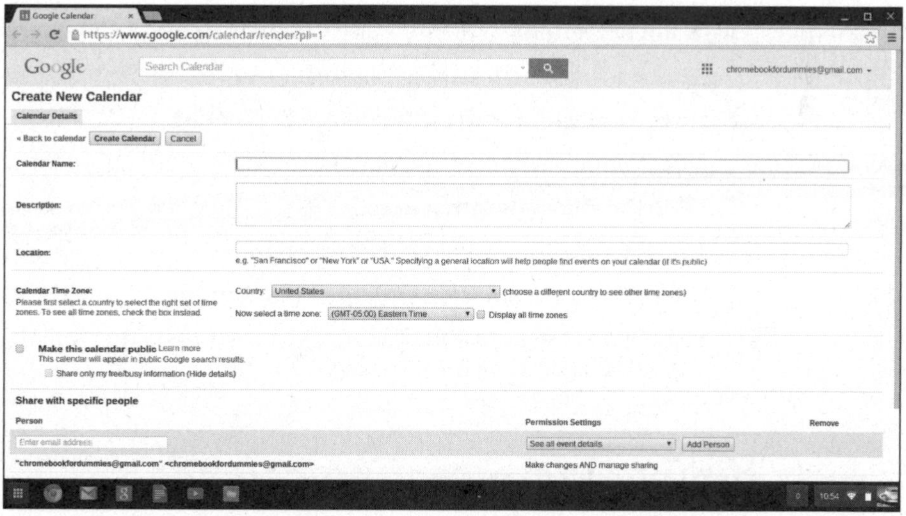

Figure 11-9:
Creating a new calendar.

3. In the Calendar Name text box, name your calendar.

Keep the name short and to the point.

4. **Enter a description for your calendar in the Description text box.**

5. **Enter the location for your new calendar in the Location text box.**

6. **Choose a time zone for your calendar from the Now Select a Time Zone drop-down list.**

The time zone for your calendar is important because Google Calendar will schedule all of your events with this time zone. When you travel to different time zones, Google maintains your calendar based on the default time zone of your calendar events.

You have other options to make your calendar public or share it with others, discussed in the section "Sharing Calendars," later in this chapter. For now, don't touch these fields.

7. **Scroll to the bottom of the screen and click Create Calendar.**

Calendar view reappears, and your newly created calendar appears in the My Calendars collapsible menu.

Color-coding calendars

As you add multiple calendars, you can avoid confusion by assigning a color to each calendar so that events on different calendars are easy to identify. You can color-code your calendars by following these steps:

1. **In the left sidebar, open the My Calendars collapsible menu.**

All of your calendars appear in this menu.

2. **Move your pointer over the desired calendar.**

A down-pointing arrow appears to the right of the calendar name.

3. **Click the down-pointing arrow.**

A menu appears, revealing multiple options.

4. **Select a color from the available color palette.**

The color of your calendar changes to the selected color. All events for this calendar will be in the associated color.

Hiding and revealing calendars

Having the option to add multiple calendars should make it easier for you to keep your events organized by grouping them into categories. However, if all of the events and activities of your busy life are visible on your calendar at all times, the value of organizing them into separate calendars may be lost. The good news is that you can hide and reveal your calendars so that you can quickly view activities specific to a particular calendar. To hide or reveal calendars, follow these steps:

1. **In the left sidebar, open the My Calendars collapsible menu.**

   The menu expands, revealing your calendars.

   On the left side of each calendar name is a box. An uncolored box indicates that calendar is currently hidden. A box filled with the calendar color indicates the calendar is currently visible.

2. **Click the calendar you wish to hide or reveal.**

   The box fills or un-fills, depending on whether it was hidden or visible, and the events appear or vanish accordingly.

If you add multiple calendars to your Google Calendar account, it may be tedious to turn off all your calendars in the event you want to isolate a single calendar. To isolate a single calendar, follow these steps:

1. **In the left sidebar, open the My Calendars collapsible menu.**

   The menu expands, revealing your calendars.

2. **Move your pointer over the desired calendar.**

   This reveals a down-pointing arrow to the right of the calendar name.

3. **Click the down-pointing arrow.**

   A menu appears, revealing multiple options.

4. **Click Display Only This Calendar.**

   All calendars except the selected calendar vanish from sight.

Creating Calendar Events

Your Calendar is an organized collection of activities called events. Each event you create contains the following information that describes the event:

- ✔ Date
- ✔ Start and stop time
- ✔ Time zone
- ✔ Event location

✔ Calendar

✔ Event description

✔ Reminders

✔ Event guests

Aside from the date, you can create events with as little or as much of the remaining information outlined above as you want. However, the more information that you include, the more helpful your calendar becomes.

To create a calendar event, follow these steps:

1. **With Google Calendar open, click the Create button in the top-right corner of the window.**

   The New Event page, shown in Figure 11-10, appears.

Figure 11-10:
The New
Event page.

2. **Complete the fields on the New Event page.**

   These fields include

   • **Event Title:** This text box displays Untitled Event by default. Click in it and enter the title you want to give the event.

   • **Date & Time:** Starting and ending dates and times of the event.

   • **Where:** Location of the event.

- **Calendar:** The calendar on which you want to place the event.

- **Description:** Notes for your event.

- **Reminders:** Set a reminder.

- **Show Me As:** Indicate yourself as busy or available.

3. **When you're satisfied with your entries, click the Save button at the top of the page.**

   The calendar entry is saved at the date and time location in your calendar.

If you're on the move and you need to quickly add an event to your calendar, you can do so by taking these steps:

1. **In your calendar, click the desired date and time.**

   A pop-up window appears, as shown in Figure 11-11.

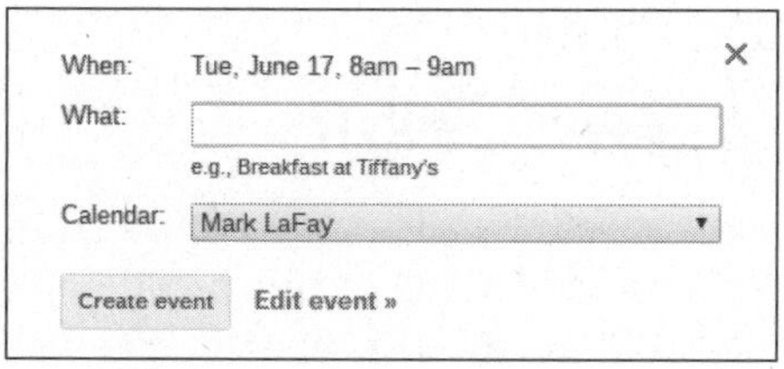

Figure 11-11:
Quickly adding an event.

When:	Tue, June 17, 8am – 9am	✕
What:		
	e.g., Breakfast at Tiffany's	
Calendar:	Mark LaFay ▾	

Create event   Edit event »

2. **Enter a title for your event in the What text box.**

3. **Select a calendar for your new event from the Calendar drop-down list.**

4. **Click Create Event.**

   Your new event is saved to your calendar.

Editing and deleting an event

After an event is created, you may find that you need to edit the event to add more notes, change the date or time, and so on. You can edit your events by following these steps:

1. **In Calendar, click the event you wish to edit.**

   A pop-up window appears, as shown in Figure 11-12, giving you the option to edit your event.

	Event1 ×
Figure 11-12: Editing an event.	Mon, June 16, 8am – 9am
	Delete Edit event »

2. Click Edit Event.

The Event Details page, where you can edit the selected event, appears.

You can quickly remove events from your calendar by clicking Delete instead of Edit Event. The selected event is removed from your calendar.

Make sure you absolutely want to delete an event before you click Delete. There's no Undelete feature in Calendar, so you have to re-add any deleted events manually.

3. When you've made your desired changes, click the Save button.

Inviting others to your event

Events, of course, involve other people. You can make sure that other event participants don't forget about your scheduled events by adding those participants to your Calendar event. When you add someone to an event, Google Calendar sends each participant an invitation to the event via email. The email invitation contains a calendar entry so that your invitees can add the event to their own calendars, as well.

You can invite others to your events when you create a new event. However, it's better to complete the creation of your event first so you can be sure it contains all the necessary information, and then go back and add invitees to the event. Your invitees receive updates every time you modify the event, and that can become annoying to some people. To invite participants to a calendar event, follow these steps:

1. Click the calendar entry to which you would like to add invitees.

A pop-up menu appears.

2. Click Edit Event.

The Event Details page loads, with the Add Guests text box on the right.

3. Enter the email address of an event invitee in the Add Guests text box and click Add.

4. **Repeat Step 3 for each invitee.**

   The invitee appears below the Add Guests field when you enter him.

5. **Click the Save button at the top of the page.**

   Upon saving, Google Calendar sends an event invitation to each invitee.

Sharing Calendars

Whether your calendar is for work or for home, sharing a calendar can alleviate the need to have to constantly communicate your availability with family and coworkers. Share one of your calendars with your coworkers or your spouse so that they can see your events and even add events directly to your calendars. Share one of your calendars by following these steps:

1. **In the left sidebar, open the My Calendars collapsible menu.**

   All of your calendars appear.

2. **Move your pointer over the desired calendar.**

   A down-pointing arrow appears to the right of the calendar name.

3. **Click the down-pointing arrow.**

   A menu appears, revealing multiple options.

4. **Click Share This Calendar.**

   The Calendar details load, as shown in Figure 11-13.

Figure 11-13:
Sharing with specific people.

5. **Enter the email address of the person with whom you wish to share your calendar in the Share with Specific People section.**

6. **Open the Permission Settings drop-down list.**

   The following options are revealed:

   - *Make Changes AND Manage Sharing:* Allow others to make changes to your calendar and invite others to access your calendar.

   - *Make Changes to Events:* Allow others to view and make changes to your events only.

   - *See All Event Details:* Allow others to see your events but not make changes.

   - *See Only Free/Busy (Hide Other Details):* Allow others to see only your events and whether you're free or busy, but do not reveal any other event details.

7. **Select the desired permission setting and click Add Person.**

8. **Click Save.**

You can un-share your calendars by following Steps 1 through 4 as outlined above, and then clicking the Trash icon in the Share with Specific People section to the right of the person you want to delete. Then click Save.

In the event you have a calendar that you would like to make public — that is, the entire world can view — follow these steps:

1. **In the left sidebar, open the My Calendars collapsible menu.**

   All of your calendars are displayed.

2. **Move your pointer over the desired calendar.**

   A down-pointing arrow to the right of the calendar name appears.

3. **Click the down-pointing arrow.**

   A menu appears, revealing multiple options.

4. **Click Share This Calendar.**

   The Calendar details load.

5. **Click Make This Calendar Public.**

6. **Click Save.**

   Your calendar is publicly accessible and completely visible in Google Search.

You can also link people to your calendar so that they can navigate to it and bookmark it. Locate the link by following these steps:

1. **In the left sidebar, open the My Calendars collapsible menu.**

   All of your calendars appear.

2. **Move your pointer over the desired calendar.**

   This reveals a down-pointing arrow to the right of the calendar name.

3. **Click the down arrow.**

   A menu appears, revealing multiple options.

4. **Click Share This Calendar.**

   The Calendar details load.

5. **Click Calendar Details at the top of the page.**

   The Calendar Details page opens.

6. **Click the HTML button in the Calendar Address section.**

   A Calendar Address pop-up window appears, as shown in Figure 11-14, containing your calendar's web address (URL). Copy the URL and paste it wherever you wish to share it.

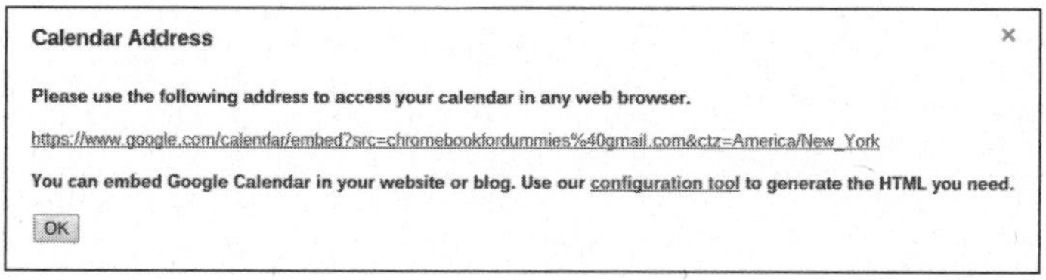

Figure 11-14:
Your cal-
endar has
a public
address.

Calendar Address   ×

Please use the following address to access your calendar in any web browser.

https://www.google.com/calendar/embed?src=chromebookfordummies%40gmail.com&ctz=America/New_York

You can embed Google Calendar in your website or blog. Use our configuration tool to generate the HTML you need.

OK

Using Calendar Offline

Google Calendar for Chromebook gives you the option to use your calendar offline. In the event you don't have Internet access, you can still access and use your calendar. To access your calendar offline with your Chromebook, follow these steps:

1. **Open the App Launcher and click the Google Calendar icon.**

   A Chrome web browser opens and loads Google Calendar.

2. **Click the Settings icon in the top-right corner of the page.**

   A drop-down list appears, revealing several options.

3. **Click Offline.**

The Enable Google Calendar Offline pop-up window appears. (See Figure 11-15.)

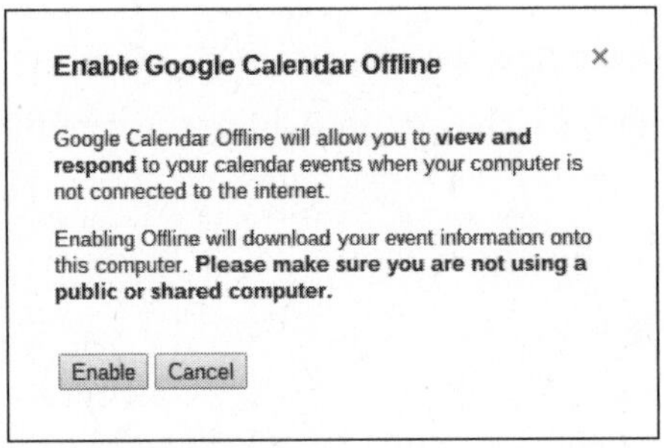

Figure 11-15:
Using
Calendar
offline.

Enable Google Calendar Offline   ×

Google Calendar Offline will allow you to **view and respond** to your calendar events when your computer is not connected to the internet.

Enabling Offline will download your event information onto this computer. **Please make sure you are not using a public or shared computer.**

[Enable] [Cancel]

4. **Click Enable.**

A status bar appears indicating the status of the offline sync.

You can verify that your Calendar is ready for offline use by clicking the Settings icon and checking whether a green circle containing a checkmark appears next to the Offline option.

Part III
The Chromebook Recreational Vehicle

Use your Chromebook as a one-stop media center. Connect Chromebook to your TV to watch movies on a bigger screen. Learn how at www.dummies.com/extras/chromebook.

In this part . . .

- ✔ Streaming albums, songs, or customized radio stations with Google Play

- ✔ Watching videos on your Chromebook or streaming them over the Internet with Google Play Video

- ✔ Staying in touch with family and friends or conducting a business meeting from around the globe with Google Hangouts

- ✔ Capturing only your best angles with your Chromebook camera

- ✔ Purchasing, renting, and reading books on your Chromebook

Chapter 12

Mustering Your Music

. . . .

. . . .

*B*efore the advent of the Internet, the primary delivery mechanism for music was radio and television. Broadcast media almost dictated what was popular simply because there was no other way to get exposed to new music unless you scoured the record bins at the local music store. Or maybe you had friends that had a cool older sibling who gave out mixtapes to broaden your musical horizons. The Internet turned the entire media industry on its head by providing access to anything, anywhere, anytime.

These days, purchasing physical music media is primarily done by collectors and super-fans. Broadcast radio is shrinking and consolidating. When was the last time MTV played a music video? The expansion of the Internet, broadband access, and wireless technology has revolutionized the way the world consumes media. Its a buyer's market in the music industry.

In this chapter, you explore the ins and outs of Google's digital music platform, Google Play Music. Upload your digital music library to Google Play and have it sync to your Chromebook and other wireless devices. Search the Google Play catalog of over 20 million songs and stream them to your Chromebook. Learn how to create playlists that can be shared with other Google Play users or simply search for radio stations that will play an endless stream of tunes to get you through the day. It's never a dull moment with Google Play.

Getting Started with Google Play

Google Play is Google's online marketplace, very similar to Apple's iTunes Store. Google Play sells videos, televisions shows, books, music, and applications for Android, Chromebook, the Chrome browser, and more.

 As is the case with all of the applications on the Google platform, access to apps is linked to your Google Account. If you have multiple Google Accounts, make sure you're logged into your Chromebook with the account that you want to be associated with Google Play. Launch Google Play by opening the App Launcher and clicking the Google Play Music icon.

If you're logging into Google Play for the first time, a Welcome screen appears. You need to decide what level of service you want. Google Play Music offers two levels of service. The free version is free indefinitely with limited functionality.

With the free version, you can

- ✔ Upload your music collection (up to 20,000 songs) and stream it to any Chromebook, Android, iOS, or web-enabled device.
- ✔ Purchase new music through Google Play, and download it or stream it to your Chromebook, Android, iOS or web-enabled device.

With the paid version, you get everything the free version offers, but you also can

- ✔ Listen to custom radio stations with personalized recommendations.
- ✔ Access the Google Play catalog of 20 million songs, completely advertisement-free.

Creating a standard account

To begin, proceed with the standard (free) version of Google Play by following these steps:

1. **Open the App Launcher menu and click the Google Play Music icon.**

   Google Play Music opens in a Chrome browser.

2. **Review the terms of service by clicking Terms of Service, and then locate and click the Agree and Next button.**

3. **To proceed with standard access, click the Use Standard button.**

   A page loads in your Chrome browser, giving you the option to keep proceeding with the standard version of Google Play Music or go back and select the premium version.

4. **Stay the course and click Next to proceed with the standard (free) service level.**

   A pop-up window appears. Google wants to confirm your country of residence by putting a credit card on file. In reality, Google can't capitalize on impulse purchases if you can't purchase songs in two clicks or less.

5. **Click Add Card.**

   The Google Wallet pop-up window appears with fields for all of the details on your preferred payment method, as shown in Figure 12-1.

6. **Complete the required fields and click Accept and Continue.**

   A pop-up window appears, asking you to confirm your purchase of $0.00.

7. **Click Buy. (See Figure 12-1.)**

   A page loads, asking you to upload music to Google Play.

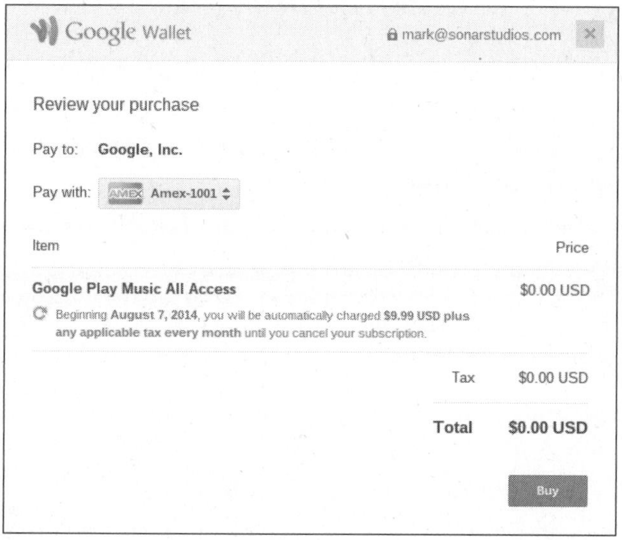

Figure 12-1: The Google Wallet pop-up window.

8. **Click Not Now to proceed to Google Play.**

   You're now taken to your Google Play Music account, as shown in Figure 12-2.

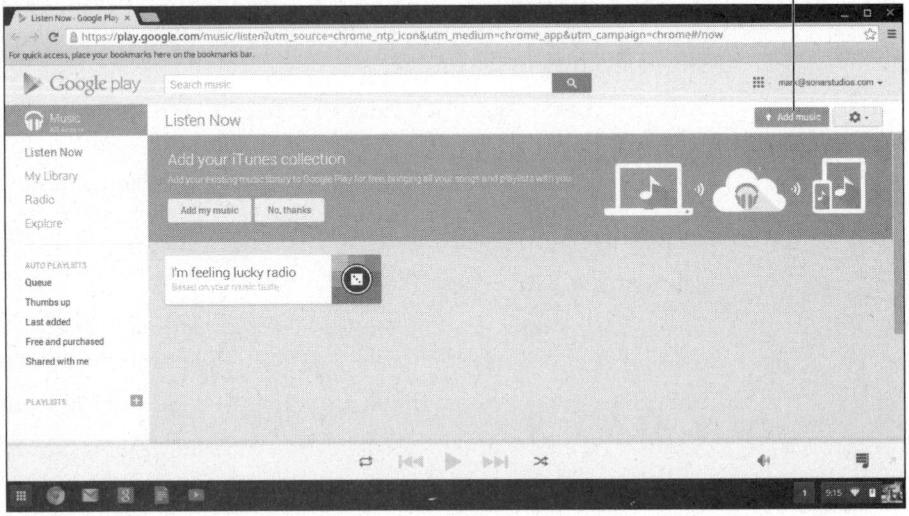

The Add Music button

Figure 12-2:
Google Play
Music.

Creating a premium account

Proceed with the premium (paid) version of Google Play by following these
steps:

1. **Review the terms of service by clicking Terms of Service, then click
   the Agree and Next button.**

2. **To proceed with premium access, click the Try All Access button.**

   If you haven't put a credit card on file with your Google Account, a
   Google Wallet pop-up window appears asking you to enter a credit card.
   Otherwise, you're asked to select a payment method.

3. **Click Add Card.**

   The Google Wallet pop-up window appears with fields for all of the
   details on your preferred payment method. (Refer to Figure 12-1.)

4. **Complete the required fields and click Buy.**

   A pop-up window appears, asking you to confirm your purchase of $0.00.
   Google Play is free for the first 30 days!

5. **Click Start Now.**

   A page loads, asking you to select the genres you like, as shown in
   Figure 12-3.

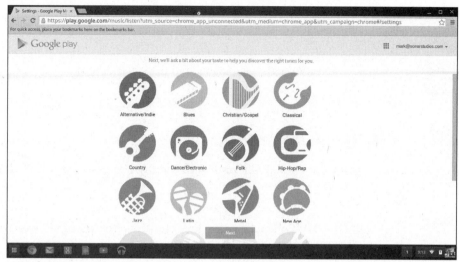

Figure 12-3:
Picking
favorite
genres.

6. **Select the genres you like and click Next.**

   A page loads, asking you to select the artists you like.

7. **Select your favorite artists and click Next.**

   Google Play loads your account, signaling the completion of the account-creation process.

Accessing the Google Play Library

The Google Play library is where all of your music uploads and music purchases reside. In the standard account, your Google Play view defaults to your music library. If you aren't in your library, you can get there by locating and clicking the My Library link on the left side of the page. Your library loads, revealing all of your music that's available to stream.

If you opted for the standard account and haven't uploaded or purchased any music, your library will be empty. Even so, you have two options for playing music (you have three if you have a premium account):

- **Try It Now:** Stream music from Google Play's catalog of over 20 million songs. (This is a premium feature, so you need to pay for a premium account to use it.)
- **Add Your Music:** Upload your music.

✔ **Shop:** Shop the Google Play store for songs that you want to purchase and add to your Google Play library.

With the standard account, Google Play allows you to upload up to 20,000 songs. If your collection is bigger than that, just upload the music you listen to most and leave the back catalog on a jump drive.

Uploading music

1. **Click the Add Music button in the top-right corner of the Google Play window (refer to Figure 12-2).**

   The Add Music screen appears.

2. **If Files isn't already open, launch it by clicking the Files icon in the App Launcher.**

3. **Navigate to the folders on your Chromebook that contain the music you want to upload.**

4. **Select the file(s) or folder(s) that you wish to upload and then drag-and-drop them in the Google Play window.**

   Google Play queues the files and uploads them in the background as long as Google Play is open.

⊙ Processing music... You can monitor the progress of your file upload by clicking the Processing Music button (which displays the flashing upload indicator icon) in the bottom-left of the Google Play window.

Purchasing music

Google Play's music library is vast like the ocean. If you have a standard account, you can expand your music selection by purchasing songs from the Google Play store. If you have a premium account, you also have the option to purchase songs, but there's little reason to do so because you can stream any song in the Google Play database for no additional charge.

If you want to purchase songs, you can do so by following these steps:

1. **With Google Play Music open, click the Shop button on the left side of the page.**

   The Google Play Music store opens.

2. **Begin your search for the music you want to buy by using the Search bar at the top of the screen.**

   Just type in the name of the band, album, or song, and then click the Search button located at the right side of the Search bar.

   Google Play serves up search results categorized by Artist, Album, and Track.

3. **Locate the artist in the Artist section and click their picture.**

   The Artist Profile page appears.

4. **In the Artist Profile page, click the album you're looking for.**

   The Album Profile page loads. You have the option to purchase the entire album or individual songs, as shown in Figure 12-4.

   It's always a good idea to select the artist first. Many variations of songs are available today, so it's easy to accidentally select the wrong version. First select the artist, and then locate the album from the artist's Google Play profile. You can then purchase the entire album or a singular track.

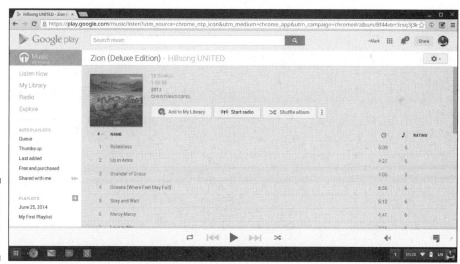

Figure 12-4:
A Google
Play Album
Profile page.

5. **Make your purchase.**

   You can buy the entire album by clicking the price located next to the album artwork at the top of the page or purchase just a song by clicking the Price button associated with the desired song.

   A pop-up window appears, asking you to confirm your payment method and the purchase price.

6. **Click Buy to complete your purchase.**

   Google charges your payment source and adds the song(s) to your library.

Streaming Music

With a premium Google Play Music account, you have the keys to the kingdom. Google boasts of over 20 million songs in its music catalog, all available to you with just a stroke of the finger. To stream music, follow these steps:

1. **With Google Play Music open, click the Listen Now button on the left side of the screen.**

   Google Play loads the Listen Now section, populated with musical suggestions and past selections.

2. **Begin your search for music by using the Search bar.**

   Just type the name of an artist that you would like to stream and then click the Search button on the right side of the Search bar.

   Google displays search results with the best matches appearing at the top, as shown in Figure 12-5.

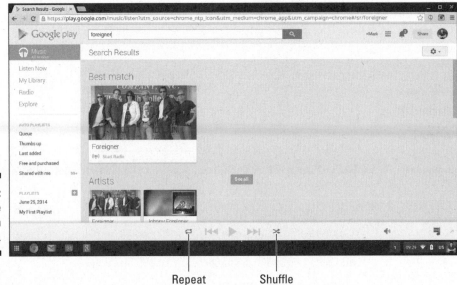

Figure 12-5: Google Play search results.

Repeat   Shuffle

Google does its best to match your search query with the correct result. However, the Best Match may not be the correct match. Be sure to scroll down to search through the Artists, Albums, and Songs if you don't think the right results are showing in the Best Match section. Worst case scenario: Retry your search.

3. **Click the Artist who matches your search and, in the Artist Profile page that appears, click the album you're looking for.**

   The Album Profile page loads, giving you the option to stream the entire album or play a single song.

4. **Move your cursor over the desired song and click the Play button that appears.**

   The selected song begins playing. Google Play then plays through the entire album in order.

To play a song or album repeatedly, click the Repeat icon on the left side of the play controls. To play the album in random order, click the Shuffle button. (Refer to Figure 12-5.)

Creating Playlists

Playlists are a convenient way to group together songs you want to play in a specific or randomized order. Google Play gives you the ability to build playlists comprised of songs that you've uploaded to your library or, if you have an All Access account, with songs available in the Google Play catalog. Google allows you to have up to 1,000 songs in a playlist!

All your playlists are listed on the bottom-left of your Google Play window. To create your first playlist, follow these steps:

1. **In the Playlists section on the left sidebar of your Google Play Music window, click the plus sign (+) button located to the right of the word Playlists.**

   The New Playlist pop-up window appears, presenting you with fields that describe your new playlist. (See Figure 12-6.)

2. **Enter the name of your playlist in the Name text box and give it a nice description in the Description text box.**

3. **For now, make the playlist available only to you by checking the Only Me radio button.**

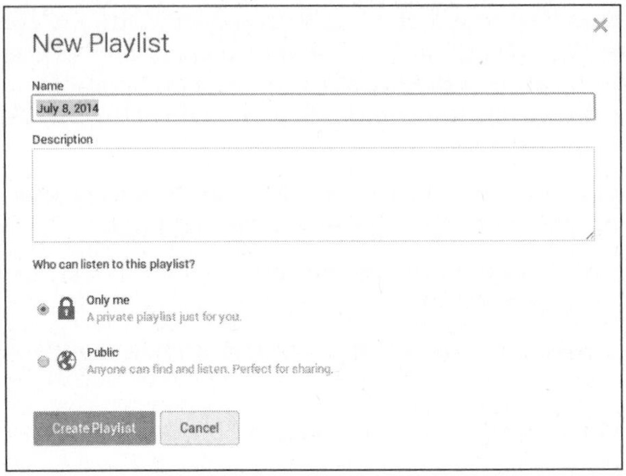

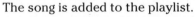

New Playlist

Name

July 8, 2014

Description

Who can listen to this playlist?

○ 🔒 **Only me**
A private playlist just for you.

○ 🌐 **Public**
Anyone can find and listen. Perfect for sharing.

Create Playlist   Cancel

Figure 12-6:
Creating a
new playlist.

4. **Click Create Playlist.**

Your new creation appears in the list on the bottom-left of your Google Play window.

Adding music to playlists

To add music from your library to your playlist, follow these steps:

1. **With Google Play Music open, click My Library.**

Your library loads in the main window.

2. **Browse for the song you wish to add to your playlist and, when you locate it, right-click the title.**

A pop-up menu appears.

3. **Hover over Add to Playlist.**

A submenu appears, revealing all available playlists.

4. **Select the playlist to which you'd like to add your selected song.**

The song is added to the playlist.

If you want to create a new playlist on the fly, follow Steps 1 through 3 and then select New Playlist.

If you want to add songs to your playlist from the Google Play catalog of songs, follow these steps (you must have a premium account):

1. **With Google Play Music open, click Listen Now.**

   A window appears filled with recently played music and bands that fit your preferences.

2. **Begin your search for music by using the Search bar.**

   Just type the name of the artist of the song or songs that you wish to add to your playlist, and then click the Search button to the right of the Search bar.

   Google Play loads your search results.

3. **Click the artist who matches your search query and, in the Artist Profile page that appears, click the album you're looking for.**

   The Album Profile page loads and lists the contents of the album.

4. **Right-click the desired song and, in the resulting menu, hover over Add to Playlist.**

   A submenu appears, revealing all available playlists.

5. **Select the playlist in which you want to place your selected song.**

   The song is added to the playlist.

Sharing playlists

Chances are good you'll create an epic playlist that will be remembered for ages. There's no sense in keeping that playlist to yourself. You need to share it! To share a playlist, follow these steps:

1. **In the bottom-left corner of the Google Play Music window, click the playlist you want to share.**

   Your playlist loads.

2. **Find and click the Playlist Settings button located next to the Share Playlist button.**

   The Playlist Settings button looks like three vertical dots.

   A menu appears, revealing several options.

3. **Choose Edit Playlist.**

   The Edit Playlist pop-up window appears, revealing the playlist details. (See Figure 12-7.)

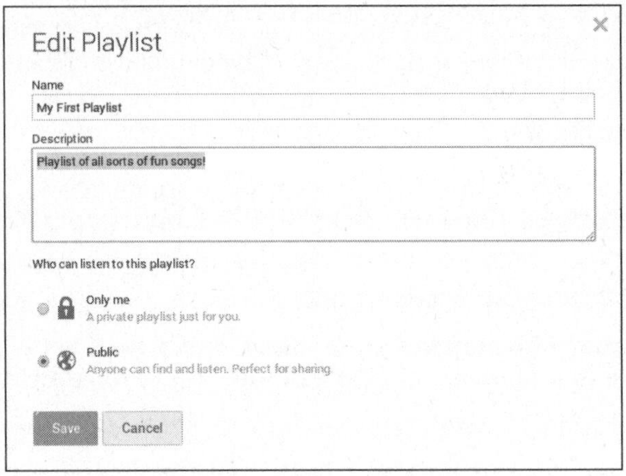

Edit Playlist   ✕

Name
My First Playlist

Description
Playlist of all sorts of fun songs!

Who can listen to this playlist?

🔒 Only me
    A private playlist just for you.

🌐 Public
    Anyone can find and listen. Perfect for sharing.

Save   Cancel

Figure 12-7:
The Edit
Playlist
pop-up
window.

4. **At the bottom of the window, click the Public radio button.**

5. **Click Save.**

   Your playlist is now searchable in Google Play and available to all users.

If you wish to share your playlist with friends through email or on social media, you can generate a link to your playlist and send it out to every deserving soul in your network. Locate your playlist link by following these steps:

1. **In the bottom-left corner of the Google Play Music window, click the playlist you want to share.**

   Your playlist loads.

2. **Click the Share Playlist button.**

   A drop-down list appears.

3. **Choose Get Link.**

   The Get Link pop-up window appears, as pictured in Figure 12-8.

4. **Ensure that the Public radio button is checked.**

5. **Select the link in the text box below the radio buttons and copy it by pressing Ctrl+C; then click Done.**

   The link to your playlist is copied to your Clipboard.

6. **Paste the link in an email, in a Google+ status update, or elsewhere by pressing Ctrl+V.**

   Google Play users who click the link can access your playlist and share in the fun!

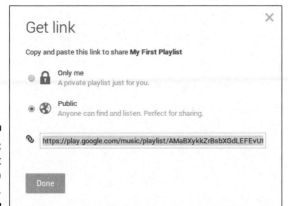

Figure 12-8:
The Get
Link pop-up
window.

Listening to a Radio Station

Google Play allows you to create or listen to existing "radio" stations —
essentially playlists of songs generated on the fly by Google Play. The songs
are chosen according to their similarity to a song, artist, or album you
specify.

You must have a premium Google Play account to create a radio station. If you
have a premium account, follow these steps to create your first radio station:

1. **Click the Listen Now link on the top-left of the Google Play Music
   window.**

   The Listen Now window loads.

2. **Specify the song, album, or artist on which your radio station will be
   based.**

   In the Search bar, enter the name of this song, album, or artist, then click
   the Search button to the right of the Search bar.

   The search results are calculated and loaded into the window.

3. **Click the desired result and, in the associated Profile page that loads,
   find the song, album, or artist you're looking for and click the Start
   Radio button.**

   If you're searching for a song rather than an artist or album, you must
   right-click the song to reveal the Start Radio option.

   The radio station is created, and a playlist of related songs begins to play.

Chapter 13

Chromebook Video

*W*atching video used to be relegated to televisions and video playback devices like VHS players, DVD, and Blu-ray. However, thanks to the prevalence of high-speed Internet access, increasingly powerful computers, and wireless broadband, the Internet has become a primary delivery mechanism for video.

You can't argue that streaming video has become one of the major consumers of Internet bandwidth in the 21st century. As of the end of 2013, streaming video accounted for nearly 53 percent of all Internet traffic. Recent statistics show that more than 1 billion unique users visit YouTube each month. Over 6 billion hours of video are watched each month, and nearly 100 hours of video are uploaded to YouTube every minute. Nielsen recently reported that YouTube reaches more U.S. adults ages 18 to 34 than any cable network.

In this chapter, you learn how to play videos on your Chromebook with the internal video player and how to browse for and stream videos through Google Play Video. Lastly, you learn how to navigate Google's YouTube network and how to create, edit, and share videos using YouTube.

Watching Video on Chromebook

Video files tend to be much larger than pictures and audio files, largely due to the length of the videos, the quality of the video, and even the quality of the embedded audio. Chromebooks come with dramatically less internal storage than traditional PCs and Apple computers. Although Chromebooks allow you to download video from the Internet, doing so can fill up the available storage rather quickly. Instead, store video files (along with other media files) on external storage devices like USB memory sticks or SD cards.

Chromebook has a video player that plays most video files. To access video files on your Chromebook, follow these steps:

1. **Insert the USB memory stick or SD card that contains the video file you want to play into your Chromebook.**

   Chromebook launches Files and loads data from your external storage device, as shown in Figure 13-1.

2. **Double-click the video file you wish to play.**

   Your selected video loads and begins playing in the Chromebook video player, as shown in Figure 13-2.

Figure 13-1:
A Files window showing an external storage device.

Figure 13-2:
Playing video in the Chromebook video player.

Navigating the Chromebook Video Player

The Chromebook video player is very barebones. There's a window control bar across the top of the window where you can minimize, maximize, and close the video player window.

Your video occupies the majority of the window space. If you move your pointer over the bottom of the video window, an overlay appears, containing the controls for the video player, which include

- ✔ Pause and Play buttons
- ✔ Status bar with time indicator
- ✔ Volume control
- ✔ Full Screen mode control

By default, the Chromebook video player starts your video as soon as that video loads. If you wish to pause your video, follow these steps:

1. **While the video is playing, move your pointer to the bottom of the video player window.**

   The video control overlay briefly appears, revealing several options.

2. **Click the Pause button on the left side of the pop-up window.**

   The Pause button looks like two vertical bars.

   The video pauses playback at its current location.

3. **To restart the video, move your pointer over the bottom of the video once again, and when the overlay reappears, click the Play button.**

   The Play button looks like a triangle pointing to the right.

   The video resumes playing.

Skipping around a video

If you want to skip ahead to your favorite part of a video — or maybe just pick up where you left off — you can do so with the Chromebook video player. To skip around in a video, follow these steps:

1. **While your video is open and playing, move your pointer over the bottom of the video player.**

   The video control overlay appears, revealing several video control options.

2. **Locate the position indicator in the status bar.**

   The position indicator is a rounded object that moves left to right as the video plays.

3. **Click and drag the position indicator forward or backward to the place in your video where you would like to start watching.**

   The video skips to the selected location in the timeline.

You don't have to pause your video to skip around in the video. However, you can pause the video to ensure that the video doesn't keep playing when you skip to different locations in the video.

Activating Full Screen mode

By default, the Chromebook video player plays the video at the optimal viewing size. You can, however, make the video occupy the entire screen by using Full Screen mode. To engage Full Screen mode, follow these steps:

1. **While your video is open and playing, move your pointer over the bottom of the video player.**

   The video control overlay appears, revealing several video control options.

2. **Click the Full Screen button on the right side of the overlay.**

   The video player enlarges to fill the screen, as shown in Figure 13-3.

3. **To exit Full Screen mode, press the Esc key.**

Figure 13-3:
Full Screen
mode.

Adjusting the volume

To control the volume in the Chromebook video player, follow these steps:

1. **Move your pointer over the bottom of the video player.**

   The video control overlay appears, revealing several video control options.

2. **Locate the volume control slider on the right side of the overlay.**

3. **To mute the volume, click the Speaker icon.**

   When muted, the icon appears with a slash through it, indicating volume has been reduced to zero.

4. **Increase or decrease the volume by moving the slider — to the right to increase and to the left to decrease.**

   The volume changes in accordance with the direction you move the volume slider.

Getting Started with Google Play Video

Google Play is Google's online marketplace. Google Play is very similar to Apple's iTunes store. Google Play sells videos, televisions shows, books, music, and applications for Android, Chromebook, the Chrome browsers, and more.

As is the case with all of the applications on the Google platform, access to Google Play Video is linked to your Google Account. If you have multiple Google Accounts, make sure you're logged into your Chromebook with the account that you want to be associated with Google Play Video.

 You can launch Google Play Video by opening the App Launcher and clicking the Google Play Movies & TV icon. When you do, Google Play Video launches in a Chrome web browser.

Navigating Google Play Video

Google Play gives you the ability to purchase movies and television shows for download, as well as for streaming. Any purchases you make are tracked in the My Movies & TV section of Google Play, as shown in Figure 13-4.

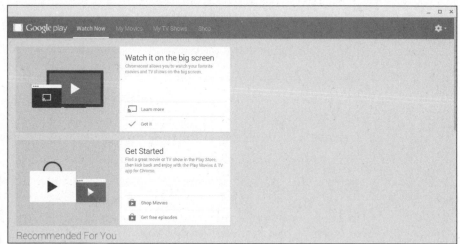

Figure 13-4:
My Movies
& TV.

Before you can purchase movies or TV shows, you need to first know how to navigate through Google Play's vast database. You can search for movies and TV shows using the Search bar at the top of the window or by browsing the Google Play charts. For example, to browse for a movie, click Movies on the left side of the Google Play window to open the Movies page, as shown in Figure 13-5 and then click Shop.

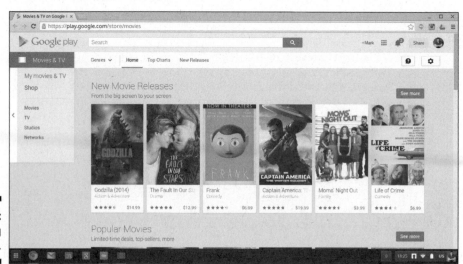

Figure 13-5:
Browsing
movies.

On the Movies page, you can browse movies by category. Categories might include

✔ New Releases

✔ Most Popular

✔ Top Charts

✔ Recommendations

✔ Deals

✔ Seasonal

Browsing videos by category is a great way to discover great thought-provoking cinema and mindless entertainment alike.

Purchasing movies and TV shows

Google Play gives you several options to view movies and television shows. You can either purchase content and access that content for an indefinite amount of time, or rent content that's available for viewing for a specified amount of time. Renting is definitely a cheaper option, but if you like to watch movies over and over again, or if you want to build a database of flicks you can dial up whenever you want, purchasing may be the way to go.

To purchase or rent a movie on Google Play, follow these steps:

1. **With Google Play Video open, in the Search bar, enter the name of the movie or TV show (for example,** Ghostbusters**), and then click the Search button.**

   Google Play loads the search results.

2. **Click the video you want to watch (see Figure 13-6).**

   The Movie Profile page loads.

3. **Click the Buy button at the top of the screen. (To rent, click Rent.)**

   A pop-up window appears, presenting you with the option to buy your movie.

   Newer movies and televisions shows are typically available for purchase or rent in high definition (HD) or standard definition (SD). HD has a much greater picture quality than standard definition. For this reason, Google asks you to pay more for HD during the checkout process.

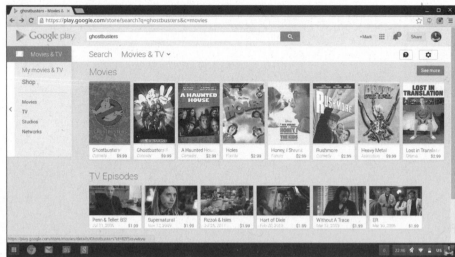

Figure 13-6:
Who you
gonna call?

Figure 13-6:
Who you
gonna call?

4. **Click the Buy button.**

   A Google Wallet pop-up window appears, as shown in Figure 13-7, asking you to review your purchase before confirming.

   If you haven't set up your Google Wallet, you need to do so at this point. Follow the prompts to add the desired payment method to your Google Account. Once set up, you can quickly conduct purchases on the Google network!

5. **If you're satisfied with your purchase decision, click Buy.**

   The movie or TV show you purchased appears in My Movies & TV and is available to play. If you rented the content, it's available in My Movies & TV for only a limited period of time before it's removed.

Figure 13-7:
The Google
Wallet
pop-up
window.

Playing movies and TV shows

After you purchase movies or TV shows in Google Play, they appear in the My Movies & TV section and are available for playing. To play your movies and TV shows, follow these steps:

1. **With Google Play Video open, click My Movies & TV on the left side of the page.**

   Your movies and TV shows are loaded.

2. **Move your pointer over the desired content and click Play.**

   A pop-up window appears, and your video content begins playing.

By default, the video plays in a pop-up window that's centered over the Google Play window. You can pause the video by following these steps:

1. **While the video content is playing, move your cursor over the bottom of the video pop-up window.**

   The video control overlay, containing several video controls, appears.

2. **Click the Pause button on the bottom-left of the overlay.**

   The Pause button looks like two vertical bars.

   The video playback pauses.

3. **To resume playing your video, move your pointer back over the video control overlay and click the Play button.**

   The Play button displays a sideways triangle.

Activating Full Screen mode

By default, Google Play Video plays the video at the optimal viewing size. You can, however, make the video occupy the entire screen by using Full Screen mode. To engage Full Screen mode, follow these steps:

1. **While your video is open and playing, move your pointer over the bottom of the video player.**

   The video control overlay appears, revealing several video control options.

2. **Click the Full Screen button on the right side of the overlay.**

   The video player enlarges to fill the screen.

3. **To exit Full Screen mode, press the Esc key.**

Adjusting the volume

To control the volume in the Google Play Video player, follow these steps:

1. **Move your pointer over the bottom of the video player.**

   The video control overlay appears, revealing several video control options.

2. **Locate the Volume icon on the left side of the overlay.**

3. **To mute the volume, click the Speaker icon.**

   When muted, the icon appears with a slash through it, indicating volume has been reduced to zero.

4. **Increase or decrease the volume by moving the slider — to the right to increase and to the left to decrease.**

   The volume changes in accordance with the direction you move the volume slider.

Ditching the Boob Tube for YouTube

YouTube is a free video-sharing website that has grown over the past few years into one of the most trafficked sites on the Internet. YouTube's video database is completely user-generated. Recent statistics provided by YouTube say that users upload an average of 100 hours of video footage every minute!

YouTube has become a go-to source for all kinds of video: unfiltered field-reporting, documentation of conflict, music videos, self-help and how-to, thought-provoking documentaries, family archives, humorous interpretations, chance happenings, and more. Users have the ability to create channels to store and categorize endless minutes of video. With YouTube, you can upload and edit videos, share video content around the web, keep track of video views, and so much more.

 YouTube is a great tool for Chromebook users as it can serve as a bottomless repository for captured video footage. In order to access YouTube, you must have a Google Account. To access YouTube, open the App Launcher and click the YouTube icon. When you do so, YouTube loads in a Chrome web browser.

Navigating YouTube

When YouTube has loaded, it can be sensory overload with all of the available options. It would take an entire book to cover all of the intricacies of YouTube. This section gives you a few tips to get you started.

The main page of YouTube contains several video options for suggested viewing. Much of what YouTube suggests is driven by your viewing habits. If you like videos of smiling kittens, for instance, YouTube suggests videos of kittens to capture your attention. YouTube also sells placements to businesses, so you may see an advertisement or two. Along the left side of the screen are options for finding videos you've seen and videos you haven't seen yet.

The most useful way to find new videos is by using the Search bar at the top of the screen. YouTube has over 1 billion unique visitors every month, and those visitors typically search for video content just as they would search for a web page by using Google's search engine. This search functionality has made YouTube the second-largest search engine in the world.

Enter a term in the Search bar, click the Search button (which looks like a magnifying glass), and then scroll through the pages of search results to find the video you're searching for. To aid in your search, YouTube ranks the results by relevance to your search query. If you haven't found the video you're looking for by the third or fourth page of search results, you may want to refine your search.

Playing and pausing video

Playing a video on YouTube is as straightforward as searching for it. Just find the video you want to play in YouTube's search results and click the title. YouTube loads the Video Profile page and begins playing your selection automatically.

The bottom bar of the video, pictured in Figure 13-8, contains all of your play controls, status bar audio controls, and viewing settings.

To pause the video, click the Pause button on the left side of the control bar. (The Pause button looks like two vertical bars.) When video is paused, pressing Pause again (or the Play button) resumes playback.

Activating Full Screen mode

By default, YouTube plays the video at the optimal viewing size. You can, however, make the video occupy the entire screen by using Full Screen mode. To engage Full Screen mode, click the Full Screen button on the right side of the video's control bar. To exit Full Screen mode, press the Esc key.

Figure 13-8:
YouTube's
control bar.

Control bar

Adjusting the volume

To control the volume in the YouTube player, follow these steps:

1. **Locate the Volume icon on the left side of the control bar.**

2. **To mute the volume, click the Speaker icon.**

   When muted, the icon appears with an X through it, indicating volume has been reduced to zero.

3. **Increase or decrease the volume by moving your pointer over the volume icon and clicking and dragging the volume slider that appears.**

   Move the slider left to decrease volume, right to increase it.

Chapter 14

Chatting with Friends and Family

● ●

● ●

*G*oogle Hangouts is an application that allows you to connect with your friends by sending messages, as well as making video calls and voice calls. You can even share your screen to show others what you're working on or how to navigate a particular application. Collaborate with a team of people by conducting a group call with video, voice, and group texts. Or use the Hangouts Chat plug-in in Chrome to have one-on-one text conversations with your contacts.

Regardless of how you intend to use it, Hangouts is a wonderful tool for staying connected to family, friends, and coworkers. Chromebook includes the Hangout system as a native application — it's built-in, in other words, so you don't access it in the cloud.

In this chapter, you learn how to launch Hangouts and invite your contacts to a video call. Conduct a one-on-one video chat or invite several people for a group video chat. Take and share pictures with Hangouts and even call phone numbers in the U.S. and Canada. Lastly, you learn how to use the Hangouts app to share your screen.

Getting Started with Hangouts

Like the majority of applications on the Google platform, Hangouts is a web-based application that makes it easy for you to connect with people all over the world. Hangouts makes it possible to video chat or send short text messages to other users through Google+, Gmail, or a slew of Chrome browser plug-ins. With your Chromebook, however, Google has upped the ante and created an application that resides on your Chromebook and taps into the Hangouts system, giving you a better experience all around.

 You can launch Hangouts by opening the App Launcher and clicking the Hangouts call icon.

Navigating Hangouts on Chromebook

Hangouts gives you several ways to connect with others around the globe. After all, without someone to talk with, Hangouts is a pretty boring application! Therefore, after opening Hangouts, you're immediately presented with a dialog box that gives you several ways that you can invite others. (See Figure 14-1.)

You can copy the URL address at the top of the dialog box and paste it into emails, Facebook, Twitter, or elsewhere. Users who click the address are taken to a website where they can participate in your hangout.

If you prefer, you can invite your friends via email by using the Send an Invite text box. Just add the email addresses of everyone you want to invite. If these email addresses appear in your Gmail address book, just enter the name, and Gmail adds the appropriate email address automatically. Lastly, if you're a Google+ user, you can list Google+ circles to invite entire groups of people to hang out.

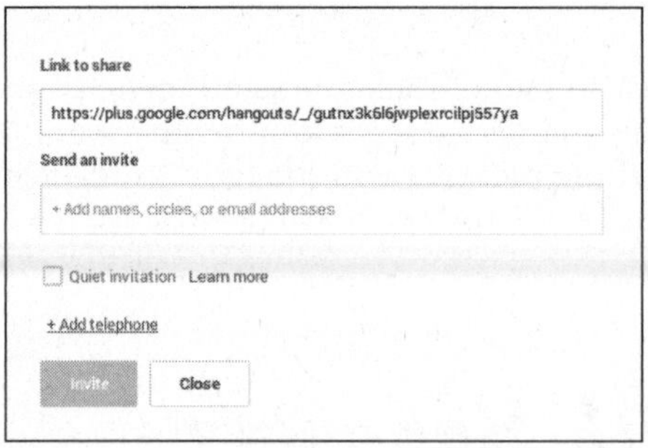

Figure 14-1:
Inviting
others to
Hangouts.

Link to share

https://plus.google.com/hangouts/_/gutnx3k6l6jwplexrcilpj557ya

Send an invite

+ Add names, circles, or email addresses

☐ Quiet invitation   Learn more

+ Add telephone

Invite   Close

 Hangouts permits a maximum of 100 participants in a video hangout. If you want to conduct a digital family reunion, you won't have an excuse for excluding your weird in-laws!

Hangouts is nothing if not inclusive. Even if the people you invite don't have a webcam — or even a computer — you can still invite them to dial in from their phones.

For now, click the Close button at the bottom of the dialog box. The dialog box closes, and the Hangouts application home screen appears, as shown in Figure 14-2.

Figure 14-2:
The Hangouts home screen.

By default, Hangouts initializes the video camera on your Chromebook. Now's the time to fix your hair! If you're not ready, you can turn the video camera off by following these steps:

1. **Move your pointer toward the top of the Hangouts window.**

   Menu options appear. (See Figure 14-3.)

2. **Click the icon that looks like a video camera with a slash through it.**

   Your video camera turns off.

The menu across the top of the Hangouts app contains all the controls you need to conduct a hangout. From this menu, you can

  ✔ Invite users to participate in your hangout.

  ✔ Mute your audio.

✔ Turn video on and off.

✔ Adjust the volume of your hangout.

✔ Tweak settings that control your video camera and audio source.

✔ End a call.

The menu on the left side of the Hangouts app contains options for your hangout:

✔ Turn on chatting for typing out text to your group.

✔ Share your screen with the group.

✔ Take pictures to send and share.

✔ Remote Desktop (access another user's desktop).

✔ Stream to YouTube.

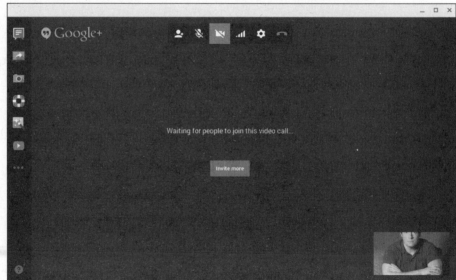

Figure 14-3:
The Hangouts menu system.

Video chatting with Hangouts

Conducting a video chat with Hangouts is pretty straightforward with these steps:

1. **Launch Hangouts.**

2. **Invite others to your video chat either by providing them with the URL address at the top of the dialog box or by entering the email address of each person you wish to invite and then clicking the Invite button.**

   The dialog box closes, revealing the Hangouts app and a video of yourself while you wait for your invitees to join the hangout.

   Even if you've closed this dialog box, you can still invite people to the call by clicking the Invite People button in the control menu at the top of the Hangouts window.

   As your invitees join the hangout, video thumbnails begin to populate the bottom of the Hangouts window, as shown in Figure 14-4. You can change the person who appears in the main part of the window by clicking her associated thumbnail.

3. **Enjoy your video chat!**

Figure 14-4:
Multiple
users in a
hangout.

4. **When you're ready to end the hangout session, click the Leave Call button in the control menu at the top of the Hangouts window.**

   The hangout session ends, and the controls all disappear.

5. **Close Google Hangouts by clicking the X in the top-right of the window.**

Making a phone call

If you don't want to make a video call, or if you simply want to give someone a ring and don't have your phone handy, you can call them by following these steps:

1. **Launch Hangouts.**

2. **Click the Add Telephone link that appears above the Invite button.**

   The Call A Phone Number dialog box appears.

3. **Enter the phone number you wish to call and click Call.**

   Hangouts calls the number entered.

   If you're in the U. S. or Canada, calls within the U. S. and Canada are free. Calls outside the U. S. or Canada may incur long-distance charges, which are charged to the credit card you have on file with Google Wallet.

4. **Click the icon in the control menu that looks like a video camera with a slash through it.**

   The video camera turns off. If you're making a phone call, there's no sense in burning extra battery by having your video camera on.

5. **Enjoy your call!**

6. **When you're ready to disconnect, click the Leave Call button at the Top of the Hangouts window.**

Taking and sharing photos

During a hangout, you may decide that you want to capture an image to share with your hangout attendees at a later time. You can do that with ease by using the Photo feature in Hangouts. To take a photo and share it with your hangout companions, use the following steps:

1. **While you're in an active hangout, move your pointer to the left side of the Hangouts window and click the Camera icon.**

   Hangouts loads the video coming from your webcam.

2. **Click the camera button at the bottom of the window.**

   Hangouts captures a picture using your web camera and loads the picture on the right side of the Hangouts window, as shown in Figure 14-5. The video is also automatically uploaded to your Google+ account (whether you use it or not) and shared with the attendees of your hangout.

Figure 14-5:
Check out
your photo
(nice hair).

3. **Click the image thumbnail on the bottom of the Hangouts window.**

   Hangouts loads an image navigator on the right side of the window for your review. Everyone participating in the hangout will be able to view the images captured during your session.

4. **View an image by clicking on a thumbnail located in the image navigator.**

   The image loads in the hangout window. Close the photo by clicking the X in the top-right corner.

5. **(Optional) To share the image with anyone not participating in the hangout, Alt-click the image, and select Copy Image URL.**

   The image's URL is copied and made available to paste into an email or elsewhere.

6. **Exit Photo mode by clicking the Photo icon on the left side of the Hangouts window once again.**

   The main Hangouts window reappears.

Sharing your screen

Sharing your screen on a hangout is a great way to remotely demonstrate an activity on your Chromebook. Or maybe you just want to show someone a bunch of photos or videos without having to package them up and email them. Sharing your screen is great for a number of scenarios. You can share your screen by following these steps:

1. **While you're in an active hangout, click the Screenshare icon on the left side of the Hangouts window.**

   A dialog box appears, asking you to confirm that you want to present your entire screen to everyone participating in your hangout.

2. **Click Share.**

   In place of your video stream at the bottom-right corner of the Hangouts window, an image of your desktop appears, as shown in Figure 14-6. Anyone who joins your hangout can see your computer screen.

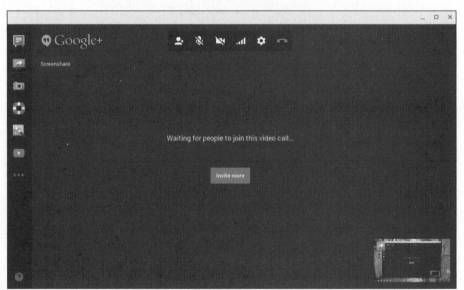

Figure 14-6:
Sharing your
screen.

3. **Exit Screensharing mode by clicking the Screenshare icon on the left side of the Hangouts window once again.**

   The main Hangouts window reappears.

Using Hangouts Remote Desktop

If you ever need to help a friend with something on his computer, you can take control of his or her machine by using the Hangouts Remote Desktop feature. To use Remote Desktop, follow these steps:

1. **While you're in an active hangout, click the Remote Desktop icon on the left side of the Hangouts window.**

   You are asked to refresh your Hangouts connection to load Remote Desktop, as shown in Figure 14-7. Meanwhile, the other user must approve the request and refresh his or her Hangouts session, as well.

Figure 14-7:
Refresh your hangouts session to load Remote Desktop.

2. **Refresh your Hangouts session by pressing the Refresh button**

   Hangouts reloads and you are presented with the option to "help" the other user. Click the Help button. When the other user accepts the Control Desktop request, you have control over his or her computer.

3. **Exit Remote Desktop mode by clicking the End button at the top of the Hangouts window.**

   The main Hangouts window reappears.

Texting with the Hangouts Chat App

If you don't want to have a full-fledged video conference with your friends, you can swap text messages with your contacts using the Hangouts chat client. If you want to turn your chat into a video hangout, you can do so with just a quick click of a button. To use the Hangouts Chat app, you first need to install it by following these steps:

1. **Open the App Launcher and click the Store icon.**

   The Chrome Web Store launches.

2. **Type** Hangouts **into the Search bar and press Enter.**

   Search results load in the Web Store window.

3. **Click the Free button to install the Hangouts application, as shown in Figure 14-8.**

   After you install the app, the Hangouts icon appears in the top-right corner of your Chrome browser, waiting to be pressed.

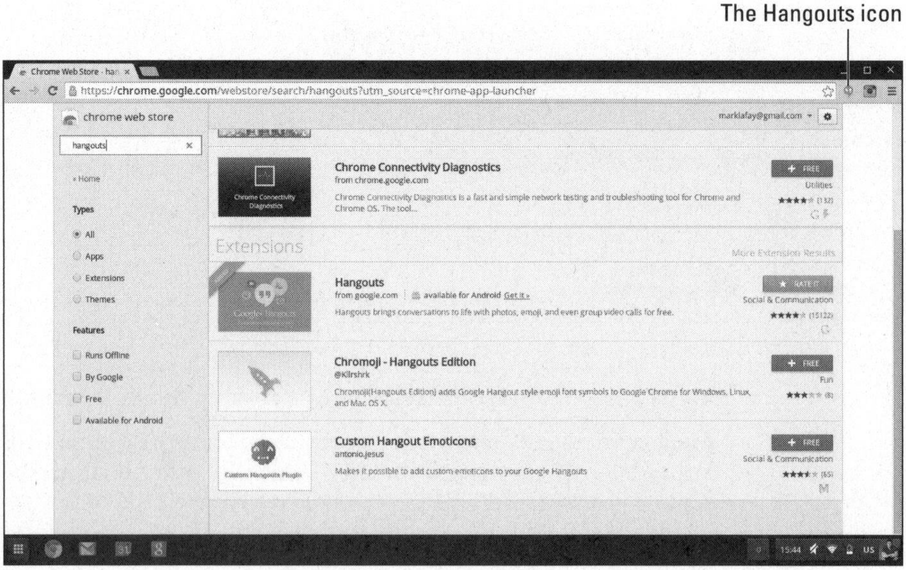

The Hangouts icon

Figure 14-8: Installing the Hangouts Chat application.

After you install the Hangouts Chat application, you can chat with your friends by following these steps:

1. **Open a Chrome browser and click the Hangouts icon in the top-right corner.**

   A Hangouts Chat menu pops up from the bottom-right corner of your Chromebook Shelf.

2. **To start a new hangout conversation, enter the name or email address of the person with whom you wish to chat, and then press Enter.**

   A Chat window appears, giving you the option to enter a message.

3. **Type any message you wish to send and press Enter.**

   The message is sent to that user. If he isn't currently online, he receives the message when he next logs on.

4. **If you wish to launch a video chat from your Hangouts Chat window, click the Video icon in the Chat window.**

   The Hangouts app launches and initiates a video chat with your contact.

Chapter 15

Fun with Photos

In This Chapter

▶ Using your Chromebook to take photos

▶ Editing photos

▶ Sharing photos with others

▶ Viewing photos on external media

*T*he Chromebook is a great multimedia device. With it, you can take photos, listen to music, watch videos, share media files, surf the web, and more. Every Chromebook currently on the market comes with a built-in camera that gives you the ability to video chat and to capture photos for sharing on the web. In addition, you can load photos from external media, edit the pictures, and share them across the web. The Chromebook is definitely no slouch when it comes to multimedia!

In this chapter, you learn how to access the built-in camera to take pictures. You also find out how to edit your pictures by resizing, rotating, adding color filters, and more. I also show you how to access and manipulate photos on removable storage like SD cards.

Navigating Chromebook Camera

The application that runs your Chromebook's camera is a native application, meaning that you don't need Internet access to connect to it because it resides on your Chromebook itself. This is handy if you ever want to take pictures while you're in an Internet desert.

 To launch your Chromebook Camera app, open the App Launcher and click the Camera icon.

When the Camera app is open, your Chromebook camera becomes engaged. Two things indicate that your Chromebook camera is on:

- ✔ In the Camera app, a video appears of yourself sitting in front of your Chromebook.

- ✔ The green light next to your Chromebook camera turns on.

The Camera app window has a few distinct areas that you should be aware of. In the top-right corner, you have the window controls. You can make the camera application fill the screen by clicking the square in the top-right corner. Click it again to restore the application to its default size. If you wish to close the application altogether, simply click the X in the top-right corner.

On the bottom of the application window, a large red button and several smaller icons appear. (See Figure 15-1.) This is your *camera control area*. In this area, you can take photos, access recent photos, and turn features on and off.

Figure 15-1:
The Camera app.

Toggle filters   Toggle mirroring   Toggle timer   Toggle multi-shot

Take a picture   Go to gallery

Taking a Picture

To take a picture, launch the Camera app and follow these steps:

1. **Hover your mouse pointer over the red Picture button in the camera control bar. (Don't click it yet.)**

2. **Look at the green dot next to your Chromebook camera.**

   This ensures you're looking straight ahead in your photo.

3. **Click the red Picture button.**

   Your Chromebook makes a camera noise and takes your picture. It briefly displays the picture onscreen, as shown in Figure 15-2.

Figure 15-2: Say, "Cheese!"

Picture quality depends largely on the quality of the camera and the operator. Granted, Chromebook cameras are pretty good, given the size and application, but they struggle to deliver the goods in certain settings. Here are some suggestions to take a good photo with your Chromebook camera:

- ✔ If you're taking a photo of yourself, make sure you're as bright as or brighter than what's behind you. Avoid backlighting: Try to not take photos in front of windows or with the sun or any bright lights behind you.

- ✔ Make sure you're lit well. Your background may be dim, but if you don't have light shining on you, the camera will struggle to capture a nice photo. (Can you tell that light is a big deal?)

- ✔ Most of the time, your Chromebook will be positioned lower than you, and therefore, the majority of photos appear as though someone shorter than you took them. Try to take a photo with your Chromebook angled straight-on with you.

Using the camera timer

The camera timer is the family vacation's best friend. Remember your mom or dad positioning the camera, hitting the timer button, and then running back into frame for the awkward family photo in front of *every* monument in Washington D.C.? Well, some things never change. The camera timer is here to stay, at least for the time being, and it's as functional as it ever was.

To take pictures using a timer, follow these steps:

1. **In the Camera app, locate the Timer. If the Timer button (directly to the right of the red Picture button) is grayed-out, click it.**

   A message appears in the middle of the application, shown in Figure 15-3, indicating the status of the Timer feature.

Figure 15-3: The Timer activation indicator.

2. **If you're ready to take a picture, click the red Picture button.**

   Your Chromebook beeps five times before taking the picture. You'll know the picture was taken when you hear a camera sound and the picture briefly appears on the screen.

Whenever you take a photo with the camera, with or without the timer, always look at the green dot to ensure that you're looking directly into the camera. Unless you go for an arty pose, looking into the camera delivers the best results. Say, "Cheese!"

Enabling Multi-Shot mode

If you're the type who typically blinks in every photo, you might want to consider turning on Multi-Shot mode. In this mode, the Camera app takes three photos with one click of the Photo button. To enable Multi-Shot mode and take a picture (or three), follow these steps:

1. **In the Camera app, locate the Multi-Shot button (two buttons to the right of the red Picture button). If it's grayed out, click it.**

   A message appears in the middle of the application, shown in Figure 15-4, indicating the status of the Multi-Shot feature.

2. **If you're ready to take a picture, click the red Picture button.**

   Your Chromebook quickly takes three pictures. Your Chromebook makes multiple camera noises, and the individual photos briefly appear on screen.

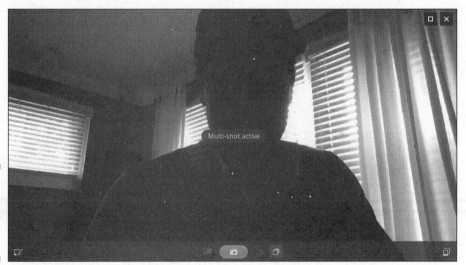

Multi-shot active

Figure 15-4:
The Multi-
Shot
activation
indicator.

If you're taking a group photo with your Chromebook, turn on both the Timer and the Multi-Shot features so that you can increase your chances of capturing a photo in which no one looked away, frowned, or blinked.

Taking a picture with a filter

Thanks to Hipstamatic and Instagram, the world has gone crazy over taking photos that appear aged or vintage. Google hasn't missed the boat with this latest craze: A slew of filters are built in to change the appearance of the photos you capture with the Chromebook Camera app. Take photos with a filtered effect by following these steps:

1. **Launch the Chromebook Camera app.**

2. **Click the Toggle Filters button, located on the far-left of the camera control bar.**

   The camera control bar slides up to reveal several different filters. (See Figure 15-5.)

Figure 15-5: Choosing a filter.

3. **Select a filter to apply to your picture by clicking that filter's thumbnail. (See Figure 15-6.)**

4. **If you're ready to take a picture, click the red Picture button.**

   Your Chromebook snaps a photo with your filter applied. Chromebook makes a camera noise, and your photo briefly appears onscreen.

Figure 15-6:
The Big
Head filter.

Viewing Photos

After you take all the photos you desire, the photos are stored in the Camera app's gallery, which is inaccessible outside of the Camera app. If you wish to view your photos, follow these steps:

1. **Launch the Chromebook Camera app.**

2. **Click the Gallery button on the far-right of the camera control bar.**

   The gallery loads, as shown in Figure 15-7.

Figure 15-7:
The gallery.

3. **To view a particular photo, double-click the image thumbnail.**

The photo loads, as shown in Figure 15-8.

Figure 15-8:
Reviewing
your Renoir.

Saving and Deleting Photos

Photos captured using the Camera feature aren't saved directly to your Chromebook hard drive. These photos are stored within the Camera app, and you need to save them to your hard drive, removable storage, or Google Drive before you can share them. To save a photo, follow these steps:

1. **Launch the Chromebook Camera app.**

2. **Click the Gallery button on the far-right of the camera control bar.**

The gallery loads.

3. **Click the photo you wish to save.**

The photo enlarges ever-so-slightly and becomes highlighted.

4. **Click the Save to Disk button, located in the bottom-right of the window, as pictured in Figure 15-9.**

A Files window appears, giving you the ability to name the image file and select the location for your photo.

Figure 15-9:
Saving to
disk.

5. **Navigate to the location where you wish to store your photo, rename the file, and click Save.**

The Files window disappears.

You can save only one photo at a time, so saving several photos can be a time-consuming process.

Editing Photos

You don't have to capture photos with the Chromebook Camera to be able to work with and otherwise edit, manipulate, or distribute your photos. Most major digital cameras today store your photos on removable storage devices called *SD cards*. (See Figure 15-10.) The majority of Chromebooks on the market today have an SD-card slot for quickly accessing your data, such as photos, among other things.

Figure 15-10:
A standard
SD card.

To access photos on an SD card, follow these steps:

1. **Place your SD card into the SD-card slot on your Chromebook.**

   Chromebook may automatically load an application for importing all of your photos to Google+. If this happens, simply click Do Not Import and close the application.

2. **Launch the Chromebook Camera app.**

   Your SD card appears in the list of media options on the left side of the Files window.

3. **Click the SD card in Files to begin browsing its contents.**

Whether you're accessing photos on an SD card or on your Chromebook hard drive, you can edit the photos by following these steps:

1. **In the Files window, browse to the photo you wish to edit and double-click the photo file.**

   Chromebook opens the photo in a photo viewer.

2. **Move your mouse to the bottom-right of the photo viewer.**

   A control bar containing several options is revealed.

3. **Click the Edit icon, which looks like a pencil.**

   Several editing controls are revealed.

   The Chromebook Picture Editor gives you the ability to make minor modifications to your photos. These edit features include:

   • *Crop:* Isolate a portion of the photo that you wish to keep and discard the rest.

   • *Brightness:* Make your picture darker or lighter. You can make colors in your picture pop by adjusting the contrast, as well.

   • *Rotation:* If your picture is in the wrong orientation, rotate it to the left or the right using this feature.

4. **When you're satisfied with your edits, press Enter to save your changes.**

   Your original file is overwritten with the changes that you make using the Photo Editor. If you wish to save your modified photo to a different file and preserve the original, you must uncheck the Overwrite Original box located in the bottom-left of the control bar in the Photo Editor.

Chapter 16

eBooks on Chromebooks

*e**Book** is short for electronic book. Over the past decade, several devices were created specifically for serving up entire libraries of novels in a single device. Amazon created the Kindle, Barnes & Nobles created the Nook, and Apple created iBooks, which is the book platform that resides on all of their iDevices. The benefits of eBooks are numerous, but perhaps the biggest is convenience. With eBooks, you no longer have to lug around heavy paper books; now you can store hundreds of books on a single slim device.

Although eBooks will never entirely replace the analog experience of turning pages, reading books on your Chromebook is an excellent way to enjoy a good novel. The Google Play store is home to over 5 million titles, and that number continues to grow!

In this chapter, you learn how to load Google Play Books on your Chromebook and how to navigate the Play Bookstore. I show you how to add new books to your library — and some books in the Play Bookstore are available for free! Using your Chromebook, you can read your books online and offline, regardless of where you are.

Navigating Google Play Books

The majority of your book reading on the Chromebook happens with Google Play Books. Google Play Books is where you search for and purchase titles and where you can find all of your book purchases and uploaded books.

 To launch Google Play Books, open the App Launcher and click the Google Play Books icon.

If Google Play Books doesn't appear among the choices in your App Launcher, add it by following these steps:

1. **Open the App Launcher and click the Store icon.**

   The Chrome Web Store opens in a Chrome browser.

2. **Type the words** Google Play Books **into the Search bar and press Enter.**

   Google Play Books appears as the first search result.

3. **Click the Free button and follow the prompts to add Google Play Books to your Chromebook App Launcher.**

Searching and purchasing books

If this is the first time you've worked with Google Play Books, there may not be much to see. However, you can change that quickly! Open Google Play Books and click the Shop Books link in the top-right corner of the window. The Google Play Bookstore loads, giving you the option to search for and purchase books.

To purchase a book, follow these steps:

1. **In the Search bar at the top of the Google Play Bookstore, enter the name of the book for which you're searching. Press Enter.**

   The search results populate the screen, as shown in Figure 16-1.

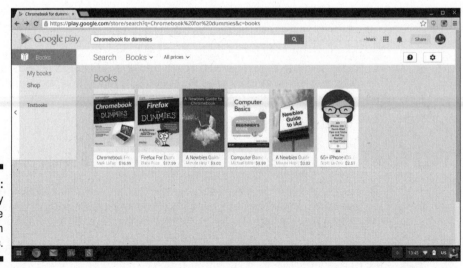

Figure 16-1:
Google Play Bookstore search results.

2. **Browse through the search results to locate the desired book and click the thumbnail of the cover.**

   If the book you're looking for doesn't appear in the search results, revise your search to use fewer words and thus expand your search results.

   The book profile page loads. In this page, you can read a description of the book, read reviews, search for similar texts, and purchase the book for reading on your Chromebook.

3. **If you're ready to purchase the book, click the Buy button located to the right of the book thumbnail.**

   A Google Wallet pop-up window appears, as shown in Figure 16-2, asking you to confirm your purchase. If you don't have a payment method on file, you must first add one before you can purchase the book.

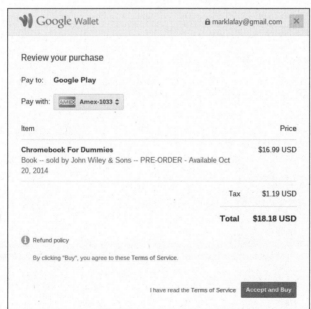

Figure 16-2:
Buying a
book in
Google
Wallet.

4. **Click Accept and Buy.**

   The purchase is completed, and the book is added to your Google Play Books library.

Even if you don't want to spend money, you can still add new books to your library by choosing one of the free books available in the Google Play

Bookstore. The free books are mixed into Google Play, but you can get access to a list of the top free books by following these steps:

1. **Click the Top Charts link at the top of the Google Play Bookstore window.**

   The top-selling charts appear.

2. **Locate the Top Free Books chart and click the See More link.**

   The complete Top Free Books chart loads.

3. **Browse through the list and click the thumbnail of a book you're interested in.**

   The book's profile page loads.

4. **If you want to read the book, click the Free button next to the book cover thumbnail at the top of the window.**

   A Google Wallet pop-up window appears, asking you to confirm your free purchase.

5. **Click Accept and Buy to complete your free purchase.**

   A notification appears to confirm the addition of the free book to your library. (See Figure 16-3.)

Figure 16-3:
Adding a
new book to
your library.

Renting a book

Not only is Google Play Books one of the largest bookstores in the world, it's also a larger-than-life library. Many books are also available for rent. A book is typically available for rent when you see the price listed as *from* a certain price. When you click the book price, the options to rent the book or purchase the book appear. Rental books are available in your library only for the period of time indicated. Once the rental period has passed, Google automatically removes the rented book.

To rent a book, follow these steps:

1. **Type** Adobe Photoshop Classroom **into the Search bar at the top of the Google Play Bookstore window and press Enter.**

   Google Play serves up several search results.

2. **Click the thumbnail for Classroom in a Book.**

   Google Play loads the book's profile page.

3. **Click the Price button next to the thumbnail at the top of the window.**

   Notice that the price starts with the word From, indicating this book can be rented.

   Your purchase and rental options appear in a pop-up window, pictured in Figure 16-4.

Figure 16-4:
Renting a
book.

4. **Click the Rent button to rent the book for the time indicated.**

   A Google Wallet pop-up window appears.

5. **Click Buy to confirm the rental.**

   A confirmation pop-up window appears, and the book is added to your library.

Uploading a book

Google Play gives you the ability to upload PDF and ePub files to your Google Play Books library. You can upload up to 1,000 files to your Google Play Books library as long as they are smaller than 100MB in size. Files that you upload are stored in your library and available to view whenever you're online. To upload a PDF or ePub file, follow these steps:

1. **Click the My Books link on the left side of the Google Play Bookstore window.**

   Your Books library loads.

2. **Click the Upload Files link in the top-right corner of the window. (See Figure 16-5.)**

   A pop-up window appears, giving you the option to browse for the files you wish to upload.

The Upload Files button

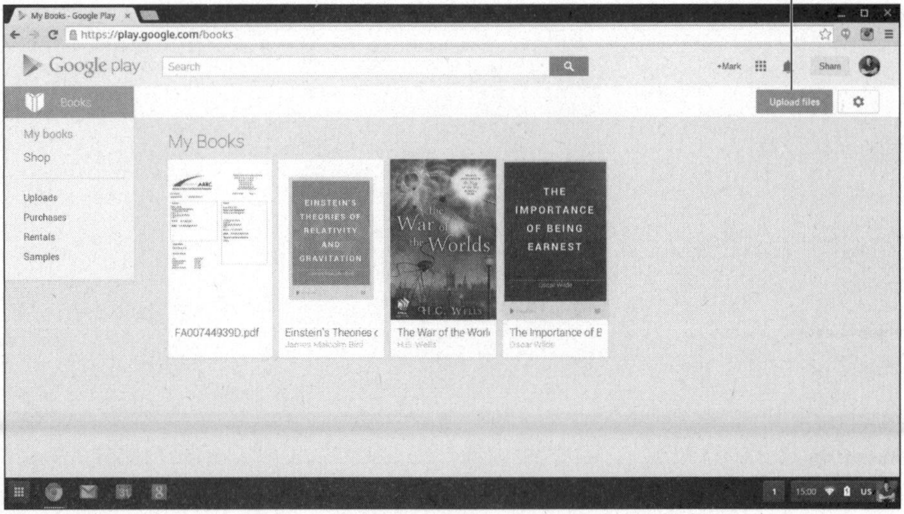

Figure 16-5:
The Upload
Files button.

3. **Choose the files you wish to upload and click Select.**

   The files are uploaded to your Google Play Books library.

Reading eBooks with Your Chromebook

Every book that you upload, purchase, or rent through Google Play Books is stored in your Google Play Books library in the cloud and is accessible from any device that has an Internet connection. This is a great feature, allowing you to access your library on any number of devices.

To start reading a book, just click that book's thumbnail image in your Google Play Books library. As you read, you can advance through pages by *scrolling* — using finger gestures on the touchpad of your Chromebook — or by clicking the left or right arrows on the screen. Scrolling is a great way to advance quickly to a spot in the book, but the arrow buttons are ideal for turning pages.

Customizing your view

While you're reading your book, you can customize the density of the lines of text, increase or decrease the size of the letters, and even change the typeface of the eBook text. To customize your view, follow these steps:

1. **In your Google Play Books library, click the book you wish to read.**

   The book is loaded into the window.

2. **Click the Aa icon in the top-right of the window.**

   The Display Options pop-up window appears, revealing several options for customizing your eBook view. (See Figure 16-6.)

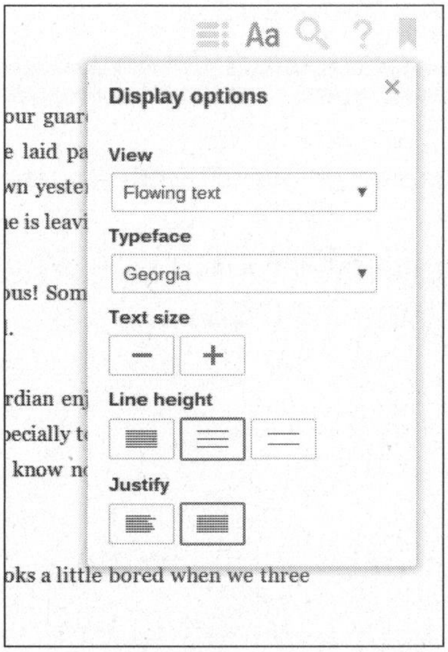

Figure 16-6:
The Display
Options
window.

3. **Make changes in the menu.**

   Google applies those changes to the text in real-time.

4. **When you're finished making changes, click outside of the Display Options pop-up window.**

   The pop-up window disappears.

Using bookmarks

As you're reading through your eBooks, you may want to place a bookmark to remember your place. With Google Play Books, you can place multiple bookmarks so that you can quickly return to sections of a book. Place a bookmark by following these steps:

1. **In your Google Play Books library, click the book you wish to read.**

   The book is loaded into the window.

2. **Click the icon that looks like a bookmark in the top-right corner of the window.**

   The bookmark enlarges and turns red, as shown in Figure 16-7, indicating that the page has been bookmarked.

Figure 16-7:
A book-marked page.

3. **Quickly navigate to your bookmarked pages by clicking the Contents icon in the top-right corner of your eBook.**

4. **In the resulting pop-up menu, choose Bookmarks.**

   All available bookmarks appear in the pop-up menu.

5. **Click the desired bookmark.**

   The saved location opens immediately.

Defining words

As you're reading, you may come to a word that you don't know. If you're reading the book while connected to the Internet, you can quickly define the word by double-clicking it. A pop-up window appears, shown in Figure 16-8, containing the popular definitions of the word. Click anywhere outside of the definition window to make it disappear.

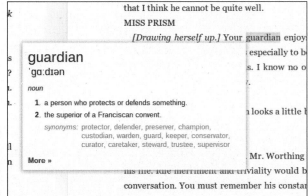

Figure 16-8:
Defining a word.

Reading offline

As is the case with most of what you do on a Chromebook, all of your books are stored in the cloud in your Google Play Books library. So, you must have an Internet connection to read your books unless you prepare your books for reading offline. To read your Google Play Books offline, follow these steps:

1. **Launch Google Play Books.**

   Your Google Play Books library opens in a Chrome browser.

2. **Hover your pointer over the thumbnail of the book you wish to read offline.**

   A pop-up window appears, containing basic information about the book and a check box for reading the book offline.

3. **Click the Make Available Offline check box.**

The book is downloaded to your Chromebook, and you can see the book's offline availability under its thumbnail in your library, as shown in Figure 16-9.

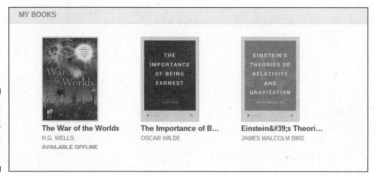

Figure 16-9:
Your book
is available
offline.

Part IV
Advanced Chromebook Settings

In this part . . .

- ✔ Customizing the look and feel of your Chromebook
- ✔ Adjusting Chromebook security options to set your perfect balance of convenience and security
- ✔ Diagnosing common problems before calling in reinforcements

Chapter 17

Customizing Your Chromebook

*E*ase of use is baked into the DNA of the Chromebook. Out of the box, the Chromebook user can be up and running in less than five minutes. By default, the features and functionality of the Chromebook make the user experience top notch without much customization. However, Google recognizes that all people are different, and although their user-experience designers are some of the best in the world, there's no one-size-fits-all when it comes to the way people use technology. For that reason, you have the ability to customize several aspects of your Chromebook.

In this chapter, you learn how to customize your display with your own wallpaper images, change the resolution of your display, and add an additional monitor to your Chromebook. You also find out how to customize the appearance and position of your Shelf. Also, I explain how to utilize cloud printing to print documents from your Chromebook by using printers all over the world.

Customizing Your Display Settings

Out of the box, your Chromebook's default settings are what the manufacturer found to be the optimal settings for viewing, computing, and so on. Your display defaults to the best screen resolution for the masses. Your Chromebook likely also comes with some standard background images, called *wallpaper,* that you can use to change up the look of your desktop area. However, if you would like to customize your display so that it better matches your taste, you can do so in a number of ways.

To view your settings, go to the settings menu. Find settings area in the bottom-right corner of the shelf. Click the area to reveal a menu of options — the settings panel — and choose Settings. Your settings will open within a Chrome browser.

Changing your wallpaper

When you start up your Chromebook, the image that fills your desktop background is called *wallpaper*. Your device manufacturer provides several options for wallpaper that you can try out. You also have the option to change the wallpaper to almost any photo that you desire. To change your Chromebook wallpaper, follow these steps:

1. **Open the settings panel in your Shelf and choose Settings.**

   Your Chromebook settings appear in a Chrome browser. (See Figure 17-1.)

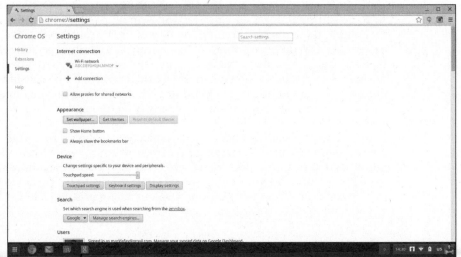

Figure 17-1: Chromebook settings.

2. **In the Chromebook Settings window, click the Set Wallpaper button in the Appearance section.**

   The Settings window minimizes, revealing the Wallpaper pop-up window with several image options, as shown in Figure 17-2.

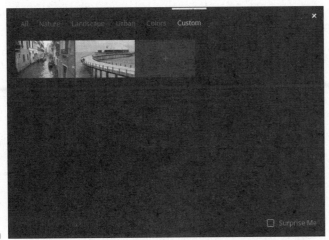

3. **Select an option by clicking the thumbnail.**

   Your Chromebook's wallpaper changes to match your selection.

   If you don't find a stock image that you like, you can also use one of your own. To do so, click the Custom link on the Wallpaper pop-up window, then click the blank thumbnail image containing a plus sign (+). A window appears in which you can browse to find your custom image. Select it and then click Open.

4. **Click the X in the top-right corner of the Wallpaper window.**

   The window closes, and the Chromebook Settings window reappears.

Changing your screen resolution

Screen resolution, simply put, is the measure of the sharpness and clarity of the image that can be shown on your screen. Resolution is expressed in terms of horizontal rows and vertical columns of pixels. A *pixel* is a very small area of illumination in a screen. For instance, the typical flat screen television may have a resolution of 1920x1080, which means that the image is 1920 pixels wide and 1080 pixels tall. When you increase or decrease your resolution, the physical size of your screen doesn't change. What changes is the number of pixels you're packing into that physical area. High resolution equals more pixels, which equals greater clarity.

Now that you have a general idea of what screen resolution is, customize your Chromebook's screen resolution by following these steps:

1. **Open the settings panel on your Shelf and click Settings.**

   Your Chromebook settings open in a Chrome browser.

2. **In your Chromebook Settings window, click the Display Settings button in the Device section.**

   The Manage Displays pop-up window appears, as shown in Figure 17-3.

Figure 17-3: Chrome-book's Manage Displays pop-up window.

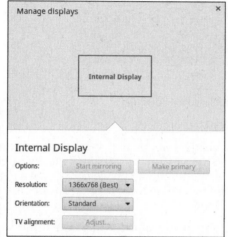

3. **Open the Resolution drop-down list and choose a new resolution.**

   Your Chromebook display automatically adjusts to match your selection. Figure 17-4 shows what the screen might look like at an extremely low resolution.

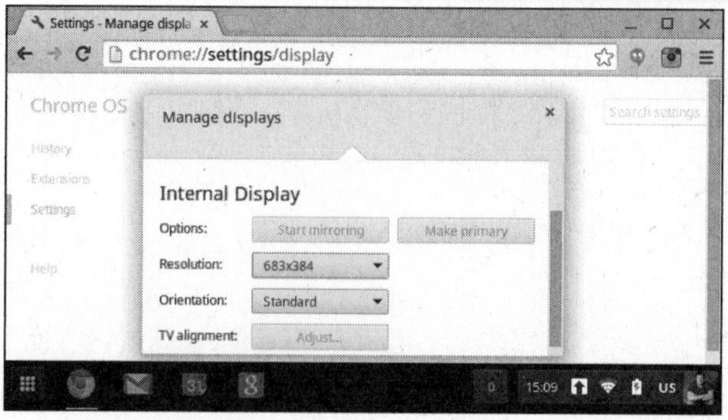

Figure 17-4: Chrome-book's display with a low resolution.

4. **When you're satisfied with your selection, click the X located in the top-right corner of the window.**

   The Chromebook Manage Displays pop-up window closes.

Using an external display

Working with a laptop all day long can be a grueling task for your eyes. Thankfully, you have the option to use an external display device with your Chromebook. To add and customize an external display device, follow these steps:

1. **Locate the display (HDMI) port on your Chromebook.**

   The majority of Chromebooks on the market come with at least one HDMI port, such as the one shown in Figure 17-5.

Figure 17-5: Chrome-book's HDMI port.

2. **Ensure that your external display device is powered on.**

3. **Connect the external display device to your Chromebook using an HDMI cable.**

   Your Chromebook screen flickers briefly as it auto-configures the new display. At length, the external display device shows the image from your Chromebook.

   You can now begin working from your Chromebook using both screens.

By default, Chromebook extends your desktop so that you have two screens to work with. You can, however, mirror your Chromebook display onto the external display device so that you have a single (but possibly bigger) display. Mirror your display and otherwise customize your external display device by following these steps:

1. **Open the Settings panel on your Shelf and click Settings.**

   Your Chromebook settings appear in a Chrome browser.

2. **In your Chromebook Settings window, click the Display Settings button in the Device section.**

   The Manage Displays pop-up window appears, as shown in Figure 17-6.

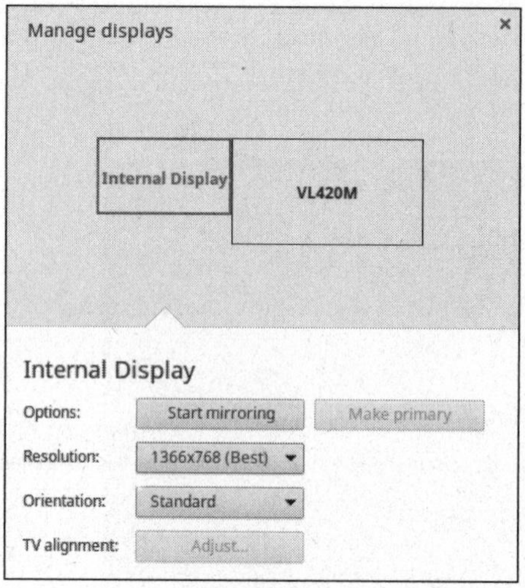

> **Manage displays** ✕
>
> | Internal Display | VL420M |
>
> **Internal Display**
>
> Options: [Start mirroring] [Make primary]
>
> Resolution: [1366x768 (Best) ▼]
>
> Orientation: [Standard ▼]
>
> TV alignment: [Adjust...]

Figure 17-6: Manage your displays.

3. **You can Mirror your displays by clicking the Start Mirroring button located next to Options.**

   The image on your Chromebook screen now appears on the external display device.

Mirroring your Chromebook display onto an external display device is helpful when presenting or demonstrating a task to a larger audience. Display devices can be televisions, monitors, or even projectors.

Customizing Your Shelf

Your Shelf is the home base for everything that happens on your Chromebook. By default, the Shelf is located along the bottom of your screen. Your app menu (similar to the Start button on a Windows PC) appears on the left side of your Shelf. Next to the app-launcher icon are shortcuts to your favorite apps. You can find your notification panel and status area on the right side of your Shelf.

Hiding your Shelf

By default, your Shelf is always visible. You can, however, set the Shelf to hide when you're not using it. To auto-hide your Shelf, follow these steps:

1. **Alt-click the background of your Chromebook.**

2. **In the pop-up menu that appears, select Autohide Shelf.**

   Your Shelf appears with a partially opaque background, indicating that it's set to Auto-Hide mode, as shown in Figure 17-7.

Figure 17-7: The Chromebook Shelf in Auto-Hide mode.

Now, whenever you launch an application, the Shelf hides to give you more usable space on your screen. To reveal the Shelf when you're working in a browser window, simply move your pointer so that it hovers over the Shelf area at the bottom of the screen.

Changing the position of your Shelf

By default, your Shelf is located along the bottom of your screen. To move the Shelf to the left or right side of your screen, follow these steps:

1. **Alt-click the background of your Chromebook.**

2. **In the menu that appears, hover your cursor over Shelf Position.**

   A submenu appears.

3. **Select the option that corresponds with the side of the screen to which you'd like to move your Shelf.**

   The Shelf relocates to the designated side, as shown in Figure 17-8.

Figure 17-8:
Relocating
your Shelf.

Cloud Printing

Part of what makes the Chromebook operating system so fast is that it offers only limited support for the vast assortment of peripheral devices on the market, including printers. But what does that mean for Chromebook users who need to print? Thankfully, Google has rolled out a way to print over the web called *cloud printing*. Cloud printing allows you to connect a printer to the Internet and access it using your Google Account. Several printers on the market are cloud-printing–enabled, but in the event your printer isn't, don't fret. You can still set it up for printing.

In order to set up cloud printing with a classic (that is, not cloud-printing–enabled) printer, you need a computer that's not a Chromebook and an Internet connection. Then follow these steps:

1. **Plug your printer into your non-Chromebook computer and power it on.**

2. **Open Chrome on the computer.**

   Ensure you're logged into Chrome with the same Google Account that you use to access your Chromebook. If you're not, click the Disconnect your Google Account button and then log in with the correct credentials before proceeding!

3. **After Chrome loads, click the Settings button in the top-right corner of the browser.**

   A menu appears.

4. **Click Settings.**

   Your Chrome settings load into the Chrome browser.

5. **Click Show Advanced Settings.**

   Several additional options appear.

6. **In the Google Cloud Print section, choose Manage.**

   A list appears, displaying the devices on your network available to register with Google Cloud Print.

7. **Locate the Classic Printers section and click Add Printers.**

   A page loads, giving you the option to add every printer installed on your device.

8. **Uncheck every printer except for the printer you just connected to your non-Chromebook computer, and then click Add Printer.**

   A confirmation page appears.

   At this point, you can print from your Chromebook as long as the computer to which your classic printer is connected is on and connected to the Internet.

To test that you successfully set up your printer for cloud printing, follow these steps:

1. **With your Chromebook, open a Chrome web browser.**

2. **Click the Settings button in the top-right corner.**

   A menu appears.

3. **Click Print.**

    Print options appear in a window.

4. **Click the Change button in the Destination section on the left side of the screen.**

    The Select a Destination pop-up window appears, giving you the option to select a different printer destination, as shown in Figure 17-9.

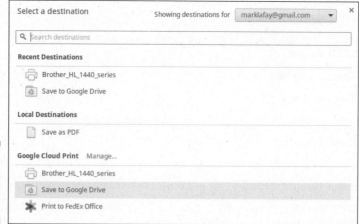

Select a destination   Showing destinations for   marklafay@gmail.com ▼   ×

Q Search destinations

Recent Destinations

    Brother_HL_1440_series

    Save to Google Drive

Local Destinations

    Save as PDF

Google Cloud Print   Manage...

    Brother_HL_1440_series

    Save to Google Drive

    Print to FedEx Office

Figure 17-9:
Selecting
your cloud
printer.

5. **Select your cloud printer.**

    The pop-up window disappears, and your selection is indicated in the Destination area of the print window.

6. **Click Print.**

    Your document prints to the selected printer.

If your document didn't print, ensure the following:

✔ The printer to which you're printing is turned on.

✔ The computer that's connected to your printer is turned on.

✔ The computer that's connected to your printer is connected to the Internet.

✔ Chrome is open on the computer that's connected to your printer.

Chapter 18

Supersizing Security

*B*efore the Internet, when you heard discussions of security, it usually included physically locking doors, safes, cabinets, and so on. Increased security meant bigger safes with more complex locks. In today's age, security is similar, only it involves ones and zeros. Everything must be password-protected and encrypted. Firewalls protect intruders from getting to your computer at home. SSL encryption ensures that the data you send over the Internet can't be read if it's intercepted. As our lives increasingly intersect with the Internet, security will increasingly become important.

The good news is that the Chromebook is an extremely secure device. It has to be! Chromebook is designed to ensure that the hardware and software are not compromised. When you turn on your Chromebook, the hardware checks itself to ensure no alterations have been made. As Chrome OS loads, it runs checks against the hardware and itself to ensure there have been no critical alterations made to the OS that could compromise your security when you log in. Chromebooks give you complete access to your Google Accounts, so it's important that Google took security seriously when extending your access to their platform through a mobile device!

In this chapter, you learn how to manage access to your Chromebook with user accounts and Guest mode. Add more peace of mind by locking your screen and managing your passwords. Ensure you aren't leaving valuable information around by managing your privacy settings. Concerned something is amiss with your Chromebook? Power-wash it to ensure it's as clean as can be and start fresh!

Conducting User Management

Google takes security seriously, and thus the Chromebook is no slouch when it comes to security, as well. In order to access a Chromebook, you must have a Google Account. This requirement is just as much about enhancing your interaction with the Chromebook and the Google platform as it is securing your interaction. By default, when you first use your Chromebook, you have the option to log in with a Google Account, or you can use the Chromebook as a guest. Guest users don't get any of the privileges that registered users get. In fact, Guest mode is a lot like surfing the web incognito because none of your traffic is tracked, stored, or otherwise logged.

When you log in to your Chromebook with a Google Account, that user account becomes the master account, or *Owner account,* of the Chromebook. With this account, you can administer and manage all other users that access the Chromebook, or you can restrict users whom you don't want to access the Chromebook.

Adding and deleting users

Account management is a very important part of securing your Chromebook. By default, anyone with a Google Account can log in and utilize your Chromebook. The good news is that Chromebook doesn't allow each user to access other users' data; however, you may not want your computer to be accessible to everyone on the planet. If you would like to limit access to your Chromebook to specific users, follow these steps:

1. **Log in to your Chromebook with the Owner account's username and password.**

2. **Open the settings panel on your Shelf and click Settings.**

   Your Chromebook settings open in a Chrome browser window.

3. **Click the Manage Other Users button in the Users section.**

   The Users pop-up window appears, as shown in Figure 18-1.

4. **Select the Restrict Sign-In to the Following Users check box.**

   The box located below this check box activates, revealing all the users who have logged into your device already, as shown in Figure 18-2.

Figure 18-1:
Managing
users.

Figure 18-2:
Viewing
active users.

If you're the only person who has accessed the Chromebook up until this point, then the only account you see in this box is yours. Notice that next to your account name is the word Owner, which means that your account is the owner of the Chromebook. With the Restrict Sign-In to the Following Users box checked, the only users who can access your Chromebook are listed with your account.

5. **To add additional users, in the Add Users text box at the bottom of the window, enter the email addresses for the Google Accounts to which you wish to grant access. Press Enter.**

   The names are added to the list of approved accounts, as shown in Figure 18-3.

Figure 18-3: Adding names to the list.

The Add Users text box calls for either a name or an email address. To save on headaches or errors, use only the email addresses assigned to the Google Accounts that will access your Chromebook.

To delete an added user, simply click the X to the right of the user's name in the list. No X appears to the right of the owner's name because the owner's access can't be revoked. Users who aren't listed as owner can't modify the user settings for your Chromebook. If they attempt to, a notification appears, like the one shown in Figure 18-4.

Users ✕

⊖ These settings may only be modified by the owner: marklafay@gmail.com

☑ Enable Guest browsing

☑ Show usernames and photos on the sign-in screen

☑ Restrict sign-in to the following users:

Add users
Enter names or addresses.

Done

Figure 18-4:
Changing
user set-
tings is
reserved for
the owner
only.

Hiding users at login

When you add new users to your Chromebook, their names and profile pictures are shown on the login screen. This can make access for frequent users easy and convenient. However, it also reduces security: The approved user accounts are in plain sight, so potential intruders don't have to work so hard. Instead of having to guess both a username and a password, intruders need only guess a password. To hide users so they don't appear on the login screen, follow these steps:

1. **Log in to your Chromebook with the Owner account's username and password.**

2. **Open the settings panel on your Shelf and click Settings.**

   Your Chromebook settings open in a Chrome browser window.

3. **In the Settings window, click the Manage Other Users button in the Users section.**

4. **In the Users window, uncheck the Show Usernames and Photos on the Sign-In Screen check box.**

5. **Click Done.**

The Users window closes.

6. **Verify your settings were applied by logging out.**

To log out, reopen the Settings menu in your Shelf and click Sign Out.

You're signed out of your Chromebook, and the usernames and photos disappear from the sign-in screen. Instead, a generic login box appears, requiring you to enter your account username and password.

Guest mode

Guest mode is an easy way to allow anyone to use your Chromebook without putting your personal account at risk. Key features like saving data to the device, changing settings, or otherwise modifying the Chromebook are disabled. Any changes, downloads, or tweaks done to the Chromebook while in Guest mode are deleted when the Chromebook is powered off or when the guest logs out. If you ever want to give someone quick access without having to create a user account, Guest mode is the way to go!

Even so, you may find that Guest mode leaves you more vulnerable than you like. In that case, you can revoke guest browsing by following these steps:

1. **Log in to your Chromebook with the Owner account's username and password.**

2. **Open the settings panel on your Shelf and click Settings.**

3. **Click the Manage Other Users button in the Users section.**

4. **In the Users window that appears, uncheck the Enable Guest Browsing check box.**

5. **Click Done.**

The Users window closes.

6. **Verify your settings were applied by logging out.**

To log out, reopen the Settings menu in your Shelf and click Sign Out.

You're signed out of your Chromebook.

If you successfully disabled Guest mode, the option to use the Chromebook as a guest disappears from the login screen. If you'd like to turn Guest mode back on, simply log back in and follow the steps above, selecting the check box in Step 5.

Locking Your Screen

Walking away from your Chromebook without first logging out or shutting it off can leave you vulnerable, even for only a brief moment. Locking your screen is a great way to ensure that your device isn't messed with while you're away. There are two ways that you can lock your Chromebook screen:

✔ Press and hold your Power button for four-tenths of a second. You know your computer is locking because the windows begin to fade.

Be sure to take your finger off the Power button at the right time. Holding the Power button for longer than four-tenths of a second can force your Chromebook to shut down!

✔ Open the Settings menu on your Shelf and click the Lock button. (See Figure 18-5.)

Figure 18-5:
Locking your
screen with
the Lock
button.

The Lock button

To add a little more security to your Chromebook, you can require a password to wake your Chromebook from Sleep mode. *Sleep mode* is a mode that your Chromebook goes into in order to conserve power when not in use. Your Chromebook automatically goes into Sleep mode after eight minutes of inactivity when plugged in and six minutes of inactivity when not plugged in, but you can put the Chromebook into Sleep mode immediately simply by closing the lid.

By default, a sleeping Chromebook is still vulnerable. Entering Sleep mode doesn't log you out or lock your screen. So if you rarely turn off your computer, enabling a wake-from-sleep password is probably a good idea. To set this feature, log in to your Chromebook and then follow these steps:

1. **Open the settings panel on your Shelf and click Settings.**

2. **Check the Require Password to Wake from Sleep check box in the Users section, as shown in Figure 18-6.**

   From here on out, you'll need your account password to bring your computer out of Sleep mode!

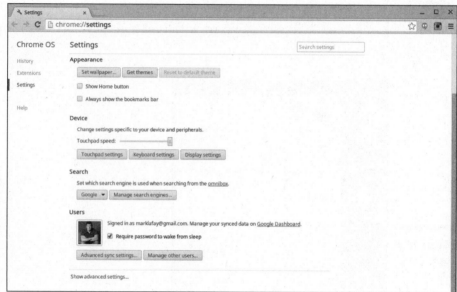

Figure 18-6:
Enabling the wake-from-sleep password requirement.

Power-washing

Sometimes it's nice to have a clean start. Your Chromebook makes it easy for you to wipe the slate clean and start over. You may find this useful when you have too much junk on your device. Or maybe you want to simply reset your Chromebook to its default settings because you're giving your Chromebook to another person. You can wipe your device quickly, easily, and securely by using Chromebook's built-in Powerwash feature.

To power-wash your Chromebook, log in to your Chromebook and follow these steps:

1. **Open the settings panel on your Shelf and click Settings.**

2. **Scroll to the bottom of the screen and click Show Advanced Settings.**

3. **Click the Powerwash button in the Powerwash section at the bottom of the screen. (See Figure 18-7.)**

   A confirmation dialog box appears.

Figure 18-7:
The
Powerwash
button.

The Powerwash button

4. **If you're positive you want to wipe your Chromebook clean, click the Restart button shown in Figure 18-8.**

   You can't undo power-washing. Once you click Restart, your Chromebook turns into a secure, power-cleaning machine. Nothing on the device will be left. The good news is that it won't touch anything on your Google Drive or other web services. But anything stored locally on your Chromebook will be gone forever.

   Your Chromebook restarts, clean as can be.

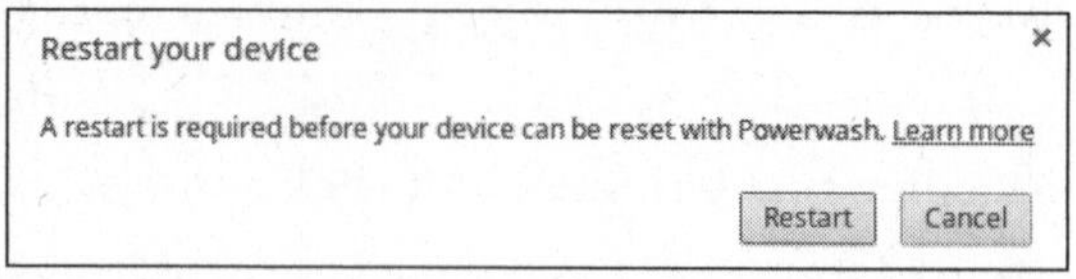

Figure 18-8:
Are you
sure?!

> Restart your device   ✕
>
> A restart is required before your device can be reset with Powerwash. Learn more
>
>   [Restart] [Cancel]

Protecting with Passwords

Sometimes increased usability can mean increased security concerns. Face it: The more protection you put in place, the more hassle there is. The airport is a great example of that. To ensure that nothing bad can happen on a plane, we endure the hassle of taking off shoes, belts, jackets, and hats and removing computers and metal objects as we walk through x-ray machines and body-image scanners. Chromebook security is the same way. You can add or remove as much security as you want, but there are consequences both ways — and unfortunately, security isn't convenient.

Your Chromebook has a default feature for storing and managing your passwords for you. This is a feature of the Chrome browser that made it into the Chromebook, and it's great if you have several passwords for several online products.

Don't worry, your passwords aren't stored without your permission. You have to approve the storage of a password the first time you enter it on a particular webpage, as shown in Figure 18-9.

If you choose to store your password, Chrome encrypts the password and stores it in your account for later. If you ever want to delete the password from Chrome's memory, you can do so by following these steps:

1. **Ensure you're logged in, and then open the settings panel on your Shelf and click Settings.**

2. **Scroll to the bottom of the Settings window that appears and click Show Advanced Settings.**

3. **Click Manage Passwords in the Passwords and Forms section.**

   The Password Manager pop-up window appears, revealing every stored password.

4. **To delete a password, click the X to the right of that password.**

If you ever forget a password, you can come to the Password Manager and simply click the password you've forgotten. A Show button appears that reveals your password when clicked.

Chromebook asks for your permission to store a password

Figure 18-9:
Store your
password?

You don't have to save passwords; however, you may find that saving them makes your web-browsing experience better. If you opt not to save a password but change your mind later, you'll need to delete the website from the Never Saved section of your Password Manager. To do so, follow these steps:

1. **Ensure you're logged in, and then open the settings panel on your Shelf and click Settings.**

2. **Scroll to the bottom of the Settings window that appears and click Show Advanced Settings.**

3. **In the Passwords and Forms section, click Manage Passwords.**

   The Password Manager pop-up window appears, revealing every stored password.

4. **In the Never Saved section, click the X to the right of the website you want to remove from this list.**

   Now, the next time you return to that website and enter your login credentials, you're prompted with the option to save your password, at which point you can approve saving it.

Chapter 19

Troubleshooting and Disaster Preparation

*T*echnology is great until it breaks. Right? That saying probably goes all the way back to the cavemen who discovered fire. The reality is, we live in an imperfect world, and nothing works perfectly all the time. For that reason, it's always good to consider those areas where life with your Chromebook could go sideways.

You can't use your Chromebook to the fullest without Internet access. For that reason, this chapter shows you how to troubleshoot network connectivity issues. You also learn how to troubleshoot and possibly remedy issues with your battery. In the event the sky starts falling and your Chromebook operating system becomes corrupt, you'll want to be sure that you have a restore disk so you can reinstall Chrome OS and get back to work as fast as possible. If all else fails, Google has a vast database of help resources online to provide solutions for any Chromebook problem. By the end of this chapter, you'll know where to go and how to search through these resources to get answers fast!

Resolving Internet-Connectivity Problems

Chromebooks require a connection to the Internet to be able to serve their purpose in the portable-computing ecosystem. For that reason, every Chromebook comes equipped with high-speed Wi-Fi. Some Chromebooks even come with cellular connectivity, allowing them to get online wherever a cell connection is present. If you're having trouble connecting to a wireless network, check these possible solutions before calling tech support:

✔ **Ensure your Wi-Fi controller is turned on.** Check the Wi-Fi indicator in the settings panel of your Shelf. If the Wi-Fi indicator is crossed out with an \, as shown in Figure 19-1, then your wireless adapter has been shut off. Turn it on by following these steps:

Figure 19-1:
The wireless adapter is turned off.

The X here means that no wi-fi access is present.

1. *Open the settings panel on your Shelf and click No Network.*

2. *In the menu that appears, click Turn Wi-Fi On.*

   Your wireless adapter turns on, giving you the option to select from all available networks.

✔ **Make sure your Chromebook is connected to a network.** Look at the Wi-Fi indicator that appears in the settings area of your shelf: If you have bars and no X and you still can't connect, verify you're connected to the correct network by following these steps:

1. *Click anywhere in the settings panel on your Shelf.*

   The settings menu appears, revealing several options. Second from the top is an option that also indicates the network to which you are connected.

2. *If the connected network isn't the network you want to connect to, click the network option that's second from the top.*

The Wireless Network menu appears.

3. *Scroll through the list, shown in Figure 19-2, to find the desired network, and then select it.*

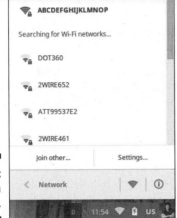

Figure 19-2:
Selecting a
network.

If your wireless controller is turned on and you're connected to a network but you still can't connect to the Internet, try restarting your Chromebook. This restart flushes your Chromebook memory and power cycles all of your Chromebook hardware, giving them a chance to start fresh. Restarting devices is the easiest and most common fix for glitches like connecting to a network or the Internet.

If you've restarted your Chromebook and you're connected to the network but you still can't connect to the Internet, ask the owner of the network to restart the Internet gateway. The gateway may be a home Internet router, cable modem, or DSL modem. If you're in an office or school, you may want to first check with other users to see if they are having connectivity issues.

Resolving Power Problems

Sometimes batteries go bad. Sometimes they go out in a literal blaze of glory. Don't worry, the odds of that happening with your Chromebook battery are slim. However, Chromebooks can have several kinds of power problems:

✔ **Your battery's charge doesn't last nearly as long as it should, or its ability to stay charged decreases with each use.** Refer to your device manual or look online to identify estimated battery life based on your level of device usage. Then verify your Chromebook's battery consumption by following these steps:

1. *Plug your Chromebook into the power charger until you hit a 100-percent charge.*

2. *Verify the charge level of your battery by opening the settings panel on your Shelf and examining the battery indicator at the bottom.*

3. *Verify that the battery indicator says Battery Full before disconnecting your power charger.*

Take note of the time and begin working with your Chromebook. Refer back to the battery indicator to monitor how quickly it reduces in charge. Once the battery is low enough to justify plugging in, take note of the time again to see how long the battery lasted. If it's within normal usage limits as defined by the manufacturer of your Chromebook, then you may want to adjust your usage.

On the other hand, if your battery loses charge faster than your manufacturer's specifications, follow these steps before returning to the manufacturer or point of purchase:

1. *Plug your Chromebook into a power source and charge the battery to 100-percent full.*

2. *When the Chromebook has reached 100 percent, unplug it and use the device until power dwindles down to 5 percent or less but not until it shuts off.*

3. *Repeat this process at least ten times before testing to see if the battery life has extended.*

If your battery still won't maintain a charge, return to the point of purchase or contact the manufacturer for service.

✔ **The battery won't charge at all so your Chromebook must stay connected to the power adapter, or your Chromebook won't turn on when plugged in.** Attempt to use another power adapter. If the symptoms persist with the alternate power adapter, your battery is likely toast. If the alternate power adapter rectifies the situation, you likely have a bad power adapter.

Using the Chromebook Recovery Utility

Chrome OS is great, but it's not an infallible operating system. It's possible for things to go awry with your Chromebook. If your Chromebook ever gives you a message that says Chrome OS Is Missing or Damaged, you may have to reinstall the operating system. Reinstalling the operating system removes all data from your Chromebook, but if you're getting the missing-or-damaged error, chances are you've already lost your data anyway.

Nevertheless, reinstalling the operating system requires a recovery drive (like a USB jump drive) to get you back up and running. To create a recovery drive, follow these steps:

1. **Open the App Launcher and click the Chrome Web Store icon.**

   The Chrome Web Store loads.

2. **Search for** Chromebook Recovery Utility **and then add it to your Chromebook.**

   The app is shown in Figure 19-3.

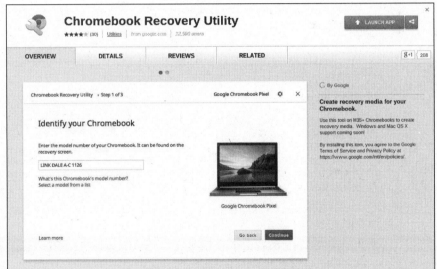

Figure 19-3:
The
Chromebook
Recovery
Utility.

3. **When the app has been added, click the green Launch App button.**

   The Chromebook Recovery Utility launches.

4. **Follow the prompts until you're asked to enter the model number of your Chromebook.**

5. **Click the What's This Chromebook's Model Number link.**

   Your Chromebook's model number appears in the field.

6. **Click Continue.**

   The Utility asks you to insert a USB drive or SD card, as shown in Figure 19-4.

Insert your USB flash drive or SD card

Select the media you'd like to use.

Silicon Motion, Inc. - Taiwan (formerly Feiya Technol ⇕

Learn more   Go back   Continue

Figure 19-4:
Insert your
USB drive or
SD card.

7. **Select the media that you want to use as your recovery drive and click Continue.**

   Anything still on your USB drive or SD card will be deleted once you create the recovery image. Now is the time to ensure you used the right media.

8. **Click Create Now.**

   Your Chromebook begins downloading and installing the software needed to make your recovery drive.

   Right about now, you should be getting a cup of coffee and reviewing your stocks because this process is going to take the better part of ten minutes.

   Chromebook notifies you when your recovery media has been successfully created.

9. **Remove your SD card or USB drive from your Chromebook and click Done.**

To recover your Chromebook by reinstalling Chrome OS, follow these steps:

1. **At the Chrome OS Is Missing or Damaged screen, insert the recovery media into your USB or SD slot.**

   Your Chromebook automatically detects the recovery media.

2. **Wait for the operating system to install the OS automatically.**

   Chromebook begins recovering your system.

3. **After Chromebook finishes recovering your system, remove the recovery media.**

   Your Chromebook reboots automatically.

Finding Help Online

If you ever find yourself in a situation that you can't solve with this book or with your Chromebook's help manuals, try the Chromebook Help Center online. (See Figure 19-5.) You can visit the Help Center at https://support.google.com/chromebook. The Help Center provides answers to some of the most common Chromebook questions relating to setup, connecting a Chromebook to the Internet, printing, working with media, and more. If your question is a little more refined and technical, you also have the option to dive into the Chromebook Help Forum.

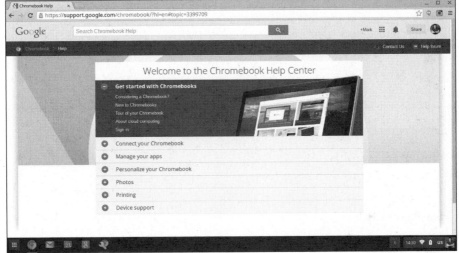

Figure 19-5:
The online
Chromebook
Help Center.

Once you arrive at the Help Forum, you can either search or browse topics. The easiest way to get started is to enter your problem in the Search bar and press Enter. For example, if you're having issues with the battery in your Chromebook 14, search with the following query: **Chromebook 14 battery problem**. Or you can get more specific: **Chromebook 14 battery will not hold charge**. Several results appear for you to browse through.

If you have a question you'd like to post, make sure you do a thorough search through the Forum prior to posting your question. Forums are websites where the general public can converse on a specific topic or range of topics. Although the Google forums (including the Chromebook Help Forum) are moderated to ensure everyone is playing nicely, you may still rub people the wrong way if you post a question that has already been asked and answered.

Part V
The Part of Tens

Compare the features of ten different Chromebooks at www.dummies.com/extras/chromebook.

In this part . . .

- ✔ Learning how to speed up your Chromebook with the fastest reboot ever

- ✔ Seeing how to quickly navigate and control your Chromebook with Chrome URLs and the Chrome browser

- ✔ Bringing Google Search to life on your Chromebook without launching a Chrome browser

- ✔ Controlling another computer with your Chromebook using Remote Desktop

Chapter 20

Ten Handy Shortcuts

C hromebook was definitely made to be easy to use right out of the box. It's not a self-driving car, but it's almost as easy. Get it out, plug it in, turn it on, and follow the prompts: You'll be up and running in less than five minutes. Still, even though Chromebook is very usable, you may want to do some further customization. This chapter contains ten tips, tricks, and shortcuts to make your Chromebook experience more productive — or at least a little more fun.

Google Search from the App Launcher

The Google platform is baked into the Chromebook and Chrome OS. That was the point when Chromebook was created: Create a tool that's powered almost exclusively by the extensive Google ecosystem of applications. Well, bravo, Google — you did it. One way in which the Google platform is integrated into Chrome OS is the Chromebook Search feature. When you open the App Launcher or press the Search button on your keyboard, a Search bar is revealed. Type a search query into the bar and press Enter. Chromebook serves you Google search results. In a Chrome browser window. It becomes second nature very quickly.

Quick Reboot

No computer is perfect, and although some manufacturers like to make you think that you'll never need to reboot your computer, you almost always will. The longer you use your Chromebook, the more gunked up the memory will become with remnant websites, applications, data, and so on. You can reboot your computer a number of ways, but the fastest way to reboot is to press the Power button and Refresh button simultaneously. Like a flash of light, your Chromebook restarts with fresh memory.

Control Chromebook with the Omnibox

If you're familiar with Chrome from using it on devices other than your Chromebook, you may already know that Chrome has several high-powered features that can be accessed by entering Chrome shortcuts into the Omnibox. Naturally, Chrome on Chromebook has the same set of features. Below is an outline of some of the shortcuts you might find the most helpful:

- ✔ **Chome://power:** View how much charge your Chromebook has and how much power you're using.

- ✔ **Chrome://settings:** Load your Chromebook settings.

- ✔ **Chrome://gesture:** Tweak your touchpad gesture settings.

- ✔ **Chrome:// quota-internals:** Quickly view how much storage space you have on your Chromebook.

- ✔ **Chrome://chrome-urls:** Check out all of the Chrome URLs you can type.

Launch Apps in Their Own Windows

The vast majority of the apps that you use on your Chromebook are web applications. That means when you launch your app menu and click an application, a Chrome browser window opens and loads the application. You may find that all the extraneous Chrome features may take away from your application experience. For that reason, you can launch the application in a non-Chrome browser window. To do so, simply launch an application by pressing Shift and clicking your touchpad. The application loads in its own window without all the other Chrome junk.

Lock Your Screen

Ever been in a public place working on your computer and need to get up to go to the bathroom in a hurry? Or maybe someone is barging into your room and you don't want him to get into your business and see what you're doing on your Chromebook? You can lock your screen by holding down your Power button for 400 milliseconds — but sometimes you need to lock your screen in 1 millisecond. Never fear, press Ctrl+Shift+L to lock your screen in an instant!

Launch Apps in Your Shelf

One way that you can save time on your Chromebook is by pinning frequently used apps to your Shelf. In doing so, you save yourself the extra click and possible swipe through the application menu. If you're serious about keyboard productivity, you can save yourself the need to even click: Simply load a pinned application by pressing Alt and the number corresponding with the placement of the application in your Shelf (left to right). No longer will you be bogged down by the lengthy journey of a mouse pointer to a click.

Do a Barrel Roll

Sometimes, you just need to have a little fun with your day. Chromebook has a few little Easter eggs hidden throughout. Make your screen do a barrel roll. That's it. No productivity, usefulness, or work-changing functionality here. It's just fun to make your screen go bananas for a brief moment. Press Ctrl+Alt+Shift+Refresh to make your screen roll around and then snap back to normal.

Google Voice Search

Google Voice Search was a new feature in 2014 added to the Chromebook. To put it simply, you no longer need to type a search query, you can merely speak it into your Chromebook, and Chromebook funnels the audio off to Google and comes back with search results loaded into a Chrome browser. To use Google Voice Search, follow these steps:

1. **While logged into your Chromebook, press the Search key on your keyboard.**

   The app menu opens and the Search bar appears in focus.

2. **Using your pointer, click the Microphone icon on the left side of the Search bar.**

   Chromebook engages your Chromebook microphone.

3. **Speak your search query.**

   Google converts the speech to text and submits the query to Google. Results are served up in a Chrome browser.

Math and Conversions with Search

Google Search is definitely a major component of the Chromebook. Have you ever used Google to perform conversions or calculations for you? You should if you haven't. Your Chromebook will give you the same service through the Search bar. Give it a try with these steps:

1. **While logged into your Chromebook, press the search key on your keyboard.**

   The app menu opens, and the Search bar appears in focus.

2. **Enter your math problem or search query into the Search bar.**

   For example, type **4+4**. The second result will be the answer: =8. You can even ask for conversions: Type **15 ounces to grams**. The second result is = 396.893324 grams.

Other features **Google search features** — such as translate, define, and the like — aren't available on Chromebook quite yet, but that's not to say they won't be in the near future!

Life without the Delete Key

It's true, your Chromebook doesn't have a Delete key. It has a Backspace key, but no Delete key (unless you're one of the fortunate few). Here's a brief explanation if you don't know the difference between Delete and Backspace. Delete removes the character to the right of your cursor. Backspace removes the character to the left of your cursor. The good news is that there's a Delete shortcut that's almost as good as the real thing.

To delete characters to the right of your cursor, press Alt+Backspace. Characters to the right are deleted one by one. You can also delete entire words to the left of your cursor by pressing Ctrl+Backspace. The words start to vanish one by one, as well.

Chapter 21

Ten Great Chrome OS Apps

●●●

Apps are all we hear about today. Apple, Microsoft, Google Play — heck, even BlackBerry has an application store. Needless to say, we are in application overload. Still, there are many extremely useful applications available for Chromebook users. In this section, you get a brief overview of ten apps that make your life on Chromebook more interesting, productive, and entertaining!

WeVideo

Just because you don't have a lot of storage or resources on your Chromebook doesn't mean you can't have a lot of fun working with video. WeVideo is a great application for editing video anywhere in the world. Work in multiple editing modes (storyboard, timeline, or an advanced mode), and connect with your Facebook, Google Drive, or Dropbox to make dragging and dropping video files and photos easy. Add effects, text, transitions, and subtitles, and record voiceovers to bring your videos to life. You can export WeVideos to various web services in standard definition and high definition. Video is serious business on the Chromebook with WeVideo.

Angry Birds

You've been living under a rock for the past five years if you haven't heard of Angry Birds. Angry Birds is a fun way to kill time with your Chromebook. Essentially, the premise of the game is to fling birds at the evil pigs that keep stealing bird eggs. There is quite a bit of strategy involved, especially in the more advanced levels, because you have to toss birds that can break through different materials to get to the evil green pigs. The one thing that makes the game truly remarkable, aside from the hilarious audio, is the fantastic physics engine that calculate trajectory, velocity, and impact force. But let's not kid ourselves, that doesn't make this a game for developing mental strength.

Remote Desktop

Sometimes you may need to get work done on a machine other than your Chromebook. Or maybe you have some files that reside on another machine that's miles and miles away. Remote Desktop is a great way to remotely access your other computers without having to be in the same room. The Remote Desktop client must be installed in the Chrome browser of each machine that you wish to control. You also have to make sure the other computers are connected to the Internet and the Chrome browser is open. The one catch is that, currently, Chromebook does not support Remote Desktop on the Chromebook. So, you can't control your Chromebook from a Mac or a PC. Give it time, that will likely change in the near future.

Gmail Offline

You can do all of your email through the Gmail client. (If you haven't read Chapter 10, give it a glance for the scoop on Gmail.) You can even use Gmail to field all of your non-Gmail email, similar to how you might use Outlook on a PC or Mail on a Mac. What makes Gmail really powerful, however, is Gmail Offline. This application makes it possible to access recent emails, draft new emails, and queue up new emails to send once you get an Internet connection. Gmail Offline is a must-have for anyone serious about being productive in between connections to the Internet.

Pixlr Editor

Pixlr is a high-powered photo editor that is 100-percent cloud-based, which means that it will work perfectly with your Chromebook. If you have any experience working with Gimp or Photoshop, Pixlr will feel like a natural leap with the Chromebook. Filter your photos, clean up red eye, adjust color levels, or create new images using the various drawing tools available. Pixlr can open Photoshop document files, and you can even paste copied images into your Pixlr projects. If you do any amount of image creation or manipulation, Pixlr is a great option.

Pandora

Chromebook comes with several options on the Google platform for listening to music. You can launch Google Play and listen to singles, albums, or random radio stations derived from performers, albums, or songs. Google Play may be overload for those of us just looking for a little background music while we work or play. Pandora is an Internet radio platform that lets you create stations from songs, performers, and albums. Pandora uses a combination of algorithm and user feedback to ensure songs that load into your radio station fit the sound you're looking for. Pandora is a free service, unlike Google Play — and that should be music to your ears!

Evernote

Evernote is a note-taking software. But really it's more than that. It's a tool for capturing your stream of consciousness. Include text, images, songs, and video clips into different notes that can be saved and synced across all of your devices. Maybe you want to save a web page, create to-do lists, or organize research for a project. Evernote has become the industry leader because of its ease of use, accessibility, and power. Share notes to social networks and invite others to participate in collaboration on specific notes. If you're serious about keeping your life organized, Evernote is the digital sticky note for you.

Word Online

There is Google Docs, and it's amazing. But if you come from a lifelong career working in Microsoft Word, Word Online may be the right option for you. Create documents of all sorts, from letters to research papers and autobiographies. Word Online is a near replica of the desktop experience, just online. Share your documents and invite collaborators to participate in the editing of documents with Word Online, then save your documents in OneDrive or download them for storing elsewhere. Word Online is a great option if you aren't ready for Google Docs.

Weatherbug

Weatherbug touts that it's the fastest, most accurate weather application currently available. Weatherbug is definitely a ray of sunshine in your App Launcher menu. Save multiple locations in your Weatherbug for quick referencing. Check current conditions or long-term forecasts. The virtual window gives you a pleasant visualization of the forecast. Weatherbug also funnels out real-time weather alerts to make sure you're in the know when severe weather is moving into your area. Also, check out local or national radar and plan a long trip with a precise weather forecast.

Hangouts Extension

If you've ever used iChat or Instant Messenger, you'll be right at home with Hangouts. Hangouts runs in the background and whenever you receive a chat message, Hangouts pops open a dialog box so you can chat away!

Google Hangouts is a default application on all Chromebooks. The Hangouts extension, however, is not. The Hangouts extension is an extension of Chrome and not a true application in the Chromebook sense. But it's a very useful extension given the integrated nature of the Chrome browser in Chromebook. You can have text conversations with your contacts using the Hangouts extension.

Index

● *T* ●

• U •

About the Author

Mark LaFay has entrepreneurialism running through his veins. Since grade school, LaFay has created and run small businesses that have taken him and his products around the world. LaFay built businesses in the music industry, producing hundreds of events in central Indiana and developing numerous musical acts into internationally touring and recognized groups. LaFay is co-founder of DCODIA (www.dcodia.com), a startup that helps people living with dyslexia; a minority owner and board member of SocialNetWatcher.com, a tech company helping schools and parents combat bullying; and a founding member and the product engineer of Conversion In A Box (https://conversioninabox.com), a marketing automation software startup. LaFay is an adjunct professor in the school of informatics at IUPUI (Indiana University–Purdue University Indianapolis). Currently, LaFay is applying his business acumen and love for all things entrepreneurial to the development of Roust, a social network for people interested in discussing real issues.

Dedication

To my wife. Your love and support fuels my desire for greatness.

Author's Acknowledgments

Thanks to my wife for putting up with my late nights in front of the computer. Many thanks to Katie Mohr at Wiley for fielding an absurd number of questions and long-winded emails about my garden. Thank you Jeff Hertzler for being a great dude and a fantastic technical editor. Thank you Jeff Krajewski reminding me that the road less traveled is the only road to be on. Countless thanks to all of my family and friends.

Publisher's Acknowledgments

Acquisitions Editor: Katie Mohr

Senior Project Editor: Christopher Morris

Copy Editor: Laura K. Miller

Technical Editor: Jeff Hertzler

Editorial Assistant: Claire Johnson

Sr. Editorial Assistant: Cherie Case

Project Coordinator: Patrick Redmond

Cover Image: Courtesy of Mark LaFay (author), ©Mark LaFay

Apple & Mac

iPad For Dummies,
6th Edition
978-1-118-72306-7

iPhone For Dummies,
7th Edition
978-1-118-69083-3

Macs All-in-One
For Dummies, 4th Edition
978-1-118-82210-4

OS X Mavericks
For Dummies
978-1-118-69188-5

Blogging & Social Media

Facebook For Dummies,
5th Edition
978-1-118-63312-0

Social Media Engagement
For Dummies
978-1-118-53019-1

WordPress For Dummies,
6th Edition
978-1-118-79161-5

Business

Stock Investing
For Dummies, 4th Edition
978-1-118-37678-2

Investing For Dummies,
6th Edition
978-0-470-90545-6

Personal Finance
For Dummies, 7th Edition
978-1-118-11785-9

QuickBooks 2014
For Dummies
978-1-118-72005-9

Small Business Marketing
Kit For Dummies,
3rd Edition
978-1-118-31183-7

Careers

Job Interviews
For Dummies, 4th Edition
978-1-118-11290-8

Job Searching with Social
Media For Dummies,
2nd Edition
978-1-118-67856-5

Personal Branding
For Dummies
978-1-118-11792-7

Resumes For Dummies,
6th Edition
978-0-470-87361-8

Starting an Etsy Business
For Dummies, 2nd Edition
978-1-118-59024-9

Diet & Nutrition

Belly Fat Diet For Dummies
978-1-118-34585-6

Mediterranean Diet
For Dummies
978-1-118-71525-3

Nutrition For Dummies,
5th Edition
978-0-470-93231-5

Digital Photography

Digital SLR Photography
All-in-One For Dummies,
2nd Edition
978-1-118-59082-9

Digital SLR Video &
Filmmaking For Dummies
978-1-118-36598-4

Photoshop Elements 12
For Dummies
978-1-118-72714-0

Gardening

Herb Gardening
For Dummies, 2nd Edition
978-0-470-61778-6

Gardening with Free-Range
Chickens For Dummies
978-1-118-54754-0

Health

Boosting Your Immunity
For Dummies
978-1-118-40200-9

Diabetes For Dummies,
4th Edition
978-1-118-29447-5

Living Paleo For Dummies
978-1-118-29405-5

Big Data

Big Data For Dummies
978-1-118-50422-2

Data Visualization
For Dummies
978-1-118-50289-1

Hadoop For Dummies
978-1-118-60755-8

Language &
Foreign Language

500 Spanish Verbs
For Dummies
978-1-118-02382-2

English Grammar
For Dummies, 2nd Edition
978-0-470-54664-2

French All-in-One
For Dummies
978-1-118-22815-9

German Essentials
For Dummies
978-1-118-18422-6

Italian For Dummies,
2nd Edition
978-1-118-00465-4

e Available in print and e-book formats.

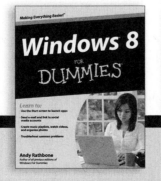

Available wherever books are sold. **For more information or to order direct visit www.dummies.com**

Math & Science

Algebra I For Dummies,
2nd Edition
978-0-470-55964-2

Anatomy and Physiology
For Dummies, 2nd Edition
978-0-470-92326-9

Astronomy For Dummies,
3rd Edition
978-1-118-37697-3

Biology For Dummies,
2nd Edition
978-0-470-59875-7

Chemistry For Dummies,
2nd Edition
978-1-118-00730-3

1001 Algebra II Practice
Problems For Dummies
978-1-118-44662-1

Microsoft Office

Excel 2013 For Dummies
978-1-118-51012-4

Office 2013 All-in-One
For Dummies
978-1-118-51636-2

PowerPoint 2013
For Dummies
978-1-118-50253-2

Word 2013 For Dummies
978-1-118-49123-2

Music

Blues Harmonica
For Dummies
978-1-118-25269-7

Guitar For Dummies,
3rd Edition
978-1-118-11554-1

iPod & iTunes
For Dummies, 10th Edition
978-1-118-50864-0

Programming

Beginning Programming
with C For Dummies
978-1-118-73763-7

Excel VBA Programming
For Dummies, 3rd Edition
978-1-118-49037-2

Java For Dummies,
6th Edition
978-1-118-40780-6

Religion & Inspiration

The Bible For Dummies
978-0-7645-5296-0

Buddhism For Dummies,
2nd Edition
978-1-118-02379-2

Catholicism For Dummies,
2nd Edition
978-1-118-07778-8

Self-Help & Relationships

Beating Sugar Addiction
For Dummies
978-1-118-54645-1

Meditation For Dummies,
3rd Edition
978-1-118-29144-3

Seniors

Laptops For Seniors
For Dummies, 3rd Edition
978-1-118-71105-7

Computers For Seniors
For Dummies, 3rd Edition
978-1-118-11553-4

iPad For Seniors
For Dummies, 6th Edition
978-1-118-72826-0

Social Security
For Dummies
978-1-118-20573-0

Smartphones & Tablets

Android Phones
For Dummies, 2nd Edition
978-1-118-72030-1

Nexus Tablets
For Dummies
978-1-118-77243-0

Samsung Galaxy S 4
For Dummies
978-1-118-64222-1

Samsung Galaxy Tabs
For Dummies
978-1-118-77294-2

Test Prep

ACT For Dummies,
5th Edition
978-1-118-01259-8

ASVAB For Dummies,
3rd Edition
978-0-470-63760-9

GRE For Dummies,
7th Edition
978-0-470-88921-3

Officer Candidate Tests
For Dummies
978-0-470-59876-4

Physician's Assistant Exam
For Dummies
978-1-118-11556-5

Series 7 Exam For Dummie
978-0-470-09932-2

Windows 8

Windows 8.1 All-in-One
For Dummies
978-1-118-82087-2

Windows 8.1 For Dummies
978-1-118-82121-3

Windows 8.1 For Dummies
Book + DVD Bundle
978-1-118-82107-7

Available in print and e-book formats.

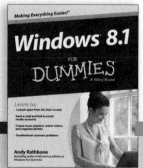